Codification Statements on Standards for Accounting and Review Services

Glen A Smith, CPA
P.O. Box 44820
Rio Rancho, NM 87174

> Numbers 1 to 20

AS OF JANUARY 2012

Copyright © 2012 by
American Institute of Certified Public Accountants, Inc.
New York, NY 10036-8775

Reprinted from
AICPA *Professional Standards*
Accounting and Review Services Parts
(as of January 2012)

All rights reserved. For information about the procedure for requesting permission to make copies of any part of this work, please e-mail copyright@aicpa.org with your request. Otherwise, requests should be written and mailed to the Permissions Department, AICPA, 220 Leigh Farm Road, Durham, NC 27707-8110.

1 2 3 4 5 6 7 8 9 0 PrP 1 9 8 7 6 5 4 3 2

ISBN 978-1-93735-021-5

PREFACE

This publication, issued by the Accounting and Review Services Committee (ARSC), is a codification of Statements on Standards for Accounting and Review Services (SSARSs), and the related accounting and review interpretations. ARSC is the senior technical committee of the AICPA designated to issue enforceable standards in connection with the unaudited financial statements or other unaudited financial information of a nonpublic entity.

SSARSs are issued by senior technical bodies of the AICPA designated to issue pronouncements on accounting and review matters. Rule 202, *Compliance With Standards* (AICPA, *Professional Standards*, ET sec. 202 par. .01), of the AICPA Code of Professional Conduct requires an AICPA member who performs compilations or reviews to comply with such pronouncements. An accountant is required to comply with an unconditional requirement in all cases in which the circumstances exist to which the unconditional requirement applies. An accountant is also required to comply with a presumptively mandatory requirement in all cases in which the circumstances exist to which the presumptively mandatory requirement applies; however, in rare circumstances, the accountant may depart from a presumptively mandatory requirement provided that the accountant documents his or her justification for the departure and how the alternative procedures performed in the circumstances were sufficient to achieve the objectives of the presumptively mandatory requirement.

Accounting and review interpretations are recommendations on the application of SSARSs in specific circumstances, including engagements for entities in specialized industries, issued under the authority of AICPA senior technical bodies. An interpretation is not as authoritative as a pronouncement; however, if an accountant does not apply an accounting and review interpretation, the accountant should be prepared to explain how he or she complied with the SSARS provisions addressed by such accounting and review interpretation. The specific terms used to define professional requirements in the SSARSs are not intended to apply to interpretations because interpretations are not accounting and review standards.

ACCOUNTING AND REVIEW
SERVICES COMMITTEE

Michael Brand, Chair
Michael P. Glynn, Senior Technical Manager—
Audit and Attest Standards

WHAT'S NEW IN THIS EDITION

Section	Change
AR Cross-References to SSARSs	Addition of new section, which contains two tables. The first table "Statements on Standards for Accounting and Review Services," has been moved from AR appendix A. The second table, "Sources of Sections in Current Text," is new.
AR 9080.63–.68	Addition of Interpretation No. 17, "Required Supplementary Information That Accompanies Compiled Financial Statements," of AR section 80, *Compilation of Financial Statements*.
AR 9090.41–.44	Addition of Interpretation No. 11, "Required Supplementary Information That Accompanies Reviewed Financial Statements," of AR section 90, *Review of Financial Statements*.
AR Appendix A	Deletion due to relocation of content from that appendix.

TABLE OF CONTENTS

Section		Page
. . .	How This Book Is Organized	1
. . .	AR Cross-References to SSARSs	3
. . .	Statements on Standards for Accounting and Review Services	7
20	Defining Professional Requirements in Statements on Standards for Accounting and Review Services [Superseded, December 2010, by the issuance of SSARS No. 19.]	15
50	Standards for Accounting and Review Services [Superseded, December 2010, by the issuance of SSARS No. 19.]	17
60	Framework for Performing and Reporting on Compilation and Review Engagements	19
80	Compilation of Financial Statements	31
9080	Compilation of Financial Statements: Accounting and Review Services Interpretations of Section 80	55
90	Review of Financial Statements	75
9090	Review of Financial Statements: Accounting and Review Services Interpretations of Section 90	111
100	Compilation and Review of Financial Statements [Superseded, December 2010, by the issuance of SSARS No. 19.]	125
110	Compilation of Specified Elements, Accounts, or Items of a Financial Statement	127
120	Compilation of Pro Forma Financial Information	137
200	Reporting on Comparative Financial Statements	149
9200	Reporting on Comparative Financial Statements: Accounting and Review Services Interpretations of Section 200	167
300	Compilation Reports on Financial Statements Included in Certain Prescribed Forms	169
9300	Compilation Reports on Financial Statements Included in Certain Prescribed Forms: Accounting and Review Services Interpretations of Section 300	173
400	Communications Between Predecessor and Successor Accountants	175
9400	Communications Between Predecessor and Successor Accountants: Accounting and Review Services Interpretations of Section 400	181

viii   Table of Contents

Section		Page
500	Reporting on Compiled Financial Statements [Deleted by the issuance of Statement on Standards for Accounting and Review Services 7, November 1992.]	183
600	Reporting on Personal Financial Statements Included in Written Personal Financial Plans	185
9600	Reporting on Personal Financial Statements Included in Written Personal Financial Plans: Accounting and Review Services Interpretation of Section 600	189
	Exhibits	191
	Appendixes	205
	Topical Index	225

Contents

HOW THIS BOOK IS ORGANIZED

The AR sections include accounting and review services standards issued through SSARS No. 20, *Revised Applicability of Statements on Standards for Accounting and Review Services*. Superseded portions have been deleted, and all applicable amendments have been included. These sections are arranged as follows:

> AR Cross-References to SSARSs
>
> Framework for Performing and Reporting on Compilation and Review Engagements
>
> Compilation of Financial Statements
>
> Review of Financial Statements
>
> Compilation of Specified Elements, Accounts, or Items of a Financial Statement
>
> Compilation of Pro Forma Financial Information
>
> Reporting on Comparative Financial Statements
>
> Compilation Reports on Financial Statements Included in Certain Prescribed Forms
>
> Communications Between Predecessor and Successor Accountants
>
> Reporting on Personal Financial Statements Included in Written Personal Financial Plans
>
> Exhibits
>
> Appendixes
>
> Topical Index

The AR Cross-References to SSARSs is a list of all issued SSARSs and a list of sources of sections in the current text.

The standards are divided into sections, each with its own section number. Each paragraph within a section is decimally numbered.

Accounting and review services interpretations are numbered in the 9000 series with the last three digits indicating the section to which the interpretation relates. Interpretations immediately follow their corresponding section. For example, interpretations related to section 200 are numbered 9200, which directly follows section 200.

There are two exhibits related to accounting and review services standards as follows:

> Exhibit A illustrates how an accountant might document expectations in a review engagement.
>
> Exhibit B helps practitioners better understand the accounting concepts of going concern in performing a compilation or review engagement.
>
> Exhibit C is reserved.

There are two appendixes related to accounting and review services standards as follows:

> Appendix A is reserved.
>
> Appendix B outlines the disposition of interpretations to section 100 as a result of changes made to conform to Statement on Standards

How This Book Is Organized

for Accounting and Review Services No. 19, *Compilation and Review Engagements*.

Appendix C provides a schedule of changes in Statements on Standards for Accounting and Review Services beginning with the issuance of Statement on Standards for Accounting and Review Services No. 1, *Compilation and Review of Financial Statements*.

The AR topical index uses the keyword method to facilitate reference to the pronouncements. The index is arranged alphabetically by topic and refers to major divisions, sections, and paragraph numbers.

AR Cross-References to SSARSs

Statements on Standards for Accounting and Review Services[*]

No.	Date Issued	Title	Section
1	Dec. 1978	Compilation and Review of Financial Statements [Superseded, December 2010, by SSARS No. 19.]	
2	**Oct. 1979**	**Reporting on Comparative Financial Statements**	**200**
3	**Dec. 1981**	**Compilation Reports on Financial Statements Included in Certain Prescribed Forms[1]**	**300**
4	**Dec. 1981**	**Communications Between Predecessor and Successor Accountants[2]**	**400**
5	July 1982	Reporting on Compiled Financial Statements [Deleted, November 1992, by SSARS No. 7.][3]	
6	**Sept. 1986**	**Reporting on Personal Financial Statements Included in Written Personal Financial Plans**	**600**
7	**Nov. 1992**	**Omnibus Statement on Standards for Accounting and Review Services—1992[4]**	
8	Oct. 2000	Amendment to Statement on Standards for Accounting and Review Services No. 1, *Compilation and Review of Financial Statements*	
9	**Nov. 2002**	**Omnibus Statement on Standards for Accounting and Review Services—2002[5]**	
10	May 2004	Performance of Review Engagements	
11	May 2004	Standards for Accounting and Review Services [Superseded, December 2010, by SSARS No. 19.][6]	

(continued)

---

[*] Pronouncements in effect are indicated in **boldface** type.

[1] SSARS No. 3 amends section 200.02.

[2] SSARS No. 4 amends section 200.16.

[3] The provisions of SSARS No. 5 have been incorporated into section 300

[4] SSARS No. 7 has been integrated to amend sections 200, 300, and 400; SSARS No. 7 also deletes SSARS No. 5.

[5] SSARS No. 9 amends sections 400.01–.06 and 400.08–.10, deletes section 400.07, and adds sections 400.11–.12.

[6] SSARS No. 11 amends section 200.17.

Statements on Standards for Accounting and Review Services

No.	Date Issued	Title	Section
12	July 2005	**Omnibus Statement on Standards for Accounting and Review Services—2005**[7]	
13	July 2005	**Compilation of Specified Elements, Accounts, or Items of a Financial Statement**	110
14	July 2005	**Compilation of Pro Forma Financial Information**	120
15	July 2007	**Elimination of Certain References to Statements on Auditing Standards and Incorporation of Appropriate Guidance Into Statements on Standards for Accounting and Review Services**[8]	
16	Dec. 2007	Defining Professional Requirements in Statements on Standards for Accounting and Review Services [Superseded, December 2010, by SSARS No. 19.]	
17	Feb. 2008	**Omnibus Statement on Standards for Accounting and Review Services—2008**[9]	
18	Feb. 2009	Applicability of Statements on Standards for Accounting and Review Services	
19	Dec. 2009	**Compilation and Review Engagements**[10]	60, 80, and 90
20	Feb. 2011	**Revised Applicability of Statements on Standards for Accounting and Review Services**[11]	

---

[7] SSARS No. 12 amends sections 200.25–.26 and adds section 200.27 (subsequent paragraphs and footnotes have been renumbered accordingly).

[8] SSARS No. 15 amends section 200.05, section 300.01, and section 400.09.

[9] SSARS No. 17 amends section 110.15; section 120.18; sections 200.01, .29, and .33; sections 300.01–.03; and section 400.01.

[10] SSARS No. 19 supersedes sections 20, 50, and 100.

[11] SSARS No. 20 amends section 90.01.

Sources of Sections in Current Text

AR Section	Contents	Source
60	Framework for Performing and Reporting on Compilation and Review Engagements	SSARS No. 19
80	Compilation of Financial Statements	SSARS No. 19
90	Review of Financial Statements	SSARS No. 19
110	Compilation of Specified Elements, Accounts, or Items of a Financial Statement	SSARS No. 13
120	Compilation of Pro Forma Financial Information	SSARS No. 14
200	Reporting on Comparative Financial Statements	SSARS No. 2
300	Compilation Reports on Financial Statements Included in Certain Prescribed Forms	SSARS No. 3
400	Communications Between Predecessor and Successor Accountants	SSARS No. 4
600	Reporting on Personal Financial Statements Included in Written Personal Financial Plans	SSARS No. 6

AR Section

STATEMENTS ON STANDARDS FOR ACCOUNTING AND REVIEW SERVICES

Statements on Standards for Accounting and Review Services (SSARS) are issued by the AICPA Accounting and Review Services Committee (ARSC), the senior technical committee of the AICPA designated to issue pronouncements in connection with the unaudited financial statements or other unaudited financial information of a nonpublic entity. Council has designated ARSC as a body to establish technical standards under Rule 202 of the AICPA's Code of Professional Conduct (ET sec. 202 par. 01).

Interpretations are issued to provide guidance on the application of SSARS. Interpretations are issued after all members of ARSC have been provided an opportunity to consider and comment on whether the proposed interpretation is consistent with SSARS. An interpretation is not as authoritative as a SSARS, but members should be aware that they may have to justify a departure from an interpretation if the quality of their work is questioned.

TABLE OF CONTENTS

Section		Paragraph
20	Defining Professional Requirements in Statements on Standards for Accounting and Review Services [Superseded, December 2010, by the issuance of SSARS No. 19.]	
50	Standards for Accounting and Review Services [Superseded, December 2010, by the issuance of SSARS No. 19.]	
60	Framework for Performing and Reporting on Compilation and Review Engagements	.01-.51
	Introduction	.01-.03
	Relevant Definitions	.04
	Objectives and Limitations of Compilation and Review Engagements	.05-.08
	Professional Requirements	.09-.14
	Requirements	.09-.11
	Explanatory Material	.12-.14
	Hierarchy of Compilation and Review Standards and Guidance	.15-.25
	Compilation and Review Standards	.15-.17

Contents

8

Table of Contents

Section		Paragraph
60	Framework for Performing and Reporting on Compilation and Review Engagements—continued	
	Interpretative Publications	.18-.19
	Other Compilation and Review Publications	.20-.21
	Ethical Principles and Quality Control Standards	.22-.25
	Elements of a Compilation or Review Engagement	.26-.47
	Three Party Relationship	.27-.36
	An Applicable Financial Reporting Framework	.37-.39
	Financial Statement or Financial Information	.40-.42
	Evidence	.43-.45
	Compilation and Review Reports	.46-.47
	Materiality	.48-.50
	Effective Date	.51
80	Compilation of Financial Statements	.01-.64
	Establishing an Understanding	.02-.05
	Compilation Performance Requirements	.06-.13
	Understanding of the Industry	.06-.07
	Knowledge of the Client	.08-.11
	Reading the Financial Statements	.12
	Other Compilation Procedures	.13
	Documentation in a Compilation Engagement	.14-.15
	Reporting on the Financial Statements	.16-.39
	Reporting on Financial Statements That Omit Substantially All Disclosures	.20
	Reporting When the Accountant Is Not Independent	.21
	Accountant's Communications With the Client When the Compiled Financial Statements Are Not Expected to Be Used by a Third Party	.22-.24
	Emphasis of a Matter	.25-.26
	Departures From the Applicable Financial Reporting Framework	.27-.29
	Restricting the Use of an Accountant's Compilation Report	.30-.39
	An Entity's Ability to Continue as a Going Concern	.40-.43
	Subsequent Events	.44-.46
	Subsequent Discovery of Facts Existing at the Date of the Report	.47-.52
	Supplementary Information	.53
	Communicating to Management and Others	.54-.55
	Change in Engagement From Audit or Review to Compilation	.56-.61
	Effective Date	.62
	Compilation Exhibit A—Illustrative Engagement Letters	.63
	Compilation Exhibit B—Illustrative Compilation Reports	.64

Contents

Table of Contents 9

Section		Paragraph
9080	Compilation of Financial Statements: Accounting and Review Services Interpretations of Section 80	
	1. Reporting When There Are Significant Departures From the Applicable Financial Reporting Framework (8/81) ...	.01-.04
	2. Reporting on Tax Returns (11/82)	.05-.06
	3. Additional Procedures Performed in a Compilation Engagement (3/83)	.07-.09
	4. Differentiating a Financial Statement Presentation From a Trial Balance (9/90)	.10-.12
	5. Submitting Draft Financial Statements (9/90)	.13-.14
	6. Reporting When Financial Statements Contain a Departure From Promulgated Accounting Principles That Prevents the Financial Statements From Being Misleading (2/91) ..	.15-.16
	7. Applicability of Statements on Standards for Accounting and Review Services to Litigation Services (5/91)	.17-.20
	8. Applicability of Statements on Standards for Accounting and Review Services When Performing Controllership or Other Management Services (7/02)	.21-.24
	9. Use of the Label "Selected Information—Substantially All Disclosures Required by [the applicable financial reporting framework] Are Not Included" in Compiled Financial Statements (12/02)	.25-.27
	10. Omission of the Display of Comprehensive Income in Compiled Financial Statements (9/03)	.28-.31
	11. Special-Purpose Financial Statements to Comply With Contractual Agreements or Regulatory Provisions (12/06)	.32-.40
	12. Reporting on an Uncertainty, Including an Uncertainty About an Entity's Ability to Continue as a Going Concern (2/07)	.41-.48
	13. Compilations of Financial Statements Prepared in Accordance With International Financial Reporting Standards (5/08)	.49-.52
	14. Compilations of Financial Statements Prepared in Accordance With a Financial Reporting Framework Generally Accepted in Another Country (5/08)	.53-.57
	15. Considerations Related to Compilations Performed in Accordance With International Standard on Related Services 4410, *Engagements to Compile Financial Statements,* Issued by the International Audit and Assurance Standards Board (5/08)	.58-.60
	16. Preparation of Financial Statements for Use by an Entity's Auditors (12/08)	.61-.62
	17. Required Supplementary Information That Accompanies Compiled Financial Statements (10/11)	.63-.68
90	Review of Financial Statements	.01-.73
	Establishing an Understanding	.03-.13
	Review Performance Requirements	.07
	Understanding of the Industry	.08-.09
	Knowledge of the Client	.10-.13

Contents

10 Table of Contents

Section		Paragraph

90 Review of Financial Statements—continued

Designing and Performing Review Procedures .... .14-.33
    Analytical Procedures .... .16-.18
    Inquiries and Other Review Procedures .... .19-.20
    Incorrect, Incomplete, or Otherwise Unsatisfactory
      Information .... .21
    Management Representations .... .22-.24
    Documentation in a Review Engagement .... .25-.26
    Reporting on the Financial Statements .... .27-.32
    Emphasis of a Matter .... .33
Departures From the Applicable Financial Reporting
  Framework .... .34-.53
    Restricting the Use of an Accountant Review Report ... .37-.44
    Limiting the Distribution of Reports .... .45-.46
    An Entity's Ability to Continue as a Going Concern .... .47-.50
    Subsequent Events .... .51-.53
Subsequent Discovery of Facts Existing at the Date
  of the Report .... .54-.59
Supplementary Information .... .60
Communicating to Management and Others .... .61-.62
Change in Engagement From Audit to Review .... .63-.68
Effective Date .... .69
Review Exhibit A—Illustrative Engagement Letter .... .70
Review Exhibit B—Illustrative Representation Letter .... .71
Review Exhibit C—Illustrative Updating Management
  Representation Letter .... .72
Review Exhibit D—Illustrative Review Reports .... .73

9090 Review of Financial Statements: Accounting and Review Services
Interpretations of Section 90

1. Reporting When There Are Significant Departures From
  the Applicable Financial Reporting Framework (8/81) ... .01-.04
2. Reporting on Tax Returns (11/82) .... .05-.06
3. Additional Procedures Performed in a Review
  Engagement (3/83) .... .07-.09
4. Submitting Draft Financial Statements (9/90) .... .10-.11
5. Reporting When Financial Statements Contain a Departure
  From Promulgated Accounting Principles That Prevents the
  Financial Statements From Being Misleading (2/91) ...... .12-.13
6. Special-Purpose Financial Statements to Comply With
  Contractual Agreements or Regulatory Provisions (11/06) .14-.22
7. Reporting on an Uncertainty, Including an Uncertainty About
  an Entity's Ability to Continue as a Going Concern (2/07) .23-.28
8. Reviews of Financial Statements Prepared in Accordance With
  International Financial Reporting Standards (5/08) .... .29-.32
9. Reviews of Financial Statements Prepared in Accordance With
  a Financial Reporting Framework Generally Accepted in
  Another Country (5/08) .... .33-.37

Contents

Table of Contents

11

Section		Paragraph

9090 Review of Financial Statements: Accounting and Review Services Interpretations of Section 90—continued

10. Considerations Related to Reviews Performed in Accordance with International Standard on Review Engagements 2400, *Engagements to Review Financial Statements*, Issued by the International Audit and Assurance Standards Board (12/08) .... .38-.40

11. Required Supplementary Information That Accompanies Reviewed Financial Statements (10/11) .... .41-.44

100 Compilation and Review of Financial Statements [Superseded, December 2010, by the issuance of SSARS No. 19.]

110 Compilation of Specified Elements, Accounts, or Items of a Financial Statement .01-.17

Conditions for Compiling Specified Elements, Accounts, or Items of a Financial Statement .... .04-.05

Understanding With the Entity .... .06-.07

Performance Requirements .... .08-.09

Documentation Requirements .... .10

Reporting Requirements .... .11-[.13]

Reporting When the Accountant Is Not Independent .... .14-.15

Exhibit A: Illustrative Engagement Letter for a Compilation of Specified Elements, Accounts, or Items of a Financial Statement .... .16

Exhibit B: Illustrative Compilation Reports on Specified Elements, Accounts, or Items of a Financial Statement .... .17

120 Compilation of Pro Forma Financial Information .01-.20

Conditions for Compiling Pro Forma Financial Information ... .06-.08

Understanding With the Entity .... .09-.10

Performance Requirements .... .11-.12

Documentation Requirements .... .13

Reporting Requirements .... .14-[.16]

Reporting When the Accountant Is Not Independent .... .17-.18

Exhibit A: Illustrative Engagement Letter for a Compilation of Pro Forma Financial Information .... .19

Exhibit B: Illustrative Compilation Report on Pro Forma Financial Information .... .20

200 Reporting on Comparative Financial Statements .01-.39

Definitions .... .07

Continuing Accountant's Standard Report .... .08-.12

Continuing Accountant's Changed Reference to a Departure From the Applicable Financial Reporting Framework ..... .13-.15

Predecessor's Compilation or Review Report .... .16-.27

Predecessor's Compilation or Review Report Not Presented .... .17-[.19]

Contents

12   **Table of Contents**

Section	*Paragraph*

200   Reporting on Comparative Financial Statements—continued
        Predecessor's Compilation or Review Report
            Reissued .... .20-.24
                Restated Prior-Period Financial Statements .... .25-[.27]
                Reporting When One Period Is Audited .... [.28]-.29
                Reporting on Financial Statements That Previously Did Not
                    Omit Substantially All Disclosures .... .30-[.33]
                Transition .... [.34-.36]
                Effective Date .... .37
                Exhibit A: Illustrative Compilation Reports on Comparative
                    Financial Statements .... .38
                Exhibit B: Illustrative Review Reports on Comparative
                    Financial Statements .... .39

9200   Reporting on Comparative Financial Statements: Accounting
        and Review Services Interpretations of Section 200
            1. Reporting on Financial Statements That Previously Did
                Not Omit Substantially All Disclosures (11/80) .... .01-.04

300   Compilation Reports on Financial Statements Included
        in Certain Prescribed Forms   .01-.06
            Exhibit: Illustrative Compilation Reports on Financial Statements
                Included in Certain Prescribed Forms .... .06

9300   Compilation Reports on Financial Statements Included in Certain
        Prescribed Forms: Accounting and Review Services
        Interpretations of Section 300
            1. Omission of Disclosures in Financial Statements Included
                in Certain Prescribed Forms (5/82) .... .01-.03

400   Communications Between Predecessor and Successor Accountants   .01-.12
            Inquiries Regarding Acceptance of an Engagement .... .03-.06
            Other Inquiries .... [.07]-.08
            Successor Accountant's Use of Communications .... .09
            Financial Statements Reported on by
                Predecessor Accountant .... .10-.11
            Exhibit: Illustrative Successor Accountant
                Acknowledgment Letter .... .12

9400   Communications Between Predecessor and Successor Accountants:
        Accounting and Review Services Interpretations
        of Section 400
            1. Reports on the Application of Accounting Principles
                (8/87) .... .01-.05

500   Reporting on Compiled Financial Statements [Deleted by the
        issuance of Statement on Standards for Accounting and
        Review Services No. 7, November 1992.]

Contents

Table of Contents **13**

Section		Paragraph

600 Reporting on Personal Financial Statements Included in Written
Personal Financial Plans .01-.08

    Effective Date .... .07

    Exhibit: Illustrative Report When the Accountant Submits a
Written Financial Plan Containing Unaudited Personal
Financial Statements That the Accountant Did Not
Compile .... .08

9600 Reporting on Personal Financial Statements Included in Written
Personal Financial Plans: Accounting and Review
Services Interpretation of Section 600

    1. Submitting a Personal Financial Plan to a Client's
Advisers (5/91) .... .01-.03

Contents

AR Section 20

Defining Professional Requirements in Statements on Standards for Accounting and Review Services

Superseded, December 2010, by the issuance of SSARS No. 19.

AR Section 50
Standards for Accounting and Review Services

Superseded, December 2010, by the issuance of SSARS No. 19.

Compilation and Review Engagements

19

AR Section 60

Framework for Performing and Reporting on Compilation and Review Engagements

Issue date, unless otherwise indicated: December 2009

Source: SSARS No. 19

> *Note:* Paragraphs 1.1–.51 of SSARS No. 19, issued in December 2009, have been codified in this section and are effective for compilations and reviews of financial statements for periods ending on or after December 15, 2010.

Introduction

.01 This section provides a framework and defines and describes the objectives and elements of compilation and review engagements. This section also sets forth the meaning of certain terms used in Statements on Standards for Accounting and Review Services (SSARSs) issued by the Accounting and Review Services Committee (ARSC) in describing the professional requirements imposed on accountants performing compilation and review engagements.

.02 The following is an overview of this section:

- "Relevant Definitions." This section defines various terms used throughout SSARSs.

- "Objectives and Limitations of Compilation and Review Engagements." This section sets forth the objectives and limitations of compilation and review engagements and identifies the differences between each engagement.

- "Professional Requirements." This section sets forth the meaning of certain terms used in SSARSs in describing the professional requirements imposed on accountants performing a compilation or review engagement.

- "Hierarchy of Compilation and Review Standards and Guidance." This section sets forth the hierarchy of SSARSs literature.

- "Elements of a Compilation or Review Engagement." This section identifies and discusses five engagement elements: a three party relationship involving management, an accountant, and intended users; an applicable financial reporting framework; financial statements; evidence (in a review engagement); and a written communication or report. It explains important distinctions between compilation engagements in which the accountant obtains no assurance and review engagements that are designed to obtain limited assurance.

- "Materiality." This section discusses the concept of materiality in the context of the preparation and presentation of financial statements.

AR §60.02

20   Statements on Standards for Accounting and Review Services

.03 This section is intended to help accountants better understand their professional responsibilities when engaged to compile or review financial statements or financial information. Additional standards of SSARSs have been established to set forth specific performance and reporting requirements. Such additional standards are based on the framework provided by this standard, and any requirements created by this standard also have been incorporated into the additional standards of SSARSs.

Relevant Definitions

.04 Terms defined for purposes of SSARSs are as follows:

Applicable financial reporting framework. The financial reporting framework adopted by management and, when appropriate, those charged with governance in the preparation of the financial statements that is acceptable in view of the nature of the entity and the objective of the financial statements, or that is required by law or regulation.

Assurance engagement. An engagement in which an accountant issues a report designed to enhance the degree of confidence of third parties and management about the outcome of an evaluation or measurement of financial statements (subject matter) against an applicable financial reporting framework (criteria).

Attest engagement. An engagement that requires independence, as defined in AICPA *Professional Standards*.

Financial reporting framework. A set of criteria used to determine measurement, recognition, presentation, and disclosure of all material items appearing in the financial statements.

Financial statements. A structured representation of historical financial information, including related notes, intended to communicate an entity's economic resources and obligations at a point in time or the changes therein for a period of time in accordance with a financial reporting framework. The related notes ordinarily comprise a summary of significant accounting policies and other explanatory information. The term *financial statements* ordinarily refers to a complete set of financial statements as determined by the requirements of the applicable financial reporting framework, but can also refer to a single financial statement or financial statements without notes.

Management. The person(s) with executive responsibility for the conduct of the entity's operations. For some entities, management includes some or all of those charged with governance (for example, executive members of a governance board or an owner-manager).

Nonissuer. All entities except for those defined in Section 3 of the Securities Exchange Act of 1934 [15 U.S.C. 78c], the securities of which are registered under Section 12 of that Act (15 U.S.C. 78l), or that is required to file reports under Section 15(d) (15 U.S.C. 78o(d)), or that files or has filed a registration statement that has not yet become effective under the Securities Act of 1933 (15 U.S.C. 77a et seq.), and that it has not withdrawn..

Other comprehensive basis of accounting (OCBOA). A definite set of criteria, other than accounting principles generally accepted in the United States of America or International Financial Reporting Standards (IFRSs), having substantial support underlying the preparation of financial statements prepared pursuant to that basis.

AR §60.03

Compilation and Review Engagements

Examples of an OCBOA are as follows:

a. A basis of accounting that the reporting entity uses to comply with the requirements or financial reporting provisions of a governmental regulatory agency to whose jurisdiction the entity is subject (for example, a basis of accounting that insurance companies use pursuant to the rules of a state insurance commission).

b. A basis of accounting that the reporting entity uses or expects to use to file its income tax return for the period covered by the financial statements.

c. The cash basis of accounting and modifications of the cash basis having substantial support (for example, recording depreciation on fixed assets). Ordinarily, a modification would have substantial support if the method is equivalent to the accrual basis of accounting for that item and if the method is not illogical.

Review evidence. Information used by the accountant to provide a reasonable basis for the obtaining of limited assurance.

Submission of financial statements. Presenting to management financial statements that an accountant has prepared.

Third party. All persons, including those charged with governance, except for members of management.

Those charged with governance. The person(s) with responsibility for overseeing the strategic direction of the entity and obligations related to the accountability of the entity. This includes overseeing the financial reporting process. Those charged with governance are specifically excluded from management, unless they perform management functions.

Objectives and Limitations of Compilation and Review Engagements

.05 A compilation is a service, the objective of which is to assist management in presenting financial information in the form of financial statements[1] without undertaking to obtain or provide any assurance that there are no material modifications that should be made to the financial statements in order for the statements to be in conformity with the applicable financial reporting framework. Although a compilation is not an assurance engagement, it is an attest engagement.

.06 A compilation differs significantly from a review or an audit of financial statements. A compilation does not contemplate performing inquiry, analytical procedures, or other procedures performed in a review. Additionally, a compilation does not contemplate obtaining an understanding of the entity's internal control; assessing fraud risk; testing accounting records by obtaining sufficient appropriate audit evidence through inspection, observation, confirmation, or the examination of source documents (for example, cancelled checks or bank images); or other procedures ordinarily performed in an audit. Therefore, a compilation does not provide a basis for obtaining or providing any assurance regarding the financial statements.

---

[1] For purposes of the Statements on Standards for Accounting and Review Services (SSARSs), with respect to compilation engagements, references to "financial statements" include, when applicable, other specified elements, accounts, or items of a financial statement and pro forma financial information.

AR §60.06

22　Statements on Standards for Accounting and Review Services

.07 A review is a service, the objective of which is to obtain limited assurance that there are no material modifications that should be made to the financial statements in order for the statements to be in conformity with the applicable financial reporting framework. In a review engagement, the accountant should accumulate review evidence to obtain a limited level of assurance. A review engagement is an assurance engagement as well as an attest engagement.

.08 A review differs significantly from an audit of financial statements in which the auditor obtains a high level of assurance (expressed in the auditor's report as obtaining reasonable assurance) that the financial statements are free of material misstatement. A review does not contemplate obtaining an understanding of the entity's internal control; assessing fraud risk; testing accounting records by obtaining sufficient appropriate audit evidence through inspection, observation, confirmation, or the examination of source documents (for example, cancelled checks or bank images); or other procedures ordinarily performed in an audit. Accordingly, in a review, the accountant does not obtain assurance that he or she will become aware of all significant matters that would be disclosed in an audit. Therefore, a review is designed to obtain only limited assurance that there are no material modifications that should be made to the financial statements in order for the statements to be in conformity with the applicable financial reporting framework.

Professional Requirements

Requirements

.09 SSARSs contain professional requirements, together with related guidance, in the form of explanatory material. Accountants performing a compilation or review have a responsibility to consider the entire text of a SSARS in carrying out their work on an engagement and in understanding and applying the professional requirements of the relevant SSARSs.

.10 Not every paragraph of a SSARS carries a professional requirement that the accountant is expected to fulfill. Rather, the professional requirements are communicated by the language and the meaning of the words used in SSARSs.

.11 SSARSs use two categories of professional requirements identified by specific terms to describe the degree of responsibility they impose on accountants. They are as follows:

- *Unconditional requirements.* The accountant is required to comply with an unconditional requirement in all cases in which the circumstances exist to which the unconditional requirement applies. SSARSs use the words *must* or *is required* to indicate an unconditional requirement.

- *Presumptively mandatory requirements.* The accountant also is required to comply with a presumptively mandatory requirement in all cases in which the circumstances exist to which the presumptively mandatory requirement applies; however, in rare circumstances, the accountant may depart from a presumptively mandatory requirement provided that the accountant documents his or her justification for the departure and how the alternative procedures performed in the circumstances were sufficient to achieve the objectives of the presumptively mandatory requirement.

AR §60.07

Compilation and Review Engagements

SSARSs use the word *should* to indicate a presumptively mandatory requirement.

If a SSARS provides that a procedure or action is one that the accountant "should consider," the consideration of the procedure or action is presumptively required, whereas carrying out the procedure or action is not. The professional requirements of a SSARS are to be understood and applied in the context of the explanatory material that provides guidance for their application. The specific terms used to define professional requirements are not intended to apply to interpretative publications issued under the authority of the ARSC because interpretative publications are not SSARSs.

Explanatory Material

.12 *Explanatory material* is defined as the text within a SSARS (excluding any related appendixes or interpretations) that may do the following:

- Provide further explanation and guidance on the professional requirements
- Identify and describe other procedures or actions relating to the activities of the accountant

.13 Explanatory material that provides further explanation and guidance on the professional requirements is intended to be descriptive rather than imperative. That is, it explains the objective of the professional requirements (when not otherwise self-evident); it explains why the accountant might consider or employ particular procedures, depending on the circumstances; and it provides additional information for the accountant to consider in exercising professional judgment in performing the engagement.

.14 Explanatory material that identifies and describes other procedures or actions relating to the activities of the accountant is not intended to impose a professional requirement for the accountant to perform the suggested procedures or actions. Rather, these procedures or actions require the accountant's attention and understanding; how and whether the accountant carries out such procedures or actions in the engagement depends on the exercise of professional judgment in the circumstances consistent with the objective of the standard. The words *may*, *might*, and *could* are used to describe these actions and procedures.

Hierarchy of Compilation and Review Standards and Guidance

Compilation and Review Standards

.15 An accountant must perform a compilation or review engagement of a nonissuer in accordance with SSARSs, except for certain reviews of interim financial information as discussed in paragraph .01 of section 90. SSARSs provide a measure of quality and the objectives to be achieved in both a compilation and review engagement.

.16 Rule 202, *Compliance With Standards* (ET sec. 202 par. .01), requires an AICPA member who performs compilations or reviews to comply with standards promulgated by the ARSC. The ARSC develops and issues standards in the form of SSARSs through a due process that includes deliberations in meetings open to the public, public exposure of proposed SSARSs, and a formal vote. Finalized SSARSs are codified.

AR §60.16

24 Statements on Standards for Accounting and Review Services

.17 The nature of SSARSs requires an accountant to exercise professional judgment in applying them.

Interpretative Publications

.18 Interpretative publications consist of compilation and review interpretations of SSARSs; appendixes to SSARSs; compilation and review guidance included in AICPA Audit and Accounting Guides; and AICPA Statements of Position, to the extent that those statements are applicable to compilation and review engagements. Interpretative publications are not standards for accounting and review services. Interpretative publications are recommendations on the application of SSARSs in specific circumstances, including engagements for entities in specialized industries. An interpretative publication is issued under the authority of the ARSC after all ARSC members have been provided an opportunity to consider and comment on whether the proposed interpretative publication is consistent with SSARSs.

.19 The accountant should be aware of and consider interpretative publications applicable to his or her compilation or review. If the accountant does not apply the guidance included in an applicable interpretative publication, the accountant should be prepared to explain how he or she complied with the provisions of SSARSs addressed by such guidance.

Other Compilation and Review Publications

.20 Other compilation and review publications include AICPA accounting and review publications not referred to previously; the AICPA's annual *Compilation and Review Alert*; compilation and review articles in the *Journal of Accountancy* and other professional journals; compilation and review articles in the AICPA's *The CPA Letter*; continuing professional education programs and other instructional materials, textbooks, guide books, compilation and review programs, and checklists; and other compilation and review publications from state CPA societies, other organizations, and individuals. Other compilation and review publications have no authoritative status; however, they may help the accountant understand and apply SSARSs. An accountant is not expected to be aware of the full body of other compilation and review publications.

.21 If an accountant applies the guidance included in an other compilation and review publication, he or she should be satisfied that, in his or her judgment, it is both relevant to the circumstances of the engagement and appropriate. In determining whether an other compilation and review publication that has not been reviewed by the AICPA Audit and Attest Standards staff is appropriate, the accountant may wish to consider the degree to which the publication is recognized as being helpful in understanding and applying SSARSs and the degree to which the issuer or author is recognized as an authority in compilation and review matters. Other compilation and review publications published by the AICPA that have been reviewed by the AICPA Audit and Attest Standards staff are presumed to be appropriate.

Ethical Principles and Quality Control Standards

.22 In addition to SSARSs, AICPA members who perform compilation and review engagements are governed by

a.   the AICPA's Code of Professional Conduct (code), which expresses the profession's recognition of its responsibilities to the public, to clients, and to colleagues. The principles of the code guide

AR §60.17

Compilation and Review Engagements

members in the performance of their professional responsibilities and express the basic tenets of ethical and professional conduct. The principles call for an unswerving commitment to honorable behavior, even at the sacrifice of personal advantage.

b.   Statements on Quality Control Standards (SQCSs), which establish standards and provide guidance on a firm's system of quality control.

.23 The code sets out the fundamental ethical principles that all AICPA members are required to observe. When performing a compilation or review engagement, the code requires an accountant to maintain objectivity and integrity and comply with all other applicable provisions.

.24 An accountant has the responsibility to adopt a system of quality control in conducting an accounting practice. Thus, a firm should establish quality control policies and procedures to provide reasonable assurance that personnel comply with SSARSs in compilation and review engagements. The nature and extent of a firm's quality control policies and procedures depend on factors such as its size, the degree of operating autonomy allowed its personnel and its practice offices, the nature of its practice, its organization, and appropriate cost-benefit considerations.

.25 SSARSs relate to the conduct of individual compilation and review engagements; SQCSs relate to the conduct of a firm's accounting practice. Thus, SSARSs and SQCSs are related, and the quality control policies and procedures that a firm adopts may affect both the conduct of an individual engagement and the firm's accounting practice as a whole. However, deficiencies in, or instances of noncompliance with, a firm's quality control policies and procedures do not, in and of themselves, indicate that a particular review or compilation engagement was not performed in accordance with SSARSs.

Elements of a Compilation or Review Engagement

.26 The following elements of a compilation and review engagement are discussed in this section:

a.   A three party relationship involving management, an accountant, and intended users

b.   An applicable financial reporting framework

c.   Financial statements or financial information

d.   In a review, sufficient appropriate review evidence

e.   A written communication or report

Three Party Relationship

.27 A compilation or review engagement involves three parties: management (or the responsible party); an accountant in the practice of public accounting, as defined by the AICPA code; and intended users of the financial statements or financial information.

.28 In some cases, management and the intended users may be the same. Intended users may be from different entities (for example, a banker or potential investor) or the same entity.

.29 If an accountant is not in the practice of public accounting, the issuance of a written communication or report under SSARSs would be inappropriate.

AR §60.29

Statements on Standards for Accounting and Review Services

Management (Responsible Party)

.30 Management responsibilities include taking responsibility for the preparation and fair presentation of the financial statements in accordance with the applicable financial reporting framework and taking responsibility for designing, implementing, and maintaining internal control.[2]

.31 A basic premise underlying the performance of a compilation or review engagement is that the accountant is performing an attest service on subject matter that is the responsibility of the client's management. Therefore, an accountant is precluded from issuing an unmodified compilation report or a review report on financial statements when management is unwilling to accept responsibility for the preparation and fair presentation of the financial statements in accordance with the applicable financial reporting framework or to take responsibility for the design, implementation, and maintenance of internal control.

.32 As part of their responsibility for the preparation and presentation of the financial statements, management and, when appropriate, those charged with governance, are responsible for the identification of the applicable financial reporting framework and the preparation and presentation of the financial statements in accordance with that framework.

.33 During the performance of a compilation or review engagement, the accountant may make suggestions about the form or content of the financial statements or prepare them, in whole or in part, based on information that is the representation of management.

Accountant in the Practice of Public Accounting

.34 The accountant should possess a level of knowledge of the accounting principles and practices of the industry in which the entity operates that will enable him or her to compile or review financial statements that are appropriate in form for an entity operating in that industry. As addressed in the firm's quality control system, an accountant should not accept an engagement if preliminary knowledge of the engagement circumstances indicates that ethical requirements regarding professional competence will not be satisfied. In some cases, this requirement can be satisfied by the accountant using the work of persons from other professional disciplines, referred to as *experts*. In such cases, the accountant should be satisfied that those persons carrying out aspects of the engagement possess the requisite skills and knowledge and that the accountant has an adequate level of involvement in the engagement and understanding of the work for which any expert is used.

---

[2] The Committee of Sponsoring Organizations of the Treadway Commission defines *internal control* as a process effected by management (or those charged with governance and other personnel) designed to provide reasonable assurance about the achievement of the entity's objectives. Internal control consists of five interrelated components:

1. Control environment sets the tone of an organization, influencing the control consciousness of its people. It is the foundation for all other components of internal control, providing discipline and structure.
2. Entity's risk assessment is the entity's identification and analysis of relevant risks to achievement of its objectives, forming a basis for determining how the risks should be managed.
3. Information and communication systems support the identification, capture, and exchange of information in a form and time frame that enables people to carry out their responsibilities.
4. Control activities are the policies and procedures that help ensure that management directives are carried out.
5. Monitoring is a process that assesses the quality of internal control performance over time.

AR §60.30

Compilation and Review Engagements

Intended Users of the Financial Statements or Financial Information

.35 The intended users are the person(s) or class of persons who understand the limitations of the compilation or review engagement and financial statements. The accountant has no responsibility to identify the intended users.

.36 In some cases, intended users (for example, bankers and regulators) may impose a requirement on or request the client to arrange for additional procedures to be performed for a specific purpose. For example, a banker may request that certain agreed-upon procedures be performed with respect to the entity's accounts receivable in addition to the financial statements being compiled. An accountant may perform additional services in conjunction with the compilation or review, as long as he or she adheres to professional standards with respect to those additional services.

An Applicable Financial Reporting Framework

.37 Management and, when applicable, those charged with governance are responsible for the selection of the entity's applicable financial reporting framework, as well as individual accounting policies when the financial reporting framework contains acceptable alternatives. The financial reporting framework encompasses financial accounting standards established by an authorized or recognized standards setting organization.

.38 The requirements of the applicable financial reporting framework determine the form and content of the financial statements. Although the framework may not specify how to account for or disclose all transactions or events, it ordinarily embodies sufficiently broad principles that can serve as a basis for developing and applying accounting policies that are consistent with the concepts underlying the requirements of the framework.

.39 Examples of financial reporting frameworks include accounting principles generally accepted in the United States of America, as promulgated by the Financial Accounting Standards Board, the Governmental Accounting Standards Board, or the Federal Accounting Standards Advisory Board; IFRSs issued by the International Accounting Standards Board; and OCBOA.

Financial Statement or Financial Information

.40 An accountant may be engaged to compile or review a complete set of financial statements or an individual financial statement (for example, balance sheet only). The financial statements may be for an annual period or for a shorter or longer period, depending on management's needs.

.41 The requirements of the applicable financial reporting framework determine what constitutes a complete set of financial statements. In the case of many frameworks, financial statements are intended to provide information about the financial position, financial performance, and cash flows of an entity. For example, a complete set of financial statements might include a balance sheet, an income statement, a statement of retained earnings, a cash flow statement, and related notes. For some other financial reporting frameworks, a single financial statement and the related notes might constitute a complete set of financial statements.

.42 The preparation of the financial statements requires management to exercise judgment in making accounting estimates that are reasonable in the circumstances, as well as to select and apply appropriate accounting policies. These judgments are made in the context of the applicable financial reporting framework.

AR §60.42

28 Statements on Standards for Accounting and Review Services

Evidence

.43 When performing a compilation engagement, the accountant has no responsibility to obtain any evidence about the accuracy or completeness of the financial statements. As a result, a compilation does not provide a basis for obtaining any level of assurance on the financial statements being compiled.

.44 When performing a review engagement, the accountant should perform procedures designed to accumulate review evidence that will provide a reasonable basis for obtaining limited assurance that there are no material modifications that should be made to the financial statements in order for the statements to be in conformity with the applicable financial reporting framework. The accountant should apply professional judgment in determining the specific nature, timing, and extent of review procedures. Such procedures should be tailored based on the accountant's understanding of the industry in which the client operates and the accountant's knowledge of the entity. The nature, timing, and extent of procedures for gathering review evidence are deliberately limited relative to an audit.

.45 Review evidence obtained through the performance of analytical procedures and inquiries ordinarily will provide the accountant with a reasonable basis for obtaining limited assurance.

Compilation and Review Reports

.46 If the accountant performs a compilation, a report or written communication is required unless the accountant withdraws from the engagement.[3] If the accountant is not independent, he or she may issue a compilation report, provided that the accountant complies with the compilation standards. In making a judgment about whether he or she is independent, the accountant should be guided by the AICPA's Code of Professional Conduct.

.47 If the accountant performs a review, a written review report is required unless the accountant withdraws from the engagement.

Materiality

.48 Financial reporting frameworks often discuss the concept of materiality in the context of the preparation and presentation of financial statements. Although financial reporting frameworks may discuss materiality in different terms, they generally explain that

- misstatements, including omissions, are considered to be material if they, individually or in the aggregate, could reasonably be expected to influence the economic decisions of users taken on the basis of the financial statements;

- judgments about materiality are made in light of surrounding circumstances and are affected by the size or nature of a misstatement or a combination of both; and

- judgments about matters that are material to users of the financial statements are based on a consideration of the common financial

---

[3] As further described in paragraphs .22–.24 of section 80, an accountant may be associated with the submission of financial statements not expected to be used by a third party. Such service does not require the accountant to issue a report on the financial statements.

AR §60.43

Compilation and Review Engagements

information needs of users as a group. The possible effect of misstatements on specific individual users, whose needs may vary widely, is not considered.

.49 Such a discussion, if present in the applicable financial reporting framework, provides a frame of reference to the accountant in determining whether there are any material modifications that should be made to the financial statements in order for the statements to be in conformity with the applicable financial reporting framework. If the applicable financial reporting framework does not include a discussion of the concept of materiality, the characteristics referred to in paragraph .48 provide the accountant with such a frame of reference.

.50 The accountant's determination of materiality is a matter of professional judgment and is affected by the accountant's perception of the financial information needs of users of the financial statements. In this context, it is reasonable for the accountant to assume that users

    a.   have a reasonable knowledge of business and economic activities and accounting and a willingness to study the information in the financial statements with reasonable diligence;

    b.   understand that financial statements are prepared, presented, and reviewed to levels of materiality;

    c.   recognize the uncertainties inherent in the measurement of amounts based on the use of estimates, judgment, and the consideration of future events; and

    d.   make reasonable economic decisions on the basis of the information in the financial statements.

Effective Date

.51 This section is effective for compilations and reviews of financial statements for periods ending on or after December 15, 2010.

AR §60.51

AR Section 80

Compilation of Financial Statements

Issue date, unless otherwise indicated: December 2009

Source: SSARS No. 19

> *Note:* Paragraphs 2.1–.64 of SSARS No. 19, issued in December 2009, have been codified in this section and are effective for compilations and reviews of financial statements for periods ending on or after December 15, 2010. Early implementation of the requirements and guidance in paragraph 2.21 (par. .21) is permitted.

.01 This section establishes standards and provides guidance on compilations of financial statements. The accountant is required to comply with the provisions of this section whenever he or she is engaged to report on compiled financial statements or submits financial statements to a client or to third parties.

Establishing an Understanding

.02 The accountant should establish an understanding with management regarding the services to be performed for compilation engagements[1] and should document the understanding through a written communication with management. Such an understanding reduces the risks that either the accountant or management may misinterpret the needs or expectations of the other party. For example, it reduces the risk that management may inappropriately rely on the accountant to protect the entity against certain risks or to perform certain functions that are management's responsibility. The accountant should ensure that the understanding includes the objectives of the engagement, management's responsibilities, the accountant's responsibilities, and the limitations of the engagement. In some cases, the accountant may establish such understanding with those charged with governance.

.03 An understanding with management and, if applicable, those charged with governance, regarding a compilation of financial statements should include the following matters:

- The objective of a compilation is to assist management in presenting financial information in the form of financial statements.

- The accountant utilizes information that is the representation of management (owners) without undertaking to obtain or provide any assurance that there are no material modifications that should be made to the financial statements in order for the statements to be in conformity with the applicable financial reporting framework.

- Management is responsible for the preparation and fair presentation of the financial statements in accordance with the applicable financial reporting framework.

---

[1] See paragraph .28 of QC section 10B, *A Firm's System of Quality Control.*

AR §80.03

32 Statements on Standards for Accounting and Review Services

- Management is responsible for designing, implementing, and maintaining internal control relevant to the preparation and fair presentation of the financial statements.

- Management is responsible to prevent and detect fraud.

- Management is responsible for identifying and ensuring that the entity complies with the laws and regulations applicable to its activities.

- Management is responsible for making all financial records and related information available to the accountant.

- The accountant is responsible for conducting the engagement in accordance with SSARSs issued by the AICPA.

- A compilation differs significantly from a review or an audit of financial statements. A compilation does not contemplate performing inquiry, analytical procedures, or other procedures performed in a review. Additionally, a compilation does not contemplate obtaining an understanding of the entity's internal control; assessing fraud risk; testing accounting records by obtaining sufficient appropriate audit evidence through inspection, observation, confirmation, or the examination of source documents (for example, cancelled checks or bank images); or other procedures ordinarily performed in an audit. Accordingly, the accountant will not express an opinion or provide any assurance regarding the financial statements.

- The engagement cannot be relied upon to disclose errors, fraud,[2] or illegal acts.[3]

- The accountant will inform the appropriate level of management of any material errors and of any evidence or information that comes to the accountant's attention during the performance of compilation procedures that fraud or an illegal act may have occurred.[4] The accountant need not report any matters regarding illegal acts that may have occurred that are clearly inconsequential and may reach agreement in advance with the entity on the nature of any such matters to be communicated.

- The effect of any independence impairments on the expected form of the accountant's compilation report, if applicable.

These matters should be communicated in the form of an engagement letter. Examples of engagement letters for a compilation of financial statements are presented in Compilation Exhibit A, "Illustrative Engagement Letters."

---

[2] For purposes of the SSARSs, *fraud* is an intentional act that results in a misstatement in compiled financial statements

[3] For purposes of the SSARSs, *illegal acts* are violations of laws or government regulations, excluding fraud.

[4] Whether an act is, in fact, fraudulent or illegal is a determination that is normally beyond the accountant's professional competence. An accountant, in reporting on financial statements, presents himself or herself as one who is proficient in accounting and compilation services. The accountant's training, experience, and understanding of the client and its industry may provide a basis for recognition that some client acts coming to his or her attention may be fraudulent or illegal. However, the determination about whether a particular act is fraudulent or illegal would generally be based on the advice of an informed expert qualified to practice law or may have to await final determination by a court of law.

AR §80.03

Compilation of Financial Statements **33**

.04 An understanding with management or, if applicable, those charged with governance, also may include other matters, such as the following:

- Fees and billings

- Any limitation of or other arrangements regarding the liability of the accountant or the client, such as indemnification to the accountant for liability arising from knowing misrepresentations to the accountant by management (regulators may restrict or prohibit such liability limitation arrangements)

- Conditions under which access to compilation documentation may be granted to others

- Additional services to be provided relating to regulatory requirements

.05 If the compiled financial statements are not expected to be used by a third party and the accountant does not expect to issue a compilation report on the financial statements, the accountant should include in the engagement letter an acknowledgment of management's representation and agreement that the financial statements are not to be used by a third party. The engagement letter also should address the following additional matters if applicable:

- Material departures from the applicable financial reporting framework may exist, and the effects of those departures, if any, on the financial statements may not be disclosed.

- Substantially all disclosures (and statement of cash flows, if applicable) required by the applicable financial reporting framework may be omitted.

- Reference to supplementary information.

Compilation Performance Requirements

Understanding of the Industry

.06 The accountant should possess an understanding of the industry in which the client operates, including the accounting principles and practices generally used in the industry sufficient to enable the accountant to compile financial statements that are appropriate in form for an entity operating in that industry.

.07 The requirement that the accountant possess a level of knowledge of the industry in which the client operates does not prevent the accountant from accepting a compilation engagement for an entity in an industry with which the accountant has no previous experience. It does, however, place upon the accountant a responsibility to obtain the required level of knowledge. The accountant may do so, for example, by consulting AICPA guides, industry publications, financial statements of other entities in the industry, textbooks and periodicals, appropriate continuing professional education, or individuals knowledgeable about the industry.

Knowledge of the Client

.08 The accountant should obtain knowledge about the client, including

- an understanding of the client's business and

- an understanding of the accounting principles and practices used by the client.

AR §80.08

34 Statements on Standards for Accounting and Review Services

.09 In obtaining an understanding of the client's business, the accountant should have a general understanding of the client's organization; its operating characteristics; and the nature of its assets, liabilities, revenues, and expenses. The accountant's understanding of the entity's business is ordinarily obtained through experience with the entity or its industry and inquiry of the entity's personnel.

.10 The accountant should obtain an understanding of the accounting principles and practices used by the client in measuring, recognizing, recording, and disclosing all significant accounts and disclosures in the financial statements. The accountant's understanding also may include matters such as changes in accounting practices and principles and differences in the client's business model as compared with normal practices within the industry.

.11 In obtaining this understanding of the client's accounting policies and practices, the accountant should be alert to unusual accounting policies and procedures that come to the accountant's attention as a result of his or her knowledge of the industry.

Reading the Financial Statements

.12 Before submission, the accountant should read the financial statements and consider whether such financial statements appear to be appropriate in form and free from obvious material errors. In this context, the term *error* refers to mistakes in the preparation of financial statements, including arithmetical or clerical mistakes, and mistakes in the application of accounting principles, including inadequate disclosure.

Other Compilation Procedures

.13 The accountant is not required to make inquiries or perform other procedures to verify, corroborate, or review information supplied by the entity. However, the accountant may have made inquiries or performed other procedures. The results of such inquiries or procedures, knowledge gained from prior engagements, or the financial statements on their face may cause the accountant to become aware that information supplied by the entity is incorrect, incomplete, or otherwise unsatisfactory or that fraud or an illegal act may have occurred. The accountant should request that management consider the effect of these matters on the financial statements and communicate the results of such consideration to the accountant. Additionally, the accountant should consider the effect of management's conclusions regarding these matters on the accountant's compilation report. In circumstances when the accountant believes that the financial statements may be materially misstated, the accountant should obtain additional or revised information. If the entity refuses to provide additional or revised information, the accountant should withdraw from the engagement.

Documentation in a Compilation Engagement

.14 The accountant should prepare documentation in connection with each compilation engagement in sufficient detail to provide a clear understanding of the work performed. Documentation provides the principal support for the representation in the accountant's compilation report that the accountant performed the compilation in accordance with SSARSs.

The accountant is not precluded from supporting the compilation report by other means in addition to the compilation documentation. Such other means

AR §80.09

Compilation of Financial Statements   **35**

might include written documentation contained in other engagement files or quality control files (for example, consultation files) and, in limited situations, oral explanations.

.15 The form, content, and extent of documentation depend on the circumstances of the engagement, the methodology and tools used, and the accountant's professional judgment. The accountant's documentation should include the following:

- *a.* The engagement letter documenting the understanding with the client

- *b.* Any findings or issues that, in the accountant's judgment, are significant (for example, the results of compilation procedures that indicate that the financial statements could be materially misstated, including actions taken to address such findings and, to the extent that the accountant had any questions or concerns as a result of his or her compilation procedures, how those issues were resolved)

- *c.* Communications, whether oral or written, to the appropriate level of management regarding fraud or illegal acts that come to the accountant's attention

Reporting on the Financial Statements

.16 When the accountant is engaged to report on compiled financial statements or submits financial statements that are reasonably expected to be used by a third party, the financial statements should be accompanied by a written report. The accountant's objective in reporting on the financial statements is to prevent misinterpretation of the degree of responsibility the accountant is assuming when his or her name is associated with the financial statements.

.17 The basic elements of the report are as follows:

- *a.* *Title.* The accountant's compilation report should have a title that clearly indicates that it is the accountant's compilation report. The accountant may indicate that he or she is independent in the title, if applicable. Appropriate titles would be "Accountant's Compilation Report" or "Independent Accountant's Compilation Report."

- *b.* *Addressee.* The accountant's report should be addressed as appropriate in the circumstances of the engagement.

- *c.* *Introductory paragraph.* The introductory paragraph in the accountant's report should

  - i. identify the entity whose financial statements have been compiled;
  - ii. state that the financial statements have been compiled;
  - iii. identify the financial statements that have been compiled;
  - iv. specify the date or period covered by the financial statements; and
  - v. include a statement that the accountant has not audited or reviewed the financial statements and, accordingly, does not express an opinion or provide any assurance about whether the financial statements are in accordance with the applicable financial reporting framework

AR §80.17

36   Statements on Standards for Accounting and Review Services

      d.   *Management's responsibility for the financial statements and for internal control over financial reporting.* A statement that management (owners) is (are) responsible for the preparation and fair presentation of the financial statements in accordance with the applicable financial reporting framework and for designing, implementing, and maintaining internal control relevant to the preparation and fair presentation of the financial statements.

      e.   *Accountant's responsibility.* A statement that the accountant's responsibility is to conduct the compilation in accordance with SSARSs issued by the AICPA.

         A statement that the objective of a compilation is to assist management in presenting financial information in the form of financial statements without undertaking to obtain or provide any assurance that there are no material modifications that should be made to the financial statements.

      f.   *Signature of the accountant.* The manual or printed signature of the accounting firm or the accountant, as appropriate.

      g.   *Date of the accountant's report.* The date of the compilation report (the date of completion of the compilation should be used as the date of the accountant's report).

Procedures that the accountant might have performed as part of the compilation engagement should not be described in the report.

See Compilation Exhibit B, "Illustrative Compilation Reports," for illustrative compilation reports.

.18 Each page of the financial statements compiled by the accountant should include a reference, such as "See accountant's compilation report" or "See independent accountant's compilation report."

.19 Financial statements prepared in accordance with an OCBOA are not considered appropriate in form unless the financial statements include:

      a.   a description of the OCBOA, including a summary of significant accounting policies and a description of the primary differences from generally accepted accounting principles (GAAP). The effects of the differences need not be quantified.

      b.   informative disclosures similar to those required by GAAP if the financial statements contain items that are the same as, or similar to, those in financial statements prepared in accordance with GAAP.

Reporting on Financial Statements That Omit Substantially All Disclosures

.20 An entity may request the accountant to compile financial statements that omit substantially all the disclosures required by an applicable financial reporting framework, including disclosures that might appear in the body of the financial statements.[5] The accountant may compile such financial statements, provided that the omission of substantially all disclosures is not, to his or her knowledge, undertaken with the intention of misleading those who might reasonably be expected to use such financial statements. When reporting

---

    [5] See paragraphs .27–.29 for the accountant's responsibilities when he or she is aware of other departures from an applicable financial reporting framework. However, see section 300, for guidance when such financial statements are included in a prescribed form, and the prescribed form or related instructions do not request the disclosures required by an applicable financial reporting framework.

AR §80.18

Compilation of Financial Statements

on financial statements that omit substantially all disclosures, the accountant should include, after the paragraph describing the accountant's responsibility, a paragraph in the compilation report that includes the following elements:

a. A statement that management has elected to omit substantially all the disclosures (and the statement of cash flows, if applicable) required by the applicable financial reporting framework (or ordinarily included in the financial statements if the financial statements are prepared in accordance with an OCBOA)

b. A statement that if the omitted disclosures (and statement of cash flows, if applicable) were included in the financial statements, they might influence the user's conclusions about the company's financial position, results of operations, and cash flows (or equivalent for presentations other than accounting principles generally accepted in the United States of America)

c. A statement that, accordingly, the financial statements are not designed for those who are not informed about such matters

When the entity wishes to include disclosures about only a few matters in the form of notes to such financial statements, such disclosures should be labeled "Selected Information—Substantially All Disclosures Required by [*identify the applicable financial reporting framework (for example "Accepted Accounting Principles Generally Accepted in the United States of America"*)] Are Not Included."

See Compilation Exhibit B for examples of compilation reports when substantially all disclosures required by an applicable financial reporting framework are omitted.

Reporting When the Accountant Is Not Independent

.21 When the accountant is issuing a report with respect to a compilation of financial statements for an entity, with respect to which the accountant is not independent, the accountant's report should be modified. In making a judgment about whether he or she is independent, the accountant should be guided by the AICPA's Code of Professional Conduct. The accountant should indicate his or her lack of independence in a final paragraph of the accountant's compilation report. An example of such a disclosure would be

I am (We are) not independent with respect to XYZ Company.

The accountant is not precluded from disclosing a description about the reason(s) that his or her independence is impaired. The following are examples of descriptions the accountant may use:

a. I am (We are) not independent with respect to XYZ Company as of and for the year ended December 31, 20XX, because I (a member of the engagement team) had a direct financial interest in XYZ Company;

b. I am (We are) not independent with respect to XYZ Company as of and for the year ended December 31, 20XX, because an individual of my immediate family (an immediate family member of one of the members of the engagement team) was employed by XYZ Company; or

c. I am (We are) not independent with respect to XYZ Company as of and for the year ended December 31, 20XX, because I (we) performed certain accounting services (the accountant may include a specific description of those services) that impaired my (our) independence.

AR §80.21

38 Statements on Standards for Accounting and Review Services

If the accountant elects to disclose a description about the reasons his or her independence is impaired, the accountant should ensure that all reasons are included in the description.

See Compilation Exhibit B for illustrative examples of accountant's compilation reports when the accountant's independence has been impaired.

Accountant's Communications With the Client When the Compiled Financial Statements Are Not Expected to Be Used by a Third Party

.22 When the accountant submits compiled financial statements to his or her client that are not expected to be used by a third party, he or she is not required to issue a compilation report.

.23 The accountant should include a reference on each page of the financial statements restricting their use, such as "Restricted for Management's Use Only," or "Solely for the information and use by the management of [*name of entity*] and not intended to be and should not be used by any other party."

.24 If the accountant becomes aware that the financial statements have been distributed to third parties, the accountant should discuss the situation with the client and determine the appropriate course of action, including considering requesting that the client have the statements returned. If the accountant requests that the financial statements be returned and the client does not comply with that request within a reasonable period of time, the accountant should notify known third parties that the financial statements are not intended for third party use, preferably in consultation with his or her attorney.

Emphasis of a Matter

.25 The accountant may emphasize, in any report on financial statements, a matter disclosed in the financial statements. Such explanatory information should be presented in a separate paragraph of the accountant's report. Emphasis paragraphs are never required; they may be added solely at the accountant's discretion.

Examples of matters that the accountant may wish to emphasize are

- uncertainties.
- that the entity is a component of a larger business enterprise.
- that the entity has had significant transactions with related parties.
- unusually important subsequent events.
- accounting matters, other than those involving a change or changes in accounting principles, affecting the comparability of the financial statements with those of the preceding period.

.26 Because an emphasis of matter paragraph should not be used in lieu of management disclosures, the accountant should not include an emphasis paragraph in a compilation report on financial statements that omit substantially all disclosures unless the matter is disclosed in the financial statements. The accountant should refer to paragraph .20 if he or she believes that a disclosure is necessary to keep the financial statements from being misleading.

AR §80.22

Compilation of Financial Statements

39

Departures From the Applicable Financial Reporting Framework

.27 An accountant who is engaged to compile financial statements may become aware of a departure from the applicable financial reporting framework (including inadequate disclosure) that is material to the financial statements. Paragraph .20 provides guidance to the accountant when the departure relates to the omission of substantially all disclosures in the financial statements that he or she has compiled. section 300, *Compilation Reports on Financial Statements Included in Certain Prescribed Forms*, provides guidance when the departure is called for by a prescribed form or related instructions. In all other circumstances, if the financial statements are not revised, the accountant should consider whether modification of the standard report is adequate to disclose the departure.

.28 If the accountant concludes that modification of the standard report is appropriate, the departure should be disclosed in a separate paragraph of the report, including disclosure of the effects of the departure on the financial statements if such effects have been determined by management or are known as the result of the accountant's procedures. The accountant is not required to determine the effects of a departure if management has not done so, provided that the accountant states in the report that such determination has not been made.

See Compilation Exhibit B for examples of compilation reports that disclose departures from the applicable financial reporting framework.

.29 If the accountant believes that modification of the standard report is not adequate to indicate the deficiencies in the financial statements as a whole, the accountant should withdraw from the compilation engagement and provide no further services with respect to those financial statements. The accountant may wish to consult with his or her legal counsel in those circumstances.

Restricting the Use of an Accountant's Compilation Report

General Use and Restricted Use Reports

.30 The term *general use* applies to accountants' reports that are not restricted to specified parties. Accountants' reports on financial statements prepared in conformity with an applicable financial reporting framework ordinarily are not restricted regarding use. However, nothing in this section precludes the accountant from restricting the use of any report.

.31 The term *restricted use* applies to accountants' reports intended only for one or more specified third parties. The need for restriction on the use of a report may result from a number of circumstances, including, but not limited to, the purpose of the report and the potential for the report to be misunderstood when taken out of the context in which it was intended to be used.

.32 The accountant should restrict the use of a report when the subject matter of the accountant's report or the presentation being reported on is based on measurement or disclosure criteria contained in contractual agreements[6] or regulatory provisions that are not in conformity with an applicable financial reporting framework.

---

[6] A *contractual agreement*, as discussed in this section, is an agreement between the client and one or more third parties other than the accountant.

AR §80.32

40 Statements on Standards for Accounting and Review Services

Reporting on Subject Matter or Presentations Based on Measurement or Disclosure Criteria Contained in Contractual Agreements or Regulatory Provisions

.33 When reports are issued on subject matter or presentations based on measurement or disclosure criteria contained in contractual agreements or regulatory provisions that are not in conformity with an applicable financial reporting framework, the accountant should restrict the report because the basis, assumptions, or purpose of such presentations (contained in such agreements or regulatory provisions) are developed for, and directed only to, the parties to the agreement or regulatory agency responsible for the provisions. The report also should be restricted because the report, the subject matter, or the presentation may be misunderstood by those who are not adequately informed of the basis, assumptions, or purpose of the presentation.

Combined Reports Covering Both Restricted Use and General Use Subject Matter or Presentations

.34 If the accountant issues a single combined report covering both (*a*) subject matter or presentations that require a restriction on use to specified parties and (*b*) subject matter or presentations that ordinarily do not require such a restriction, the use of such a single combined report should be restricted to the specified parties.

Inclusion of a Separate Restricted Use Report in the Same Document With a General Use Report

.35 When required by law or regulation, a separate restricted use report may be included in a document that also contains a general use report. The inclusion of a separate restricted use report in a document that contains a general use report does not affect the intended use of either report. The restricted use report remains restricted regarding use, and the general use report continues for general use.

Adding Other Specified Parties

.36 Subsequent to the completion of an engagement resulting in a restricted use report, or in the course of such an engagement, the accountant may be asked to consider adding other parties as specified parties.

.37 If the accountant is reporting on subject matter or a presentation based on measurement or disclosure criteria contained in contractual agreements or regulatory provisions, as described in paragraph .33, the accountant may agree to add other parties as specified parties based on the accountant's consideration of factors such as the identity of the other parties, their knowledge of the basis of the measurement or disclosure criteria, and the intended use of the report. If the accountant agrees to add other parties as specified parties, the accountant should obtain affirmative acknowledgment, preferably in writing, from the other parties of their understanding of the nature of the engagement, the measurement or disclosure criteria used in the engagement, and the related report. If the other parties are added after the accountant has issued his or her report, the report may be reissued, or the accountant may provide other written acknowledgment that the other parties have been added as specified parties. If the report is reissued, the report date should not be changed. If the accountant provides written acknowledgment that the other parties have been added as specified parties, such written acknowledgment ordinarily should state that no procedures have been performed subsequent to the date of the report.

AR §80.33

Compilation of Financial Statements

41

Limiting the Distribution of Reports

.38 Because of the reasons presented in paragraph .31, the accountant should consider informing his or her client that restricted use reports are not intended for distribution to nonspecified parties, regardless of whether they are included in a document containing a separate general use report.[7] This section does not preclude the accountant, in connection with establishing the terms of the engagement, from reaching an understanding with the client that the intended use of the report will be restricted and from obtaining the client's agreement that the client and the specified parties will not distribute the report to parties other than those identified in the report. However, the accountant is not responsible for controlling a client's distribution of restricted use reports. Accordingly, a restricted use report should alert readers to the restriction on the use of the report by indicating that the report is not intended to be and should not be used by anyone other than the specified parties.

Report Language—Restricted Use

.39 An accountant's report that is restricted should contain a separate paragraph at the end of the report that includes the following elements:

   a. A statement indicating that the report is intended solely for the information and use of the specified parties.

   b. An identification of the specified parties to whom use is restricted. The report may list the specified parties or refer the reader to the specified parties listed elsewhere in the report.

   c. A statement that the report is not intended to be and should not be used by anyone other than the specified parties.

An Entity's Ability to Continue as a Going Concern

.40 During the performance of compilation procedures, evidence or information may come to the accountant's attention indicating that an uncertainty may exist about the entity's ability to continue as a going concern for a reasonable period of time, not to exceed one year beyond the date of the financial statements being compiled (hereinafter referred to as a *reasonable period of time*). In those circumstances, the accountant should request that management consider the possible effects of the going concern uncertainty on the financial statements, including the need for related disclosure.

.41 After management communicates to the accountant the results of its consideration of the possible effects on the financial statements, the accountant should consider the reasonableness of management's conclusions, including the adequacy of the related disclosures, if applicable.

.42 If the accountant determines that management's conclusions are unreasonable or the disclosure of the uncertainty regarding the entity's ability to continue as a going concern is not adequate, he or she should follow the guidance in paragraphs .27–.29 with respect to departures from an applicable financial reporting framework.

.43 The accountant may emphasize an uncertainty about an entity's ability to continue as a going concern, provided that the uncertainty is disclosed in the

---

[7] In some cases, restricted use reports filed with regulatory agencies are required by law or regulation to be made available to the public as a matter of public record. Also, a regulatory agency, as part of its oversight responsibility for an entity, may require access to restricted use reports in which they are not named as a specified party.

AR §80.43

42 Statements on Standards for Accounting and Review Services

financial statements. In such circumstances, the accountant should follow the guidance in paragraphs .25–.26.

Subsequent Events

.44 Evidence or information that a subsequent event that has a material effect on the compiled financial statements has occurred may come to the accountant's attention in the following ways:

- *a.* During the performance of compilation procedures
- *b.* Subsequent to the date of the accountant's compilation report but prior to the release of the report [8]

In either case, the accountant should request that management consider the possible effects on the financial statements, including the adequacy of any related disclosure, if applicable.

.45 If the accountant determines that the subsequent event is not adequately accounted for in the financial statements or disclosed in the notes, he or she should follow the guidance in paragraphs .27–.29.

.46 Occasionally, a subsequent event has such a material impact on the entity that the accountant may wish to include in his or her compilation report an explanatory paragraph directing the reader's attention to the event and its effects. Such an emphasis of matter paragraph may be added at the accountant's discretion, provided that the matter is disclosed in the financial statements. See paragraphs .25–.26 for additional guidance with respect to emphasis of matter paragraphs.

Subsequent Discovery of Facts Existing at the Date of the Report

.47 Subsequent to the date of the report on the financial statements that the accountant has compiled, he or she may become aware that facts may have existed at that date that might have caused him or her to believe that information supplied by the entity was incorrect, incomplete, or otherwise unsatisfactory had the accountant then been aware of such facts.[9] Because of the variety of conditions that might be encountered, some of the procedures contained in this section are necessarily set out only in general terms; the specific actions to be taken in a particular case may vary with the circumstances. The accountant would be well advised to consult with his or her legal counsel when he or she encounters the circumstances to which this section may apply because of legal implications that may be involved in actions contemplated herein.

.48 After the date of the accountant's compilation report, the accountant has no obligation to perform other compilation procedures with respect to the financial statements, unless new information comes to his or her attention. However, when the accountant becomes aware of information that relates to financial statements previously reported on by him or her, but that was not known to the accountant at the date of the report, (and that is of such a nature and from such a source that the accountant would have investigated it had it come to his or her attention during the course of the compilation), the

---

[8] For purposes of this section, with respect to compiled financial statements in which the accountant does not report, the submission of the compiled financial statements is the equivalent of the accountant's compilation or review report date.

[9] See footnote 8.

AR §80.44

Compilation of Financial Statements

43

accountant should, as soon as practicable, undertake to determine whether the information is reliable and whether the facts existed at the date of the report. The accountant should discuss the matter with his or her client at whatever management levels the accountant deems appropriate and request cooperation in whatever investigation may be necessary. In addition to management, the accountant may deem it appropriate to discuss the matter with those charged with governance. If the nature and effect of the matter are such that (*a*) the accountant's report or the financial statements would have been affected if the information had been known to the accountant at the accountant's compilation report date and had not been reflected in the financial statements and (*b*) the accountant believes that persons are currently using or are likely to use the financial statements, and those persons would attach importance to the information, the accountant should obtain additional or revised information. Consideration should be given to, among other things, the time elapsed since the financial statements were issued.

.49 When the accountant has concluded that action should be taken to prevent further use of the accountant's report or the financial statements, the accountant should advise his or her client to make appropriate disclosure of the newly discovered facts and their impact on the financial statements to persons who are known to be currently using or who are likely to use the financial statements. When the client undertakes to make appropriate disclosure, the method used and the disclosure made will depend on the circumstances. For example

- *a.* if the effect of the subsequently discovered information on the accountant's report or the financial statements can promptly be determined, disclosure should consist of issuing, as soon as practicable, revised financial statements and, when applicable, the accountant's report. The reasons for the revision usually should be described in a note to the financial statements and, when applicable, referred to in the accountant's report. Generally, only the most recently issued compiled financial statements would need to be revised, even though the revision resulted from events that had occurred in prior years.

- *b.* when issuance of financial statements for a subsequent period is imminent, so that disclosure is not delayed, appropriate disclosure of the revision can be made in such statements instead of reissuing the earlier statements, pursuant to subparagraph (*a*).

- *c.* when the effect on the financial statements of the subsequently discovered information cannot be promptly determined, the issuance of revised financial statements would necessarily be delayed. In this circumstance, when it appears that the information will require a revision of the statements, appropriate disclosure would consist of notification by the client to persons who are known to be using or who are likely to use the financial statements that the statements should not be used; that revised financial statements will be issued; and, when applicable, that the accountant's report will be issued as soon as practicable.

.50 The accountant should take whatever steps he or she deems necessary to satisfy himself or herself that the client has made the disclosures specified in paragraph .49.

.51 If the client refuses to make the disclosures specified in paragraph .49, the accountant should notify the appropriate personnel at the highest levels within the entity, such as the manager (owner) or those charged with governance, of such refusal and of the fact that, in the absence of disclosure by the

AR §80.51

44   **Statements on Standards for Accounting and Review Services**

client, the accountant will take steps as outlined subsequently to prevent further use of the financial statements and, if applicable, the accountant's report. The steps that can appropriately be taken will depend upon the degree of certainty of the accountant's knowledge that persons exist who are currently using or who will use the financial statements and, if applicable, the accountant's report and who would attach importance to the information and the accountant's ability as a practical matter to communicate with them. Unless the accountant's attorney recommends a different course of action, the accountant should take the following steps to the extent applicable:

     a.   Notification to the client that the accountant's report must no longer be associated with the financial statements.

     b.   Notification to the regulatory agencies having jurisdiction over the client that the accountant's report should no longer be used.

     c.   Notification to each person known to the accountant to be using the financial statements that the financial statements and the accountant's report should no longer be used. In many instances, it will not be practicable for the accountant to give appropriate individual notification to stakeholders whose identities ordinarily are unknown to him or her; notification to a regulatory agency having jurisdiction over the client will usually be the only practicable way for the accountant to provide appropriate disclosure. Such notification should be accompanied by a request that the agency take whatever steps it may deem appropriate to accomplish the necessary disclosure.

    .52 The following guidelines should govern the content of any disclosure made by the accountant in accordance with paragraph .51, to persons other than his or her client:

     a.   The disclosure should include a description of the nature of the subsequently acquired information and its effect on the financial statements.

     b.   The information disclosed should be as precise and factual as possible and should not go beyond that which is reasonably necessary to accomplish the purpose mentioned in the preceding subparagraph (*a*). Comments concerning the conduct or motives of any person should be avoided.

If the client has not cooperated, the accountant's disclosure need not detail the specific information but can merely indicate that the client has not cooperated with the accountant's attempt to substantiate information that has come to the accountant's attention and that, if the information is true, the accountant believes that the compilation report must no longer be used or associated with the financial statements. No such disclosure should be made unless the accountant believes that the financial statements are likely to be misleading and that the accountant's compilation report should not be used.

Supplementary Information

    .53 When the basic financial statements are accompanied by information presented for supplementary analysis purposes, the accountant should clearly indicate the degree of responsibility, if any, he or she is taking with respect to such information. When the accountant has compiled both the basic financial statements and other data presented only for supplementary analysis purposes, the compilation report should refer to the other data, or the accountant can issue a separate report on the other data. If a separate report is issued, the report

AR §80.52

Compilation of Financial Statements **45**

should state that the other data accompanying the financial statements are presented only for the purposes of additional analysis, and that the information has been compiled from information that is the representation of management, without audit or review, and that the accountant does not express an opinion or provide any assurance on such data.

Communicating to Management and Others

.54 When evidence or information comes to the accountant's attention during the performance of compilation procedures that fraud or an illegal act may have occurred, that matter should be brought to the attention of the appropriate level of management. The accountant need not report matters regarding illegal acts that are clearly inconsequential and may reach agreement in advance with the entity on the nature of such items to be communicated. When matters regarding fraud or an illegal act involve senior management, the accountant should report the matter to an individual or group at a higher level within the entity, such as the manager (owner) or those charged with governance. The communication may be oral or written. If the communication is oral, the accountant should document it. When matters regarding fraud or an illegal act involve an owner of the business, the accountant should consider resigning from the engagement. Additionally, the accountant should consider consulting with his or her legal counsel whenever any evidence or information comes to his or her attention during the performance of compilation procedures that fraud or an illegal act may have occurred, unless such illegal act is clearly inconsequential.

.55 The disclosure of any evidence or information that comes to the accountant's attention during the performance of compilation procedures that fraud or an illegal act may have occurred to parties other than the client's senior management (or those charged with governance, if applicable) ordinarily is not part of the accountant's responsibility and, ordinarily, would be precluded by the accountant's ethical or legal obligations of confidentiality. The accountant should recognize, however, that in the following circumstances, a duty to disclose to parties outside of the entity may exist:

    a.   To comply with certain legal and regulatory requirements

    b.   To a successor accountant when the successor decides to communicate with the predecessor accountant in accordance with section 400, *Communications Between Predecessor and Successor Accountants*, regarding acceptance of an engagement to compile or review the financial statements of a nonissuer

    c.   In response to a subpoena

Because potential conflicts between the accountant's ethical and legal obligations for confidentiality of client matters may be complex, the accountant may wish to consult with legal counsel before discussing matters covered by paragraph .54 with parties outside the client.

Change in Engagement From Audit or Review to Compilation

.56 The accountant who has been engaged to audit the financial statements of a nonissuer in accordance with auditing standards generally accepted in the United States of America or the accountant who has been engaged to review the financial statements of a nonissuer in accordance with SSARSs may, before the completion of the audit or review, be requested to change the engagement to a compilation of financial statements. A request to change the engagement may

AR §80.56

46   Statements on Standards for Accounting and Review Services

result from a change in circumstances affecting the entity's requirement for an audit or review; a misunderstanding regarding the nature of an audit, review, or compilation; or a restriction on the scope of the audit or review, whether imposed by the client or caused by circumstances.

.57 Before the accountant, who was engaged to perform an audit in accordance with auditing standards generally accepted in the United States of America or a review in accordance with SSARSs, agrees to change the engagement to a compilation, at least the following should be considered:

     a.   The reason given for the client's request, particularly the implications of a restriction on the scope of the audit or review, whether imposed by the client or by circumstances

     b.   The additional audit or review effort required to complete the audit or review

     c.   The estimated additional cost to complete the audit or review

.58 A change in circumstances that affects the entity's requirement for an audit or review or a misunderstanding concerning the nature of an audit, review, or compilation would ordinarily be considered a reasonable basis for requesting a change in the engagement.

.59 In considering the implications of a restriction on the scope of the audit or review, the accountant should evaluate the possibility that information affected by the scope restriction may be incorrect, incomplete, or otherwise unsatisfactory. Nevertheless, when the accountant has been engaged to audit an entity's financial statements and has been prohibited by the client from corresponding with the entity's legal counsel, the accountant ordinarily would be precluded from issuing a compilation report on the financial statements. If in an audit or a review engagement, a client does not provide the accountant with a signed representation letter, the accountant would ordinarily be precluded from issuing a compilation report on the financial statements.

.60 In all circumstances, if the audit or review procedures are substantially complete or the cost to complete such procedures is relatively insignificant, the accountant should consider the propriety of accepting a change in the engagement.

.61 If the accountant concludes, based upon his or her professional judgment, that reasonable justification exists to change the engagement, and if he or she complies with the standards applicable to a compilation engagement, the accountant should issue an appropriate compilation report. The report should not include reference to (*a*) the original engagement, (*b*) any audit or review procedures that may have been performed, or (*c*) scope limitations that resulted in the changed engagement.

Effective Date

.62 This section is effective for compilations of financial statements for periods ending on or after December 15, 2010. Early implementation of the requirements and guidance in paragraph .21 is permitted.

AR §80.57

Compilation of Financial Statements

47

.63

Compilation Exhibit A—Illustrative Engagement Letters

Standard Engagement Letter for a Compilation

[Appropriate Salutation]

This letter is to confirm our understanding of the terms and objectives of our engagement and the nature and limitations of the services we will provide.

We will perform the following services:

We will compile, from information you provide, the annual *[and interim, if applicable]* financial statements of XYZ Company as of and for the year ended December 31, 20XX, and issue an accountant's report thereon in accordance with Statements on Standards for Accounting and Review Services (SSARSs) issued by the American Institute of Certified Public Accountants (AICPA).

The objective of a compilation is to assist you in presenting financial information in the form of financial statements. We will utilize information that is your representation without undertaking to obtain or provide any assurance that there are no material modifications that should be made to the financial statements in order for the statements to be in conformity with *[the applicable financial reporting framework (for example, accounting principles generally accepted in the United States of America)]*.

You are responsible for

- *a.*   the preparation and fair presentation of the financial statements in accordance with *[the applicable financial reporting framework (for example, accounting principles generally accepted in the United States of America)]*.
- *b.*   designing, implementing, and maintaining internal control relevant to the preparation and fair presentation of the financial statements.
- *c.*   preventing and detecting fraud
- *d.*   identifying and ensuring that the entity complies with the laws and regulations applicable to its activities.
- *e.*   making all financial records and related information available to us.

We are responsible for conducting the engagement in accordance with SSARSs issued by the AICPA.

A compilation differs significantly from a review or an audit of financial statements. A compilation does not contemplate performing inquiry, analytical procedures, or other procedures performed in a review. Additionally, a compilation does not contemplate obtaining an understanding of the entity's internal control; assessing fraud risk; testing accounting records by obtaining sufficient appropriate audit evidence through inspection, observation, confirmation, or the examination of source documents (for example, cancelled checks or bank images); or other procedures ordinarily performed in an audit. Accordingly, we will not express an opinion or provide any assurance regarding the financial statements being compiled.

Our engagement cannot be relied upon to disclose errors, fraud, or illegal acts. However, we will inform the appropriate level of management of any material errors, and of any evidence or information that comes to our attention during the performance of our compilation procedures that fraud may have occurred.

AR §80.63

48   Statements on Standards for Accounting and Review Services

In addition, we will report to you any evidence or information that comes to our attention during the performance of our compilation procedures regarding illegal acts that may have occurred, unless they are clearly inconsequential.

If, during the period covered by the engagement letter, the accountant's independence is or will be impaired, insert the following:

> We are not independent with respect to XYZ Company. We will disclose that we are not independent in our compilation report.

If, for any reason, we are unable to complete the compilation of your financial statements, we will not issue a report on such statements as a result of this engagement.

Our fees for these services...

We will be pleased to discuss this letter with you at any time. If the foregoing is in accordance with your understanding, please sign the copy of this letter in the space provided and return it to us.

Sincerely yours,

_____

[Signature of accountant]

Acknowledged:

XYZ Company

_____

President

_____

Date

AR §80.63

Compilation of Financial Statements

Engagement Letter for a Compilation of Financial Statements Not Intended for Third Party Use

[*Appropriate Salutation*]

This letter is to confirm our understanding of the terms and objectives of our engagement and the nature and limitations of the services we will provide.

We will perform the following services:

We will compile, from information you provide, the [*monthly, quarterly, or other frequency*] financial statements of XYZ Company as of and for the year ended December 31, 20XX.

The objective of a compilation is to assist you in presenting financial information in the form of financial statements. We will utilize information that is your representation without undertaking to obtain or provide any assurance that there are no material modifications that should be made to the financial statements in order for the statements to be in conformity with [*the applicable financial reporting framework (for example, accounting principles generally accepted in the United States of America)*].

You are responsible for

    a.   the preparation and fair presentation of the financial statements in accordance with [*the applicable financial reporting framework (for example, accounting principles generally accepted in the United States of America)*].

    b.   designing, implementing, and maintaining internal control relevant to the preparation and fair presentation of the financial statements.

    c.   preventing and detecting fraud.

    d.   identifying and ensuring that the entity complies with the laws and regulations applicable to its activities.

    e.   making all financial records and related information available to us.

We are responsible for conducting the engagement in accordance with Statements on Standards for Accounting and Review Services issued by the American Institute of Certified Public Accountants.

A compilation differs significantly from a review or an audit of financial statements. A compilation does not contemplate performing inquiry, analytical procedures, or other procedures performed in a review. Additionally, a compilation does not contemplate obtaining an understanding of the entity's internal control; assessing fraud risk; testing accounting records by obtaining sufficient appropriate audit evidence through inspection, observation, confirmation, or the examination of source documents (for example, cancelled checks or bank images); or other procedures ordinarily performed in an audit. Accordingly, we will not express an opinion or provide any assurance regarding the financial statements being compiled.

Our engagement cannot be relied upon to disclose errors, fraud, or illegal acts. However, we will inform the appropriate level of management of any material errors, and of any evidence or information that comes to our attention during the performance of our compilation procedures that fraud may have occurred. In addition, we will report to you any evidence or information that comes to our attention during the performance of our compilation procedures regarding illegal acts that may have occurred, unless they are clearly inconsequential.

AR §80.63

50   Statements on Standards for Accounting and Review Services

The financial statements will not be accompanied by a report and are for management's use only and are not to be used by a third party.

If, during the period covered by the engagement letter, the accountant's independence is or will be impaired, insert the following:

>   *We are not independent with respect to XYZ Company.*

Our fees for these services...

We will be pleased to discuss this letter with you at any time. If the foregoing is in accordance with your understanding, please sign the copy of this letter in the space provided and return it to us.

Sincerely yours,

_____

[*Signature of accountant*]

Acknowledged:

XYZ Company

_____

President

_____

Date

AR §80.63

.64

Compilation Exhibit B—Illustrative Compilation Reports

Standard compilation report on financial statements prepared in accordance with accounting principles generally accepted in the United States of America

Accountant's Compilation Report

[*Appropriate Salutation*]

I (we) have compiled the accompanying balance sheet of XYZ Company as of December 31, 20XX, and the related statements of income, retained earnings, and cash flows for the year then ended. I (we) have not audited or reviewed the accompanying financial statements and, accordingly, do not express an opinion or provide any assurance about whether the financial statements are in accordance with accounting principles generally accepted in the United States of America.

Management (owners) is (are) responsible for the preparation and fair presentation of the financial statements in accordance with accounting principles generally accepted in the United States of America and for designing, implementing, and maintaining internal control relevant to the preparation and fair presentation of the financial statements.

My (our) responsibility is to conduct the compilation in accordance with Statements on Standards for Accounting and Review Services issued by the American Institute of Certified Public Accountants. The objective of a compilation is to assist management in presenting financial information in the form of financial statements without undertaking to obtain or provide any assurance that there are no material modifications that should be made to the financial statements.

[*Signature of accounting firm or accountant, as appropriate*]

[*Date*]

Standard accountant's compilation report on financial statements prepared in accordance with the cash basis of accounting

Accountant's Compilation Report

[*Appropriate Salutation*]

I (we) have compiled the accompanying statement of assets and liabilities arising from cash transactions of XYZ Company as of December 31, 20XX, and the related statement of revenue collected and expenses paid for the year then ended. I (we) have not audited or reviewed the accompanying financial statements and, accordingly, do not express an opinion or provide any assurance about whether the financial statements are in accordance with the cash basis of accounting.

Management (owners) is (are) responsible for the preparation and fair presentation of the financial statements in accordance with the cash basis of accounting and for designing, implementing, and maintaining internal control relevant to the preparation and fair presentation of the financial statements.

My (our) responsibility is to conduct the compilation in accordance with Statements on Standards for Accounting and Review Services issued by the American Institute of Certified Public Accountants. The objective of a compilation is to assist management in presenting financial information in the form of financial statements without undertaking to obtain or provide any assurance that there are no material modifications that should be made to the financial statements.

AR §80.64

52   Statements on Standards for Accounting and Review Services

[*Signature of accounting firm or accountant, as appropriate*]

[*Date*]

Paragraph the accountant may add after the conclusion paragraph when management has elected to omit substantially all disclosures, but the financial statements are otherwise in conformity with accounting principles generally accepted in the United States of America

Management has elected to omit substantially all of the disclosures required by accounting principles generally accepted in the United States of America. If the omitted disclosures were included in the financial statements, they might influence the user's conclusions about the company's financial position, results of operations, and cash flows. Accordingly, the financial statements are not designed for those who are not informed about such matters.

Paragraph the accountant may add after the conclusion paragraph when management has elected to omit substantially all disclosures, but the financial statements are otherwise in conformity with the income tax basis of accounting

Management has elected to omit substantially all of the disclosures ordinarily included in financial statements prepared in accordance with the income tax basis of accounting. If the omitted disclosures were included in the financial statements, they might influence the user's conclusions about the company's assets, liabilities, equity, revenue, and expenses. Accordingly, the financial statements are not designed for those who are not informed about such matters.

Accountant's compilation report on financial statements prepared in accordance with accounting principles generally accepted in the United States of America when the accountant's independence has been impaired, and the accountant determines to not disclose the reason for the independence impairment

Accountant's Compilation Report

[*Appropriate Salutation*]

I (we) have compiled the accompanying balance sheet of XYZ Company as of December 31, 20XX, and the related statements of income, retained earnings, and cash flows for the year then ended. I (we) have not audited or reviewed the accompanying financial statements and, accordingly, do not express an opinion or provide any assurance about whether the financial statements are in accordance with accounting principles generally accepted in the United States of America.

Management (owners) is (are) responsible for the preparation and fair presentation of the financial statements in accordance with accounting principles generally accepted in the United States of America and for designing, implementing, and maintaining internal control relevant to the preparation and fair presentation of the financial statements.

My (our) responsibility is to conduct the compilation in accordance with Statements on Standards for Accounting and Review Services issued by the American Institute of Certified Public Accountants. The objective of a compilation is to assist management in presenting financial information in the form of financial statements without undertaking to obtain or provide any assurance that there are no material modifications that should be made to the financial statements.

I am (we are) not independent with respect to XYZ Company.

[*Signature of accounting firm or accountant, as appropriate*]

[*Date*]

AR §80.64

Compilation of Financial Statements

53

Accountant's compilation report on financial statements prepared in accordance with accounting principles generally accepted in the United States of America when the accountant's independence has been impaired due to the accountant having a financial interest in the client, and the accountant decides to disclose the reason for the independence impairment

Accountant's Compilation Report

[*Appropriate Salutation*]

I (we) have compiled the accompanying balance sheet of XYZ Company as of December 31, 20XX, and the related statements of income, retained earnings, and cash flows for the year then ended. I (we) have not audited or reviewed the accompanying financial statements and, accordingly, do not express an opinion or provide any assurance about whether the financial statements are in accordance with accounting principles generally accepted in the United States of America.

Management (owners) is (are) responsible for the preparation and fair presentation of the financial statements in accordance with accounting principles generally accepted in the United States of America and for designing, implementing, and maintaining internal control relevant to the preparation and fair presentation of the financial statements.

My (our) responsibility is to conduct the compilation in accordance with Statements on Standards for Accounting and Review Services issued by the American Institute of Certified Public Accountants. The objective of a compilation is to assist management in presenting financial information in the form of financial statements without undertaking to obtain or provide any assurance that there are no material modifications that should be made to the financial statements.

I am (we are) not independent with respect to XYZ Company as during the year ended December 31, 20XX, I (a member of the engagement team) had a direct financial interest in XYZ Company.

[*Signature of accounting firm or accountant, as appropriate*]

[*Date*]

Accountant's compilation report on financial statements disclosing a departure from accounting principles generally accepted in the United States of America

Accountant's Compilation Report

[*Appropriate Salutation*]

I (we) have compiled the accompanying balance sheet of XYZ Company as of December 31, 20XX, and the related statements of income, retained earnings, and cash flows for the year then ended. I (we) have not audited or reviewed the accompanying financial statements and, accordingly, do not express an opinion or provide any assurance about whether the financial statements are in accordance with accounting principles generally accepted in the United States of America.

Management (owners) is (are) responsible for the preparation and fair presentation of the financial statements in accordance with accounting principles generally accepted in the United States of America and for designing, implementing, and maintaining internal control relevant to the preparation and fair presentation of the financial statements.

My (our) responsibility is to conduct the compilation in accordance with Statements on Standards for Accounting and Review Services issued by the American Institute of Certified Public Accountants. The objective of a compilation is to assist management in presenting financial information

AR §80.64

54 Statements on Standards for Accounting and Review Services

in the form of financial statements without undertaking to obtain or provide any assurance that there are no material modifications that should be made to the financial statements. During our compilation, I (we) did become aware of a departure (certain departures) from accounting principles generally accepted in the United States of America that is (are) described in the following paragraph.

As disclosed in Note X to the financial statements, accounting principles generally accepted in the United States of America require that land be stated at cost. Management has informed me (us) that the company has stated its land at appraised value and that, if accounting principles generally accepted in the United States of America had been followed, the land account and stockholders' equity would have been decreased by $500,000.

or

A statement of cash flows for the year ended December 31, 20XX, has not been presented. Accounting principles generally accepted in the United States of America require that such a statement be presented when financial statements purport to present financial position and results of operations.[1]

[Signature of accounting firm or accountant, as appropriate]

[Date]

---

[1] If a statement of cash flows is not presented, the first paragraph of the accountant's compilation report should be modified accordingly.

AR §80.64

AR Section 9080

Compilation of Financial Statements: Accounting and Review Services Interpretations of Section 80

1. Reporting When There Are Significant Departures From the Applicable Financial Reporting Framework

.01 *Question*—When the financial statements include significant departures from the applicable financial reporting framework, may the accountant modify his or her standard report in accordance with paragraphs .27–.29 of section 80, *Compilation of Financial Statements*, to include a statement that the financial statements are not in conformity with the applicable financial reporting framework?

.02 *Interpretation*—No. Including such a statement in the accountant's compilation report would be tantamount to expressing an adverse opinion on the financial statements as a whole. Such an opinion can be expressed only in the context of an audit engagement.

.03 However, paragraph .25 of section 80 states that an accountant may emphasize, in any report on financial statements, a matter disclosed in the financial statements. The accountant may wish, therefore, to emphasize the limitations of the financial statements in a separate paragraph of his or her compilation report, depending on his or her assessment of the possible dollar magnitude of the effects of the departures, the significance of the affected items to the entity, the pervasiveness and overall impact of the misstatements, and whether disclosure has been made of the effects of the departures. Such separate paragraph, which would follow the other modifications of his or his report (see illustrations in Compilation Exhibit B), might read as follows (the illustration assumes that the accountant is reporting on financial statements in which there are significant departures from accounting principles generally accepted in the United States of America):

> Because the significance and pervasiveness of the matters previously discussed makes it difficult to assess their impact on the financial statements as a whole, users of these financial statements should recognize that they might reach different conclusions about the company's financial position, results of operations, and cash flows if they had access to revised financial statements prepared in conformity with accounting principles generally accepted in the United States of America.

.04 *Interpretation*—Inclusion of such a separate paragraph in the accountant's compilation report is not a substitute for disclosure of the specific departures or the effects of such departures when they have been determined by management or are known as a result of the accountant's procedures.

[Issue Date: August 1981; Revised: November 2002; Revised: May 2004; Revised: July 2005; Revised: December 2010 to conform to SSARS No. 19 (formerly Interpretation No. 7 to section 100).]

AR §9080.04

56 Statements on Standards for Accounting and Review Services

2. Reporting on Tax Returns

.05 *Question*—May an accountant comply with a request from a nonissuer to issue a compilation report on financial information contained in a tax return, as in Form 1040, *U.S. Individual Income Tax Return*, or Form 1120, *U.S. Corporation Income Tax Return*, or in an information return, as in Form 990, *Return of Organization Exempt from Income Tax*; Form 1065, *U.S. Partnership Return of Income*; or Form 5500, *Return of Employee Benefit Plan*?

.06 *Interpretation*—Yes. Although paragraph .01 of section 80 states that the section establishes standards and provides guidance on compilations of financial statements and financial information included in a tax return is not included in the definition of financial statements, an accountant may decide to accept an engagement to issue a compilation report on such a return. In that case, the performance and reporting requirements of section 80 would apply.

[Issue Date: November 1982; Revised: February 2008; Revised: December 2010 to conform to SSARS No. 19 (formerly Interpretation No. 10 to section 100).]

3. Additional Procedures Performed in a Compilation Engagement

.07 *Question*—If an accountant performs procedures customarily performed in a review or audit but not in a compilation, is the accountant required to change the engagement to a review or an audit?

.08 *Interpretation*—No. Paragraph .13 of section 80 states that in a compilation engagement the accountant is not required to make inquiries or perform other procedures to verify, corroborate, or review information supplied by the entity. However, the accountant is not precluded from making inquiries or performing additional procedures.

.09 The wording of confirmation requests or other communications related to additional procedures performed in the course of a compilation engagement should not use phrases such as "as part of an *audit* of the financial statements" (emphasis supplied).

[Issue Date: March 1983; Revised: October 2000; Revised: November 2002; Revised: May 2004; Revised: December 2010 to conform to SSARS No. 19 (formerly Interpretation No. 13 to section 100).]

4. Differentiating a Financial Statement Presentation From a Trial Balance

.10 *Question*—Paragraph .01 of section 80 states that the accountant is required to comply with the provisions of section 80 whenever he or she is engaged to report on compiled financial statements or submits financial statements to a client or third parties. What attributes should an accountant consider when differentiating a financial statement from a trial balance to determine if he or she is required to comply with the provisions of section 80?

.11 *Interpretation*—The accountant may consider, among other matters, the following attributes when determining whether a financial presentation is a financial statement or a trial balance:

- Generally, a financial statement features the combination of similar general ledger accounts to create classifications or account groupings with corresponding subtotals and totals of dollar amounts. Some examples of these classifications or account groupings are current assets, long-term debt, and revenues. In addition, contra accounts are generally netted against the related primary accounts in financial statement presentations (that is, "Accounts

AR §9080.05

Compilation of Financial Statements

Receivable Net of Allowance for Bad Debts"). In contrast, a trial balance consists of a listing of all of the general ledger accounts and their corresponding debit or credit balances.

- Financial statements generally contain titles that identify the presentation as one intended to present financial position, results of operations, or cash flows. Typical titles for financial statements include the following:

  — Balance Sheet

  — Statement of Income or Statement of Operations

  — Statement of Comprehensive Income

  — Statement of Retained Earnings

  — Statement of Cash Flows

  — Statement of Changes in Owners' Equity

  — Statement of Assets and Liabilities (with or without owners' equity accounts)

  — Statement of Revenue and Expenses

  — Statement of Financial Position

  — Statement of Activities

  — Summary of Operations

  — Statement of Operations by Product Lines

  — Statement of Cash Receipts and Disbursements

  Examples of typical titles for trial balance presentations are as follows:

  — Trial Balance

  — Working Trial Balance

  — Adjusted Trial Balance

  — Listing of General Ledger Accounts

- The balance sheet in a set of financial statements segregates asset, liability, and owners' equity accounts and presents these three elements based on the following basic example equation:

  Assets = Liabilities + Owners' Equity

  The elements of the income statement and their relationship to net income are presented based on the following basic example equation:

  Revenues – Expenses + Gains – Losses = Net Income

  In a trial balance, no attempt is made to establish a mathematical relationship among the elements except that total debits equal total credits.

- The income statement in a set of financial statements generally contains a caption such as "Net Income" or "Net Revenues Over Expenses" that identifies the net results of operations. Trial balance presentations generally do not contain similar captions.

AR §9080.11

58   Statements on Standards for Accounting and Review Services

- The balance sheet in a set of financial statements usually presents assets in the order of their liquidity and liabilities in the order of their maturity. In a trial balance, the accounts are generally listed in account number order as they appear in the general ledger.

- In a set of financial statements, the income statement articulates with the balance sheet because the net results of operations are added to or subtracted from opening retained earnings. In a trial balance, the net results of operations are generally not closed out to retained earnings.

.12 The accountant's use of judgment is important when considering these attributes to determine whether the financial presentation constitutes a financial statement or a trial balance. When making this determination, the accountant may consider the preponderance of the attributes of the financial presentation. For example, a trial balance that contains one or two attributes of a financial statement may, in the accountant's judgment, still constitute a trial balance. When the presentation is deemed to be a financial statement, the accountant, at a minimum, should compile the financial statements in accordance with section 80 when he or she submits such financial statements to his or her client or third parties.

[Issue Date: September 1990; Revised: October 2000; Revised: February 2008; Revised: December 2010 to conform to SSARS No. 19 (formerly Interpretation No. 15 to section 100).]

5. Submitting Draft Financial Statements

.13 *Question*—Accountants frequently submit draft financial statements (*a*) because information needed to complete a compilation of the financial statements will not be available until a later date, or (*b*) to provide the client with the opportunity to read and analyze the financial statements prior to their final issuance. Is it permissible for the accountant to submit draft financial statements without intending to comply with the reporting provisions of section 80?

.14 *Interpretation*—Except in those instances in which the financial statements are not expected to be used by a third party, as permitted under paragraphs .22–.24 of section 80, an accountant is precluded from submitting draft financial statements unless he or she intends to submit those financial statements in final form accompanied by an appropriate compilation report prescribed by section 80. However, as long as the accountant intends to issue a compilation report on the financial statements in final form and labels each page of draft financial statements with words such as "Draft," "Preliminary Draft," "Draft—Subject to Changes," or "Working Draft," the accountant is not required to comply with the reporting provisions of section 80 with respect to those draft financial statements. In the rare circumstance in which the accountant intended to but never submitted final financial statements, the accountant may want to document the reasons why he or she was unable to submit financial statements in final form accompanied by an appropriate compilation report.

[Issue Date: September 1990; Revised: October 2000; Revised: December 2010 to conform to SSARS No. 19 (formerly Interpretation No. 17 to section 100).]

6. Reporting When Financial Statements Contain a Departure From Promulgated Accounting Principles That Prevents the Financial Statements From Being Misleading

.15 *Question*—Rule 203, *Accounting Principles* (ET sec. 203 par. .01), of the AICPA Code of Professional Conduct states

AR §9080.12

Compilation of Financial Statements

> A member shall not (1) express an opinion or state affirmatively that the financial statements or other financial data of any entity are presented in conformity with generally accepted accounting principles or (2) state that he or she is not aware of any material modifications that should be made to such statements or data in order for them to be in conformity with generally accepted accounting principles, if such statements or data contain any departure from an accounting principle promulgated by bodies designated by Council to establish such principles that has a material effect on the statements or data taken as a whole. If, however, the statements or data contain such a departure and the member can demonstrate that due to unusual circumstances the financial statements or data would otherwise have been misleading, the member can comply with the rule by describing the departure, its approximate effects, if practicable, and the reasons why compliance with the principle would result in a misleading statement.

Paragraphs .27–.29 of section 80 do not address the Rule 203 circumstances. When the circumstances contemplated by Rule 203 are present, how should the accountant report on the information described in the rule?

.16 *Interpretation*—Rule 203 does not apply to engagements to report on a compiled financial statements. Accordingly, when the accountant is reporting on a compiled financial statements and is confronted with the circumstances contemplated by Rule 203, the guidance in paragraphs .27–.29 of section 80 pertaining to departures from generally accepted accounting principles (GAAP) should be followed.

[Issue Date: February 1991; Revised: October 2000; Revised: November 2002; Revised: May 2004; Revised: July 2005; Revised: December 2010 to conform to SSARS No. 19 (formerly Interpretation No. 19 to section 100).]

7. Applicability of Statements on Standards for Accounting and Review Services to Litigation Services

.17 *Question*—When are litigation services excluded from the applicability of Statements on Standards for Accounting and Review Services (SSARSs)?

.18 *Interpretation*—SSARSs do not apply to financial statements submitted in conjunction with litigation services that involve pending or potential formal legal or regulatory proceedings before a "trier of fact" in connection with the resolution of a dispute between two or more parties when the

    a. service consists of being an expert witness.

    b. service consists of being a "trier of fact" or acting on behalf of one.

    c. accountant's work under the rules of the proceedings is subject to detailed analysis and challenge by each party to the dispute.

    d. accountant is engaged by an attorney to do work that will be protected by the attorney's work product privilege, and such work is not intended to be used for other purposes.

When performing such litigation services, the accountant should comply with Rule 201, *General Standards* (ET sec. 201 par. .01).

.19 *Question*—When do SSARSs apply to litigation service engagements?

.20 *Interpretation*—SSARSs apply to litigation service engagements when the accountant

    a. submits unaudited financial statements of a nonissuer that are the representation of management (owners) to others who,

AR §9080.20

60 Statements on Standards for Accounting and Review Services

under the rules of the proceedings, do not have the opportunity to analyze and challenge the accountant's work, or

b.   is specifically engaged to submit, in accordance with SSARSs, financial statements that are the representation of management (owners).

[Issue Date: May 1991; Revised: October 2000; Revised: February 2008; Revised: December 2010 to conform to SSARS No. 19 (formerly Interpretation No. 20 to section 100).]

8. Applicability of Statements on Standards for Accounting and Review Services When Performing Controllership or Other Management Services

.21 *Question*—If the accountant is in the practice of public accounting and provides an entity with controllership or other management services that entail the submission of financial statements, is the accountant required to follow the requirements of section 80?

.22 *Interpretation*—If the accountant is in the practice of public accounting as defined by the AICPA's Code of Conduct (ET sec. 92 par. .29) and is not a stockholder, partner, director, officer, or employee of the entity, the accountant is required to follow the performance and communication requirements of section 80, including any requirement to disclose a lack of independence.

.23 If the accountant is in the practice of public accounting and is also a stockholder, partner, director, officer, or employee of the entity, the accountant may either (a) comply with the requirements of section 80, or (b) communicate, preferably in writing, the accountant's relationship to the entity (for example, stockholder, partner, director, officer, or employee). The following is an example of the type of communication that may be used by the accountant:

> The accompanying balance sheet of Company X as of December 31, 20XX, and the related statements of income and cash flows for the year then ended have been prepared by [*name of accountant*], CPA. I have prepared such financial statements in my capacity [*describe capacity, for example, as a director*] of Company X.

.24 If an accountant is not in the practice of public accounting, the issuance of a report under SSARSs would be inappropriate; however, the previously mentioned communication may be used.

[Issue Date: July 2002; Revised: December 2010 to conform to SSARS No. 19 (formerly Interpretation No. 21 to section 100).]

9. Use of the Label "Selected Information—Substantially All Disclosures Required by [the applicable financial reporting framework] Are Not Included" in Compiled Financial Statements

.25 *Question*—Can an accountant label notes to the financial statements "Selected Information—Substantially All Disclosures Required by [*identify the applicable financial reporting framework (for example, accounting principles generally accepted in the United States of America")*] Are Not Included" when the client includes more than a few required disclosures?

.26 *Interpretation*—No. As discussed in paragraph .20 of section 80, when the entity wishes to include disclosures about only a few matters in the form of notes to the financial statements, such disclosures should be labeled "Selected Information—Substantially All Disclosures Required by [*identify the applicable financial reporting framework (for example "accounting principles generally accepted in the United States of America")*] Are Not Included."

AR §9080.21

Compilation of Financial Statements 61

.27 When the financial statements include more than a few disclosures, this guidance is not appropriate. The omission of one or more notes, when substantially all other disclosures are presented, should be treated in a compilation report like any other departure from the applicable financial reporting framework, and the nature of the departure and its effects, if known, should be disclosed in accordance with paragraphs .27–.29 of section 80. The label "Selected Information—Substantially All Disclosures Required by [*identify the applicable financial reporting framework (for example "accounting principles generally accepted in the United States of America"*)] Are Not Included" is not intended to be used for the omission of (intentionally or unintentionally) one or more specific disclosures. In determining whether use of the label is appropriate, the accountant needs to apply professional judgment to all the facts and circumstances.

[Issue Date: December 2002; Revised: December 2010 to conform to SSARS No. 19 (formerly Interpretation No. 22 to section 100).]

10. Omission of the Display of Comprehensive Income in Compiled Financial Statements

.28 *Question*—When an element of comprehensive income is present, can the display of comprehensive income be omitted when issuing a compilation report on financial statements that omit substantially all disclosures required by accounting principles generally accepted in the United States of America?

.29 *Interpretation*—Yes. Financial Accounting Standards Board (FASB) *Accounting Standards Codification* (ASC) 220, *Comprehensive Income*, requires the display of comprehensive income when a full set of financial statements is presented in conformity with accounting principles generally accepted in the United States of America. However, the display of comprehensive income may be omitted by identifying the omission in the compilation report or, if the engagement is to compile financial statements that are not expected to be used by a third party and the accountant does not report on those financial statements, in the engagement letter. The following is suggested modified wording (shown in *italic*) to the paragraph in the compilation report:

> Management has elected to omit substantially all the disclosures, (the statement of cash flows, if applicable,) *and the display of comprehensive income* required by accounting principles generally accepted in the United States of America. If the omitted disclosures, (the statement of cash flows, if applicable,) *and the display of comprehensive income* were included in the financial statements, they might influence the user's conclusions about the company's financial position, results of operations, and cash flows. Accordingly, these financial statements are not designed for those who are not informed about such matters.

.30 If the accountant compiles financial statements that include substantially all disclosures required by accounting principles generally accepted in the United States of America but omit the display of comprehensive income, the omission is a departure from accounting principles generally accepted in the United States of America.

.31 Additionally, if an element of comprehensive income has not been computed, for example, unrealized gains and losses arising from investments in marketable securities classified as "available for sale," then the accountant should consider a departure from accounting principles generally accepted in the United States of America and follow the guidance in paragraphs .27–.29 of section 80.

AR §9080.31

62 Statements on Standards for Accounting and Review Services

[Issue Date: September 2003; Revised: May 2004; Revised: July 2005; Revised: June 2009; Revised: December 2010 to conform to SSARS No. 19 (formerly Interpretation No. 25 to section 100).]

11. Special-Purpose Financial Statements to Comply With Contractual Agreements or Regulatory Provisions

.32 *Question*—An accountant may be asked to compile special-purpose financial statements prepared to comply with a contractual agreement or regulatory provision that specifies a special basis of presentation. In most circumstances, these financial statements are intended solely for the use of the parties to the agreement, regulatory bodies, or other specified parties. How should the accountant modify the standard compilation report when reporting on these compiled special-purpose financial statements?

.33 *Interpretation*—An accountant who is asked to compile special-purpose financial statements prepared to comply with a contractual agreement or a regulatory provision that specifies a special basis of presentation may issue a compilation report on those financial statements in accordance with section 80 as described in this interpretation. This interpretation describes reporting on

    a.   special-purpose financial statements prepared in compliance with a contractual agreement or regulatory provision that does not constitute a complete presentation of the entity's assets, liabilities, revenues, and expenses, but is otherwise prepared in conformity with GAAP or an other comprehensive basis of accounting (OCBOA), or

    b.   a special-purpose financial presentation (may be a complete set of financial statements or a single financial statement) prepared on a basis of accounting prescribed in an agreement that does not result in a presentation in conformity with GAAP or an OCBOA.

Financial Statements Prepared on a Basis of Accounting Prescribed in a Contractual Agreement or Regulatory Provision That Results in an Incomplete Presentation but One That Is Otherwise in Conformity With GAAP or an OCBOA

.34 An entity may engage an accountant to compile a special-purpose financial statement prepared in compliance with a contractual agreement or regulatory provision that does not constitute a complete presentation of the entity's assets, liabilities, revenues, or expenses, but is otherwise prepared in conformity with GAAP or an OCBOA. For example, a governmental agency may require a statement of gross income and certain expenses of an entity's real estate operation in which income and expenses are measured in conformity with GAAP, but expenses are defined to exclude certain items such as interest, depreciation, and income taxes. Such a statement may also present the excess of gross income over defined expenses. Also, a buy-sell agreement may specify a statement of gross assets and liabilities of the entity measured in conformity with GAAP, but limited to the assets to be sold and liabilities to be transferred pursuant to the agreement.

.35 When the accountant submits compiled special-purpose financial statements prepared on a basis of accounting prescribed in a contractual agreement or regulatory provision that results in an incomplete presentation but one that is otherwise prepared in conformity with GAAP or an OCBOA, the

AR §9080.32

Compilation of Financial Statements

accountant's report should be modified to include a separate paragraph with the following information:

- An explanation of what the financial statement is intended to present and a reference to the note to the special-purpose financial statement that describes the basis of presentation

- If the basis of presentation is in conformity with GAAP or an OCBOA, a statement that the presentation is not intended to be a complete presentation of the entity's assets, liabilities, revenues, and expenses

- A separate paragraph at the end of the report stating that the report is intended solely for the information and use of those within the entity, the parties to the contract or agreement, the regulatory agency with which the report is being filed, or those with whom the entity is negotiating directly, and is not intended to be and should not be used by anyone other than these specified parties

.36 The following is an illustrative example of a compilation report on special-purpose financial statements:

> I (we) have compiled the accompanying statement of net assets sold of XYZ Company as of December 31, 20X1. I (we) have not audited or reviewed the accompanying statement of net assets sold and, accordingly, do not express an opinion or provide any assurance about whether the statement of net assets sold is in accordance with the purchase agreement described in Note A.
>
> Management (owners) is (are) responsible for the preparation and fair presentation of the statement of net assets sold in accordance with the purchase agreement described in Note A and for designing, implementing, and maintaining internal control relevant to the preparation and fair presentation of the statement of net assets sold.
>
> My (our) responsibility is to conduct the compilation in accordance with Statements on Standards for Accounting and Review Services issued by the American Institute of Certified Public Accountants. The objective of a compilation is to assist management in presenting financial information in the form of financial statements without undertaking to obtain or provide any assurance that there are no material modifications that should be made to the financial statements.
>
> The accompanying statement was prepared for the purpose of presenting the net assets of XYZ Company sold to ABC Company pursuant to the purchase agreement described in Note A, and is not intended to be a complete presentation of XYZ Company's assets and liabilities.
>
> This report is intended solely for the information and use of [*the specified parties*] and is not intended to be and should not be used by anyone other than these specified parties.

Financial Statements Prepared on a Basis of Accounting Prescribed in an Agreement That Results in a Presentation That Is Not in Conformity With GAAP or an OCBOA

.37 An entity may engage an accountant to compile a special-purpose financial statement prepared in conformity with a basis of accounting that departs from GAAP or an OCBOA. A loan agreement, for example, may require the borrower to prepare consolidated financial statements in which assets, such as inventory, are presented on a basis that is not in conformity with GAAP or an OCBOA. Also, an acquisition agreement may require the financial statements of the entity being acquired (or a segment of it) to be prepared in conformity with

AR §9080.37

64   Statements on Standards for Accounting and Review Services

GAAP except for certain assets, such as receivables, inventories, and properties for which a valuation basis is specified in the agreement.

.38 Financial statements prepared under a basis of accounting as discussed in the preceding are not considered to be prepared in conformity with an OCBOA because the criteria used to prepare such financial statements do not meet the requirement of "having substantial support," even though the criteria are definite.

.39 When the accountant submits compiled special-purpose financial statements prepared on a basis of accounting prescribed in an agreement that results in a presentation that is not in conformity with GAAP or an OCBOA, the accountant's report should be modified to include a separate paragraph with the following information:

- An explanation of what the presentation is intended to present and a reference to the note to the special-purpose financial statements that describes the basis of presentation.

- A statement that the financial statement is not intended to be a presentation in conformity with GAAP or an OCBOA.

- A description and the source of significant interpretations, if any, made by the company's management relating to the provisions of a relevant agreement.

- A separate paragraph at the end of the report stating that the report is intended solely for the information and use of those within the entity, the parties to the contract or agreement, the regulatory agency with which the report is being filed, or those with whom the entity is negotiating directly, and is not intended to be and should not be used by anyone other than these specified parties. For example, if the financial statements have been prepared for the specified purpose of obtaining bank financing, the report's use should be restricted to the various banks with whom the entity is negotiating the proposed financing.

.40 The following is an illustrative example of a compilation report on special-purpose financial statements:

I (we) have compiled the special-purpose statement of assets and liabilities of XYZ Company as of December 31, 20X1, and the related special-purpose statements of revenue and expenses and of cash flows for the year then ended. I (we) have not audited or reviewed the accompanying financial statements and, accordingly, do not express an opinion or provide any assurance about whether the financial statements are in accordance with the acquisition agreement between ABC Company and XYZ Company as discussed in Note A.

Management (owners) is (are) responsible for the preparation and fair presentation of the financial statements in accordance with the acquisition agreement between ABC Company and XYZ Company as described in Note A and for designing, implementing, and maintaining internal control relevant to the preparation and fair presentation of the financial statements.

My (our) responsibility is to conduct the compilation in accordance with Statements on Standards for Accounting and Review Services issued by the American Institute of Certified Public Accountants. The objective of a compilation is to assist management in presenting financial information in the form of financial statements without undertaking to obtain or provide any assurance that there are no material modifications that should be made to the financial statements.

AR §9080.38

Compilation of Financial Statements

65

The accompanying special-purpose financial statements were prepared for the purpose of complying with the acquisition agreement between ABC Company and XYZ Company as discussed in Note A, and are not intended to be a presentation in conformity with GAAP.

This report is intended solely for the information and use of [*the specified parties*] and is not intended to be and should not be used by anyone other than these specified parties.

[Issue Date: December 2006; Revised: December 2010 to conform to SSARS No. 19 (formerly Interpretation No. 28 to section 100).]

12. Reporting on an Uncertainty, Including an Uncertainty About an Entity's Ability to Continue as a Going Concern

.41 *Question*—How should an accountant modify the standard compilation report when, during the performance of compilation procedures, evidence or information comes to the accountant's attention that there may be an uncertainty about the entity's ability to continue as a going concern for a reasonable period of time, not to exceed one year beyond the date of the financial statements being compiled?

.42 *Interpretation*—Disclosure requirements with respect to uncertainties are included in FASB ASC 275, *Risks and Uncertainties*; FASB ASC 450, *Contingencies*; and other authoritative accounting literature. However, the accounting literature does not provide specific guidance on disclosure of uncertainties caused by concern about an entity's ability to continue as a going concern. Continuation of an entity as a going concern is assumed in financial reporting in the absence of significant information to the contrary. The accountant should follow the guidance in paragraphs .47–.50 of section 80 with respect to his or her consideration of the entity's ability to continue as a going concern during the performance of compilation procedures.

.43 If the accountant concludes that management's disclosure of the uncertainty regarding the entity's ability to continue as a going concern is adequate but further decides to include an emphasis-of-matter paragraph with respect to the uncertainty in the accountant's compilation report, he or she may use the following language:

As discussed in Note X, certain conditions indicate that the Company may be unable to continue as a going concern. The accompanying financial statements do not include any adjustments that might be necessary should the Company be unable to continue as a going concern.

.44 *Question*—If the accountant, while performing a compilation, becomes aware of a material uncertainty other than a going concern uncertainty (for example, an uncertainty regarding pending or threatened litigation), what should the accountant consider in deciding whether a report modification is necessary?

.45 *Interpretation*—Disclosure requirements with respect to uncertainties are included in FASB ASC 275, 450, and other authoritative accounting literature. If the accountant determines that the disclosure of the uncertainty is not in accordance with the applicable financial reporting framework, he or she should follow the guidance in paragraphs .27–.29 of section 80.

.46 If the accountant concludes that management's disclosure of the uncertainty is in accordance with the applicable financial reporting framework but further decides to include an emphasis-of-matter paragraph with respect to the uncertainty in the accountant's compilation report, he or she may use the following language (the following is assuming that the financial statements

AR §9080.46

66　　　Statements on Standards for Accounting and Review Services

were prepared in accordance with accounting principles generally accepted in the United States of America):

> As discussed in Note X, the Company is currently named in a legal action. The Company has determined that it is not possible to predict the eventual outcome of the legal action but has determined that the resolution of the action will not result in an adverse judgment that would materially affect the financial statements. Accordingly, the accompanying financial statements do not include any adjustments related to the legal action under FASB ASC 450.

.47 *Question*—Paragraph .20 of section 80 allows the accountant, when he or she is requested to do so, to compile financial statements that omit substantially all of the disclosures required by an applicable financial reporting framework, provided the omission of substantially all disclosures was not, to the accountant's knowledge, undertaken with the intention of misleading those who might reasonably be expected to use such financial statements, and the accountant includes a paragraph in the accountant's compilation report regarding the omission of substantially all disclosures. Should disclosure of an uncertainty be considered so significant that it also could never be omitted?

.48 *Interpretation*—No. The user is adequately warned of the limitations of the financial statements by the report language required by paragraph .20 of section 80.

[Issue date: February 2007; Revised: February 2008; Amended: December 2008; Revised: June 2009; Revised: December 2010 to conform to SSARS No. 19 (formerly Interpretation No. 29 to section 100)]

13. Compilations of Financial Statements Prepared in Accordance With International Financial Reporting Standards

.49 *Question*—The International Accounting Standards Board (IASB) has been designated by the Council of the AICPA as the body to establish international financial reporting standards for both private and public entities pursuant to Rule 202, *Compliance With Standards* (ET sec. 202 par. .01), and Rule 203 of the AICPA Code of Professional Conduct as of May 18, 2008. As a result, how would an accountant apply the reporting guidance in section 80 when engaged to compile financial statements presented in accordance with International Financial Reporting Standards (IFRSs) as issued by the IASB?

.50 *Interpretation*—A report illustration of how an accountant would apply the reporting guidance in section 80 when reporting on financial statements presented in accordance with IFRSs is as follows:

Accountant's Compilation Report

[Appropriate Salutation]

I (we) have compiled the accompanying balance sheets of XYZ Company as of December 31, 20X2 and 20X1, and the related statements of income, retained earnings, and cash flows for the years then ended. I (we) have not audited or reviewed the accompanying financial statements and, accordingly, do not express an opinion or provide any assurance about whether the financial statements are in accordance with International Financial Reporting Standards as issued by the International Accounting Standards Board.

Management (owners) is (are) responsible for the preparation and fair presentation of the financial statements in accordance with International Financial Reporting Standards as issued by the International Accounting Standards

AR §9080.47

Compilation of Financial Statements

67

Board and for designing, implementing, and maintaining internal control relevant to the preparation and fair presentation of the financial statements.

My (our) responsibility is to conduct the compilation in accordance with Statements on Standards for Accounting and Review Services issued by the American Institute of Certified Public Accountants. The objective of a compilation is to assist management in presenting financial information in the form of financial statements without undertaking to obtain or provide any assurance that there are no material modifications that should be made to the financial statements.

[Signature of accounting firm or accountant, as appropriate]

[Date]

When the accountant compiles financial statements that omit substantially all disclosures but are otherwise in conformity with IFRSs as issued by the IASB, the accountant may wish to modify the third paragraph of the standard report as follows:

> Management has elected to omit substantially all disclosures (and the statement of cash flows) required by International Financial Reporting Standards as issued by the International Accounting Standards Board. If the omitted disclosures and statement were included in the financial statements, they might influence the user's conclusions about the company's financial position, results of operations, and cash flows. Accordingly, these financial statements are not designed for those who are not informed about such matters.

.51 *Question*—Unlike accounting principles generally accepted in the United States of America as issued by FASB, IFRSs require an entity to disclose comparative information in respect of the previous comparative period for all amounts presented in the current year's financial statements. When the accountant compiles financial statements that omit prior year information, should such omission be disclosed in the accountant's compilation report as a departure from IFRSs as issued by the IASB in accordance with paragraphs .27–.29 of section 80?

.52 *Interpretation*—Yes. Because IFRSs require an entity to disclose comparative information in respect of the previous comparative period for all amounts presented in the current year's financial statements, the failure to include such information in financial statements would be a departure from GAAP. An example of a paragraph that may be added to the accountant's compilation report is as follows:

> Comparative information with respect to the year ended December 31, 20XX-1 has not been presented. International Financial Reporting Standards [or *IFRSs for SMEs*] as issued by the International Accounting Standards Board require an entity to disclose comparative information in respect of the previous comparative period for all amounts presented in the current year's financial statements.

When the accountant compiles financial statements that omit substantially all disclosures but are otherwise in conformity with IFRSs as issued by the IASB, the accountant may wish to modify the third paragraph of the standard report as follows:

> Management has elected to omit substantially all disclosures (and the statement of cash flows and comparative financial information as of and for the year ended December 31, 20XX-1) required by International Financial Reporting Standards [or *IFRSs for SMEs*] as issued by the International Accounting Standards Board. If the omitted disclosures, statement, and comparative financial information were included in the financial statements, they might influence

AR §9080.52

68 Statements on Standards for Accounting and Review Services

the user's conclusions about the company's financial position, results of operations, and cash flows. Accordingly, these financial statements are not designed for those who are not informed about such matters.

[Issue Date: May 2008; Revised: June 2010; Revised: August 2010; Revised: December 2010 (formerly Interpretation No. 30 to section 100).]

14. Compilations of Financial Statements Prepared in Accordance With a Financial Reporting Framework Generally Accepted in Another Country

.53 *Question*—An accountant may be engaged to compile financial statements that have been prepared in conformity with a financial reporting framework generally accepted in another country (including financial statements prepared in accordance with a jurisdictional variation of IFRSs such that the entity's financial statements do not contain an explicit and unreserved statement of compliance with IFRSs as issued by the IASB). How should an accountant apply the reporting requirements of section 80 when reporting on those financial statements?

.54 *Interpretation*—If the financial statements are intended for use only outside of the United States of America, the accountant may report using the standard form of U.S. compilation report modified as appropriate to identify the applicable financial reporting framework, or alternatively, the accountant may report using the standard compilation report form and content of the other country. (See Interpretation No. 15 with respect to Considerations Related to Compilations Performed in Accordance with International Standard on Related Services [ISRS] 4410, *Engagements to Compile Financial Statements*).

.55 The standard compilation report used in another country, even when it appears similar to that used in the United States of America, may convey a different meaning and entail a different responsibility on the part of the accountant due to custom or culture. Issuing a standard compilation report of another country may require an understanding of local laws. When issuing the accountant's standard compilation report of another country, the accountant is required to obtain an understanding of applicable legal responsibilities, in addition to the compilation standards and accounting principles generally accepted in the other country, as indicated in paragraph .11 of section 80. Therefore, depending on the nature and extent of the accountant's knowledge and experience, the accountant may wish to consult with persons having expertise in the reporting practices of the other country and associated legal responsibilities to obtain the understanding needed to issue that country's standard compilation report.

.56 If the accountant's report is intended for use in the United States of America, the reporting requirements described in paragraphs .16–.19 of section 80 would apply. Additionally, paragraph .31 of AR section 80 states that a need for restriction on the use of the report may result from a number of circumstances, including, but not limited to, the purpose of the report and the potential for the report to be misunderstood when taken out of context in which it was intended to be used. Because of the nature of the basis of presentation of the financial statements there is a presumption that the report would be misunderstood or taken out of context in which it was intended to be used. In such instances, the accountant may use the following form of report:

Accountant's Compilation Report

[Appropriate Salutation]

I (we) have compiled the accompanying balance sheets of XYZ Company as of December 31, 20X2 and 20X1, and the related statements of income, retained

AR §9080.53

Compilation of Financial Statements 69

earnings, and cash flows for the years then ended. I (we) have not audited or reviewed the accompanying financial statements and, accordingly, do not express an opinion or provide any assurance about whether the financial statements are in accordance with [*the financial reporting framework generally accepted in another country, including identification of the nationality of the framework*].

Management (owners) is (are) responsible for the preparation and fair presentation of the financial statements in accordance with [*the financial reporting framework generally accepted in another country, including identification of the nationality of the framework*] and for designing, implementing, and maintaining internal control relevant to the preparation and fair presentation of the financial statements.

My (our) responsibility is to conduct the compilation in accordance with Statements on Standards for Accounting and Review Services issued by the American Institute of Certified Public Accountants. The objective of a compilation is to assist management in presenting financial information in the form of financial statements without undertaking to obtain or provide any assurance that there are no material modifications that should be made to the financial statements.

This report is intended solely for the information and the use of [*specified parties*] and is not intended to be and should not be used by anyone other than the specified parties.

[*Signature of accounting firm or accountant, as appropriate*]

[*Date*]

.57 When the financial statements will be used both outside of the United States of America as well as in the United States of America, nothing precludes the accountant from issuing two reports—a report to be used only outside of the United States of America and another report to be used in the United States of America.

[Issue Date: May 2008; Revised: June 2010; Revised: August 2010; Revised: December 2010 (formerly Interpretation No. 30 to section 100).]

15. Considerations Related to Compilations Performed in Accordance With International Standard on Related Services 4410, *Engagements to Compile Financial Statements*, Issued by the International Audit and Assurance Standards Board

.58 *Question*—May a U.S. accountant perform a compilation of historical financial statements of a U.S. entity[1] in accordance with ISRS 4410 issued by the International Audit and Assurance Standards Board (IAASB)? The financial statements may have been prepared in accordance with IFRSs or accounting principles generally accepted in the United States of America.

.59 *Interpretation*—Yes. An accountant performing a compilation of historical financial statements of a U.S. entity is required to follow the compilation standards as promulgated by the AICPA's Accounting and Review Services Committee. However, those standards do not prohibit an accountant from indicating that the compilation also was conducted in accordance with another set of compilation standards. In an engagement to compile the historical financial statements in accordance with ISRS 4410, the accountant may perform the compilation in accordance with SSARSs as well as ISRS 4410. Such a compilation report may read as follows:

---

[1] A *U.S. entity* is an entity that is either organized or domiciled in the United States of America.

AR §9080.59

70 Statements on Standards for Accounting and Review Services

I (we) have compiled the accompanying balance sheets of XYZ Company as of December 31, 20X2 and 20X1, and the related statements of income, retained earnings, and cash flows for the years then ended. I (we) have not audited or reviewed the accompanying financial statements and, accordingly, do not express an opinion or provide any assurance about whether the financial statements are in accordance with International Financial Reporting Standards as issued by the International Accounting Standards Board.

Management (owners) is (are) responsible for the preparation and fair presentation of the financial statements in accordance with International Financial Reporting Standards as issued by the International Accounting Standards Board and for designing, implementing, and maintaining internal control relevant to the preparation and fair presentation of the financial statements.

My (our) responsibility is to conduct the compilation in accordance with Statements on Standards for Accounting and Review Services issued by the American Institute of Certified Public Accountants and in accordance with the International Standard on Related Services (ISRS 4410) issued by the International Audit & Assurance Standards Board applicable to compilation engagements. The objective of a compilation is to assist management in presenting financial information in the form of financial statements without undertaking to obtain or provide any assurance that there are no material modifications that should be made to the financial statements.

.60 If the report is for use only outside of the United States of America, the accountant is still required to apply SSARSs, except for requirements related to report form and content.

[Issue Date: May 2008; Revised: June 2010; Revised: August 2010; Revised: December 2010 (formerly Interpretation No. 30 to section 100).]

16. Preparation of Financial Statements for Use by an Entity's Auditors

.61 *Question*—Paragraph .22 of section 80 states "When the accountant submits compiled financial statements to his or her client that are not expected to be used by a third party, he or she is not required to issue a compilation report." In the situation in which a client engages an accountant, other than its auditor, to prepare unaudited financial statements on behalf of management and those financial statements are provided by management to its outside auditor for the purposes of the annual audit, is the client's outside auditor deemed to be a third party using the financial statements?

.62 *Interpretation*—No. Although the client's outside auditor is a third party, the auditor is not deemed to be using the financial statements. The auditor's role is to apply auditing procedures to those statements in order to obtain sufficient appropriate audit evidence to support his or her opinion on those statements. Accordingly, the requirements in paragraphs .22–.24 of section 80 are applicable.

[Issue Date: December 2008; Revised: December 2010 to conform to SSARS No. 19 (formerly Interpretation No. 31 to section 100).]

17. Required Supplementary Information That Accompanies Compiled Financial Statements

.63 *Question*—Paragraph .53 of section 80 addresses situations when the basic financial statements are accompanied by information presented for supplementary analysis purposes. Certain information presented for supplementary analysis purposes is required by a body designated by the AICPA Council

AR §9080.60

Compilation of Financial Statements   **71**

to establish GAAP pursuant to Rule 202 and Rule 203 [2] (hereinafter referred to as "required supplementary information"). Examples of required supplementary information that may accompany compiled financial statements include the following:

- With respect to common interest realty associations, estimates of current or future costs of major repairs and replacements of common property that will be required in the future as required by FASB ASC 972-235-50-3

- Management's discussion and analysis and budgetary comparison statements as required by Governmental Accounting Standards Board Statement No. 34, *Basic Financial Statements—and Management's Discussion and Analysis—for State and Local Governments.*

Is the accountant required to apply procedures to required supplementary information that accompanies compiled financial statements?

.64 *Interpretation*—No. SSARSs do not require the accountant to apply procedures to any information presented for supplementary analysis purposes, including required supplementary information. However, nothing precludes the accountant from compiling the required supplementary information if engaged to do so.

.65 *Question*—Paragraph .53 of section 80 states that when the basic financial statements are accompanied by information presented for supplementary analysis purposes, the accountant should indicate the degree of responsibility, if any, he or she is taking with respect to such information. How may an accountant modify the accountant's compilation report to refer to the required supplementary information and explain the circumstances regarding its presentation?

.66 *Interpretation*—The accountant may modify the accountant's compilation report by including a separate paragraph that refers to the required supplementary information and explains the circumstances regarding its presentation. That separate paragraph would be presented after the paragraph describing the accountant's responsibility and may read as follows:

The Required Supplementary Information Is Included and the Accountant Did Not Compile the Required Supplementary Information

> [*Identify the applicable financial reporting framework (for example, accounting principles generally accepted in the United States of America)*] require that [*identify the required supplementary information*] on page XX be presented to supplement the basic financial statements. Such information, although not a part of the basic financial statements, is required by [*identify the designated accounting standard setter*] who considers it to be an essential part of financial reporting and for placing the basic financial statements in an appropriate operational, economic, or historical context. Such information was not audited, reviewed, or compiled by me (us) and, accordingly, I (we) do not express an opinion or provide any assurance on it.

---

[2] The bodies designated by the AICPA Council to establish professional standards with respect to financial accounting and reporting principles pursuant to these rules are the Financial Accounting Standards Board, the Governmental Accounting Standards Board, the Federal Accounting Standards Advisory Board, and the International Accounting Standards Board.

AR §9080.66

72 Statements on Standards for Accounting and Review Services

The Required Supplementary Information Is Included, the Accountant Compiled the Required Supplemental Information and No Material Departures From the Prescribed Guidelines Regarding the Required Supplementary Information Have Been Identified

[Identify the applicable financial reporting framework (for example, accounting principles generally accepted in the United States of America)] require that [identify the required supplementary information] on page XX be presented to supplement the basic financial statements. Such information, although not a part of the basic financial statements, is required by [identify the designated accounting standard setter] who considers it to be an essential part of financial reporting and for placing the basic financial statements in an appropriate operational, economic, or historical context. Such information has been compiled by me (us) without audit or review and, accordingly, I (we) do not express an opinion or provide any assurance on it.

All Required Supplementary Information Omitted

Management has omitted [describe the missing required supplementary information] that [identify the applicable financial reporting framework (for example, accounting principles generally accepted in the United States of America)] require to be presented to supplement the basic financial statements. Such missing information, although not a part of the basic financial statements, is required by [identify the designated accounting standard setter] who considers it to be an essential part of financial reporting and for placing the basic financial statements in an appropriate operational, economic, or historical context.

Some Required Supplementary Information is Omitted and Some Is Presented in Accordance With the Prescribed Guidelines Regarding the Required Supplementary Information

[Identify the applicable financial reporting framework (for example, accounting principles generally accepted in the United States of America)] require that [identify the included supplementary information] be presented to supplement the basic financial statements. Such information, although not a part of the basic financial statements, is required by [identify designated accounting standard setter] who considers it to be an essential part of financial reporting for placing the basic financial statements in an appropriate operational, economic, or historical context. Such information was not audited, reviewed, or compiled by me (us) and, accordingly, I (we) do not express an opinion or provide any assurance on it.

Management has omitted [describe the missing required supplementary information] that [identify the applicable financial reporting framework] require to be presented to supplement the basic financial statements. Such missing information, although not a part of the basic financial statements, is required by [identify designated accounting standard setter] who considers it to be an essential part of financial reporting for placing the basic financial statements in an appropriate operational, economic, or historical context.

Material Departures From the Prescribed Guidelines Regarding the Required Supplementary Information Were Identified While Compiling the Required Supplementary Information

[Identify the applicable financial reporting framework (for example, accounting principles generally accepted in the United States of America)] require that the [identify the supplementary information] on page XX be presented to supplement the basic financial statements. Such information, although not a part of the basic financial statements, is required by [identify designated accounting standard setter] who considers it to be an essential part of financial reporting for placing the basic financial statements in an appropriate operational, economic, or historical context. Such information was compiled by me (us) without

AR §9080.66

Compilation of Financial Statements

73

audit or review and, accordingly, I (we) do not express an opinion or provide any assurance on it. However, during my (our) compilation, I (we) did become aware of the following material departures from the prescribed guidelines regarding the required supplementary information [*identify the required supplementary information and describe the material departures from the prescribed guidelines regarding the required supplementary information*].

.67 *Question*—When required supplementary information is omitted from financial statements that omit substantially all the disclosures required by accounting principles generally accepted in the United States of America (U.S. GAAP), may the accountant combine the paragraph discussing the omission of substantially all the disclosures, as required by paragraph .20 of section 80, with the paragraph referring to the omission of the required supplementary information?

.68 *Interpretation*—No. Since required supplementary information is not a part of the basic financial statements and the omitted disclosures (and the statement of cash flows, if applicable) are required by U.S. GAAP to be included in the basic financial statements, the report elements required by paragraphs .20 and .53 of section 80 are not compatible.

[Issue Date: October 2011.]

AR §9080.68

Review of Financial Statements

AR Section 90

Review of Financial Statements

Issue date, unless otherwise indicated: December 2009

Source: SSARS No. 19.

> *Note:* Paragraphs 3.1–.73 of SSARS No. 19, issued in December 2009, have been codified in this section and are effective for compilations and reviews of financial statements for periods ending on or after December 15, 2010.

.01 This section establishes standards and provides guidance on reviews of financial statements. The accountant is required to comply with the provisions of this section whenever he or she has been engaged to review financial statements, except for reviews of interim financial information if the following are true:

    a. The entity's latest annual financial statements have been audited by the accountant or a predecessor.

    b. The accountant has been engaged to audit the entity's current year financial statements, or the accountant audited the entity's latest annual financial statements and expects to be engaged to audit the current year financial statements.*

    c. The client prepares its interim financial information in accordance with the same financial reporting framework as that used to prepare the annual financial statements.

---

* In February 2011, the Accounting and Review Services Committee issued Statement on Standards for Accounting and Review Services (SSARS) No. 20, *Revised Applicability of Statements on Standards for Accounting and Review Services*. SSARS No. 20 is effective for reviews of financial statements for periods beginning after December 15, 2011, with early application permitted. SSARS No. 20 revises the conditions in paragraph .01 of this section as follows (new language is shown in boldface italics; deleted language is shown by strikethrough):

This section establishes standards and provides guidance on reviews of financial statements. The accountant is required to comply with the provisions of this section whenever he or she has been engaged to review financial statements, except for reviews of interim financial information if the following are true:

    a. The entity's latest annual financial statements have been audited by the accountant or a predecessor.

    b. The accountant *either*

        i. has been engaged to audit the entity's current year financial statements, or

        ii. ~~The accountant~~ audited the entity's latest annual financial statements and*, when it is expected that the current year financial statements will be audited,* ~~expects to be engaged to audit the current year financial statements~~ *the appointment of another accountant to audit the current year financial statements is not effective prior to the beginning of the period covered by the review.*

    c. The ~~client~~ *entity* prepares its interim financial information in accordance with the same financial reporting framework as that used to prepare the annual financial statements.

Accountants engaged to perform reviews of interim financial information when the conditions in (*a*)–(*c*) are met should perform such reviews in accordance with AU section 722, *Interim Financial Information*.

AR §90.01

Statements on Standards for Accounting and Review Services

Accountants engaged to perform reviews of interim financial information when the conditions in (a)–(c) are met should perform such reviews in accordance with AU section 722, *Interim Financial Information*.

.02 The accountant is precluded from performing a review engagement if the accountant's independence is impaired for any reason. In making a judgment about whether he or she is independent, the accountant should be guided by the AICPA's Code of Professional Conduct.

Establishing an Understanding

.03 The accountant should establish an understanding with management regarding the services to be performed for review engagements[1] and should document the understanding through a written communication with management. Such an understanding reduces the risk that either the accountant or management may misinterpret the needs or expectations of the other party. For example, it reduces the risk that management may inappropriately rely on the accountant to protect the entity against certain risks or to perform certain functions that are management's responsibility. The accountant should ensure that the understanding includes the objectives of the engagement, management's responsibilities, the accountant's responsibilities, and the limitations of the engagement. In some cases, the accountant may establish such understanding with those charged with governance.

.04 An understanding with management and, if applicable, those charged with governance regarding a review of financial statements should include the following matters:

- The objective of a review is to obtain limited assurance that there are no material modifications that should be made to the financial statements in order for the statements to be in conformity with the applicable financial reporting framework.

- Management is responsible for the preparation and fair presentation of the financial statements in accordance with the applicable financial reporting framework.

- Management is responsible for designing, implementing, and maintaining internal control relevant to the preparation and fair presentation of the financial statements.

- Management is responsible to prevent and detect fraud.

- Management is responsible for identifying and ensuring that the entity complies with the laws and regulations applicable to its activities.

- Management is responsible for making all financial records and related information available to the accountant.

- Management will provide the accountant, at the conclusion of the engagement, with a letter that confirms certain representations made during the review.

- The accountant is responsible for conducting the engagement in accordance with SSARSs issued by the AICPA.

- A review includes primarily applying analytical procedures to management's financial data and making inquiries of company management.

---

[1] See paragraph .28 of QC section 10B, *A Firm's System of Quality Control*.

AR §90.02

Review of Financial Statements

- A review is substantially less in scope than an audit, the objective of which is the expression of an opinion regarding the financial statements as a whole. A review does not contemplate obtaining an understanding of the entity's internal control; assessing fraud risk; testing accounting records by obtaining sufficient appropriate audit evidence through inspection, observation, confirmation, or the examination of source documents (for example, cancelled checks or bank images); or other procedures ordinarily performed in an audit. Accordingly, the accountant will not express an opinion regarding the financial statements as a whole.

- The engagement cannot be relied upon to disclose errors, fraud,[2] or illegal acts.[3]

- The accountant will inform the appropriate level of management of any material errors and of any evidence or information that comes to the accountant's attention during the performance of review procedures that fraud or an illegal act may have occurred.[4] The accountant need not report any matters regarding illegal acts that may have occurred that are clearly inconsequential and may reach agreement in advance with the entity on the nature of any such matters to be communicated.

These matters should be communicated in the form of an engagement letter. An example of an engagement letter for a review of financial statements is presented in Review Exhibit A, "Illustrative Engagement Letter."

.05 An understanding with management or, if applicable, those charged with governance also may include other matters, such as the following:

- Fees and billings

- Any limitation of or other arrangements regarding the liability of the accountant or the client, such as indemnification to the accountant for liability arising from knowing misrepresentations to the accountant by management (regulators may restrict or prohibit such liability limitation arrangements)

- Conditions under which access to review documentation may be granted to others

- Additional services to be provided relating to regulatory requirements

.06 The engagement letter also should address the following additional matters if applicable:

- Material departures from the applicable financial reporting framework may exist, and the effects of those departures, if any, on the financial statements may not be disclosed.

- Reference to supplementary information.

---

[2] For purposes of this section, *fraud* is an intentional act that results in a misstatement in reviewed financial statements.

[3] For purposes of this section, *illegal acts* are violations of laws or government regulations, excluding fraud.

[4] Whether an act is, in fact, fraudulent or illegal is a determination that is normally beyond the accountant's professional competence. An accountant, in reporting on financial statements, presents himself or herself as one who is proficient in accounting and review services. The accountant's training, experience, and understanding of the client and its industry may provide a basis for recognition that some client acts coming to his or her attention may be fraudulent or illegal. However, the determination as to whether a particular act is fraudulent or illegal would generally be based on the advice of an informed expert qualified to practice law or may have to await final determination by a court of law.

AR §90.06

Statements on Standards for Accounting and Review Services

Review Performance Requirements

.07 The performance of a review engagement requires that the accountant perform procedures designed to accumulate review evidence that will provide a reasonable basis for obtaining limited assurance that there are no material modifications that should be made to the financial statements in order for the statements to be in conformity with the applicable financial reporting framework. The accountant should apply professional judgment in determining the specific nature, timing, and extent of review procedures. Such procedures should be tailored based on the accountant's understanding of the industry in which the client operates and the accountant's knowledge of the entity. Review evidence obtained through the performance of analytical procedures and inquiry will ordinarily provide the accountant with a reasonable basis for obtaining limited assurance. However, the accountant should perform additional procedures if the accountant determines such procedures to be necessary to obtain limited assurance that the financial statements are not materially misstated.

Understanding of the Industry

.08 The accountant should possess an understanding of the industry in which the client operates, including the accounting principles and practices generally used in the industry sufficient to assist the accountant with determining the specific nature, timing, and extent of review procedures to be performed.

.09 The requirement that the accountant possess a level of knowledge of the industry in which the entity operates does not prevent the accountant from accepting a review engagement for an entity in an industry with which the accountant has no previous experience. It does, however, place upon the accountant a responsibility to obtain the required level of knowledge. The accountant may do so, for example, by consulting AICPA guides, industry publications, financial statements of other entities in the industry, textbooks and periodicals, appropriate continuing professional education, or individuals knowledgeable about the industry.

Knowledge of the Client

.10 The accountant should obtain knowledge about the client sufficient to assist the accountant with determining the specific nature, timing, and extent of review procedures to be performed. That knowledge should include the following:

- An understanding of the client's business
- An understanding of the accounting principles and practices used by the client

.11 In obtaining an understanding of the client's business, the accountant should have a general understanding of the client's organization; its operating characteristics; and the nature of its assets, liabilities, revenues, and expenses. The accountant's understanding of an entity's business is ordinarily obtained through experience with the entity or its industry and inquiry of the entity's personnel.

.12 The accountant should understand the accounting principles and practices used by the client in measuring, recognizing, recording, and disclosing all significant accounts and disclosures in the financial statements. The accountant may obtain an understanding of the accounting policies and procedures used by management through inquiry, the review of client prepared documents, or experience with the client.

AR §90.07

Review of Financial Statements

.13 In obtaining this understanding of the client's accounting policies and practices, the accountant should be alert to unusual accounting policies and procedures that come to the accountant's attention as a result of his or her knowledge of the industry.

Designing and Performing Review Procedures

.14 Based on

    a.   the accountant's understanding of the industry,

    b.   his or her knowledge of the client, and

    c.   his or her awareness of the risk that he or she may unknowingly fail to modify the accountant's review report on financial statements that are materially misstated,

the accountant should design and perform analytical procedures and make inquiries and perform other procedures, as appropriate, to accumulate review evidence in obtaining limited assurance that there are no material modifications that should be made to the financial statements in order for the statements to be in conformity with the applicable financial reporting framework.

.15 The accountant should focus the analytical procedures and inquiries in those areas where the accountant believes there are increased risks of misstatements. The results of the accountant's analytical procedures and inquiries may modify the accountant's risk awareness. For example, the response to an inquiry that cash has not been reconciled for several months may revise the accountant's awareness of risks relative to the cash account.

Analytical Procedures

.16 Understanding financial and nonfinancial relationships is essential in evaluating the results of analytical procedures, and generally requires knowledge of the client and the industry in which the client operates. An understanding of the purposes of analytical procedures and the limitations of those procedures also is important. Accordingly, the identification of the relationships and types of data used, as well as conclusions reached when recorded amounts are compared to expectations, requires judgment by the accountant.

.17 Analytical procedures involve comparisons of expectations developed by the accountant to recorded amounts or ratios developed from recorded amounts. The accountant develops such expectations by identifying and using plausible relationships that are reasonably expected to exist based on the accountant's understanding of the industry in which the client operates and knowledge of the client. Following are examples of sources of information for developing expectations:

    a.   Financial information for comparable prior period(s), giving consideration to known changes

    b.   Anticipated results (for example, budgets or forecasts, including extrapolations from interim or annual data)

    c.   Relationships among elements of financial information within the period

    d.   Information regarding the industry in which the client operates (for example, gross margin information)

    e.   Relationships of financial information with relevant nonfinancial information (for example, payroll costs to number of employees)

AR §90.17

80 Statements on Standards for Accounting and Review Services

Analytical procedures may be performed at the financial statement level or at the detailed account level. The nature, timing, and extent of the analytical procedures are a matter of professional judgment.

.18 If analytical procedures performed identify fluctuations or relationships that are inconsistent with other relevant information or that differ from expected values by a significant amount, the accountant should investigate these differences by inquiring of management and performing other procedures as necessary in the circumstances. Review evidence relevant to management's responses may be obtained by evaluating those responses, taking into account the accountant's understanding of the entity and its environment, along with other review evidence obtained during the course of the review. Although the accountant is not required to corroborate management's responses with other evidence, the accountant may need to perform other procedures when, for example, management is unable to provide an explanation, or the explanation, together with review evidence obtained relevant to management's response, is not considered adequate.

Inquiries and Other Review Procedures

.19 The accountant should consider performing the following:

    a.   Inquire of members of management who have responsibility for financial and accounting matters concerning the following:

        i. Whether the financial statements have been prepared in conformity with the applicable financial reporting framework

        ii. The entity's accounting principles and practices and the methods followed in applying them and the entity's procedures for recording, classifying, and summarizing transactions and accumulating information for disclosure in the financial statements

        iii. Unusual or complex situations that may have an effect on the financial statements

        iv. Significant transactions occurring or recognized near the end of the reporting period

        v. The status of uncorrected misstatements identified during the previous engagement

        vi. Questions that have arisen in the course of applying the review procedures

        vii. Events subsequent to the date of the financial statements that could have a material effect on the financial statements

        viii. Their knowledge of any fraud or suspected fraud affecting the entity involving management or others where the fraud could have a material effect on the financial statements (for example, communications received from employees, former employees, or others)

        ix. Significant journal entries and other adjustments

        x. Communications from regulatory agencies

    In addition to members of management who have responsibility for financial and accounting matters, the accountant may determine to direct inquiries to others within the entity and those charged with governance, if appropriate.

AR §90.18

Review of Financial Statements

81

    b.   Inquire concerning actions taken at meetings of stockholders, the board of directors, committees of the board of directors, or comparable meetings that may affect the financial statements

    c.   Read the financial statements to consider, on the basis of information coming to the accountant's attention, whether the financial statements appear to conform with the applicable financial reporting framework

    d.   Obtain reports from other accountants, if any, who have been engaged to audit or review the financial statements of significant components of the reporting entity, its subsidiaries, and other investees[5]

.20 The accountant ordinarily is not required to corroborate management's responses with other evidence; however, the accountant should consider the reasonableness and consistency of management's responses in light of the results of other review procedures and the accountant's knowledge of the client's business and the industry in which it operates.

Incorrect, Incomplete, or Otherwise Unsatisfactory Information

.21 During the performance of review procedures, the accountant may become aware that information coming to his or her attention is incorrect, incomplete, or otherwise unsatisfactory. In such instances, the accountant should request that management consider the effect of these matters on the financial statements and communicate the results of its consideration to the accountant. The accountant should consider the results communicated to the accountant by management and the effect, if any, on the accountant's review report. If the accountant believes the financial statements may be materially misstated, the accountant should perform additional procedures deemed necessary to obtain limited assurance that there are no material modifications that should be made to the financial statements in order for the statements to be in conformity with the applicable financial reporting framework. If the accountant concludes that the financial statements are materially misstated, the accountant should follow the guidance in paragraphs .34–.36 with respect to departures from the applicable financial reporting framework.

Management Representations

.22 Written representations are required from management for all financial statements and periods covered by the accountant's review report. For example, if comparative financial statements are reported on, the representations obtained at the completion of the most recent review should address all periods being reported on. If current management was not present during all periods covered by the accountant's report, the accountant should nevertheless obtain written representations from current management for all such periods. The specific written representations obtained by the accountant will depend on the circumstances of the engagement and the nature and basis of presentation of the financial statements. Written representations from management ordinarily

---

[5] The financial statements of the reporting entity ordinarily include an accounting for all significant components, such as unconsolidated subsidiaries and investees. If other accountants are engaged to audit or review the financial statements of such components, the accountant will require reports from the other accountants as a basis, in part, for the accountant's review report with respect to the review of the financial statements of the reporting entity. The accountant may decide to make reference to the work of other accountants in the accountant's review report on the financial statements. If such reference is made, the report should indicate the magnitude of the portion of the financial statements audited or reviewed by the other accountants.

AR §90.22

82 Statements on Standards for Accounting and Review Services

confirm representations explicitly or implicitly given to the accountant, indicate and document the continuing appropriateness of such representations, and reduce the possibility of misunderstanding concerning the matters that are the subject of the representations. The accountant should request that management provide a written representation related to the following matters:

    a.   Management's acknowledgment of its responsibility for the preparation and fair presentation of the financial statements in accordance with the applicable financial reporting framework

    b.   Management's belief that the financial statements are fairly presented in accordance with the applicable financial reporting framework

    c.   Management's acknowledgement of its responsibility for designing, implementing, and maintaining internal control relevant to the preparation and fair presentation of the financial statements

    d.   Management's acknowledgement of its responsibility to prevent and detect fraud

    e.   Knowledge of any fraud or suspected fraud affecting the entity involving management or others where the fraud could have a material effect on the financial statements, including any communications received from employees, former employees, or others

    f.   Management's full and truthful response to all inquiries

    g.   Completeness of information

    h.   Information concerning subsequent events

The representation letter ordinarily should be tailored to include additional appropriate representations from management relating to matters specific to the entity's business or industry.[6] An illustrative representation letter is presented in Review Exhibit B, "Illustrative Representation Letter."

.23 Circumstances exist in which the accountant should consider obtaining an updating representation letter from management (for example, the accountant obtains a management representation letter after completion of inquiry and analytical review procedures, but does not issue the review report for a significant period of time thereafter, or a material subsequent event occurs after the completion of inquiry and analytical review procedures, including obtaining the original management representation letter, but before the issuance of the report on the reviewed financial statements). In addition, if a predecessor accountant is requested to reissue the report on the financial statements of a prior period and those financial statements are to be presented on a comparative basis with reviewed financial statements of a subsequent period, the predecessor accountant should obtain an updating representation letter from the management of the former client.[7] The updating management representation letter should state (*a*) whether any information has come to management's attention that would cause management to believe that any of the previous representations should be modified and (*b*) whether any events have occurred subsequent to the balance-sheet date of the latest financial statements reported on by the accountant that would require adjustment to or disclosure in those financial statements. An illustrative updating management representation letter is contained in Review Exhibit C, "Illustrative Updating Management Representation Letter."

---

[6] The accountant is not precluded from obtaining representations regarding services performed in addition to the review engagement.

[7] See paragraphs .20–.24 of section 200, *Reporting on Comparative Financial Statements.*

AR §90.23

Review of Financial Statements

.24 Because the accountant is concerned with events occurring through the date of the report that may require adjustment to or disclosure in the financial statements, management's representations set forth in the management representation letter should be made as of the date of the accountant's review report. The accountant need not be in physical receipt of the management representation letter as of the date of the accountant's review report, provided that management has acknowledged that they will sign the representation letter without modification and it is received prior to the release of the report. The management representation letter should be addressed to the accountant. The letter should be signed by those members of management whom the accountant believes are responsible for and knowledgeable about (directly or through others in the organization) the matters covered in the representation letter. Normally, the chief executive officer and chief financial officer or others with equivalent positions in the entity should sign the representation letter.

Documentation in a Review Engagement

.25 The accountant should prepare documentation in connection with each review engagement in sufficient detail to provide a clear understanding of the work performed (including the nature, timing, extent, and results of review procedures performed); the review evidence obtained and its source; and the conclusions reached. Documentation does the following:

a. Provides the principal support for the representation in the accountant's review report that the accountant performed the review in accordance with SSARSs

b. Provides the principal support for the conclusion that the accountant is not aware of any material modifications that should be made to the financial statements in order for them to be in conformity with the applicable financial reporting framework

.26 The form, content, and extent of documentation depend on the circumstances of the engagement, the methodology and tools used, and the accountant's professional judgment. The accountant's documentation should include the following:

- The engagement letter documenting the understanding with the client.

- The analytical procedures performed, including the following:

  — The expectations, when the expectations are not otherwise readily determinable from the documentation of the work performed, and the factors considered in the development of the expectations

  — Results of the comparison of the expectations to the recorded amounts or ratios developed from recorded amounts

  — Management's responses to the accountant's inquiries regarding fluctuations or relationships that are inconsistent with other relevant information or that differ from expected values by a significant amount

- Any additional review procedures performed in response to significant unexpected differences arising from analytical procedures and the results of such additional procedures.

- The significant matters covered in the accountant's inquiry procedures and the responses thereto. The accountant may document

AR §90.26

84   Statements on Standards for Accounting and Review Services

the matters covered by the accountant's inquiry procedures and the responses thereto through a memorandum, checklist, or other means.

- Any findings or issues that, in the accountant's judgment, are significant (for example, the results of review procedures that indicate the financial statements could be materially misstated, including actions taken to address such findings, and the basis for the final conclusions reached).

- Significant unusual matters that the accountant considered during the performance of the review procedures, including their disposition.

- Communications, whether oral or written, to the appropriate level of management regarding fraud or illegal acts that come to the accountant's attention.

- The representation letter.

The accountant is not precluded from supporting the review report by other means in addition to the review documentation. Such other means might include written documentation contained in other engagement files (for example, compilation or nonattest services) or quality control files (for example, consultation files) and, in limited situations, oral explanations. Oral explanations on their own do not represent sufficient support for the work the accountant performed or conclusions the accountant reached but may be used by the accountant to clarify or explain information contained in the documentation.

Reporting on the Financial Statements

.27 Financial statements reviewed by an accountant should be accompanied by a written report. The accountant's objective in reporting on the financial statements is to prevent misinterpretation of the degree of responsibility the accountant is assuming when his or her name is associated with the financial statements.

.28 The basic elements of the report are as follows:

a. *Title.* The accountant's review report should have a title that clearly indicates that it is the accountant's review report and includes the word *independent.* An appropriate title would be "Independent Accountant's Review Report."

b. *Addressee.* The accountant's report should be addressed as required by the circumstances of the engagement.

c. *Introductory paragraph.* The introductory paragraph in the accountant's report should

    i. identify the entity whose financial statements have been reviewed;

    ii. state that the financial statements have been reviewed;

    iii. identify the financial statements; that have been reviewed;

    iv. specify the date or period covered by the financial statements;

    v. include a statement that a review includes primarily applying analytical procedures to management's (owners') financial data and making inquiries of company management (owners); and

AR §90.27

Review of Financial Statements

85

    vi. include a statement that a review is substantially less in scope than an audit, the objective of which is the expression of an opinion regarding the financial statements as a whole, and that, accordingly, the accountant does not express such an opinion.

d.   *Management's responsibility for the financial statements.* A statement that management (owners) is (are) responsible for the preparation and fair presentation of the financial statements in accordance with the applicable financial reporting framework and for designing, implementing, and maintaining internal control relevant to the preparation and fair presentation of the financial statements.

e.   *Accountant's responsibility.* A statement that the accountant's responsibility is to conduct the review in accordance with SSARSs issued by the AICPA.

    A statement that those standards require the accountant to perform the procedures to obtain limited assurance that there are no material modifications that should be made to the financial statements.

    A statement that the accountant believes that the results of his or her procedures provide a reasonable basis for his or her report.

f.   *Results of engagement.* A statement that, based on his or her review, the accountant is not aware of any material modifications that should be made to the financial statements in order for them to be in conformity with the applicable financial reporting framework, other than those modifications, if any, indicated in the report.

g.   *Signature of the accountant.* The manual or printed signature of the accounting firm or the accountant as appropriate.

h.   *Date of the accountant's report.* The date of the review report (the accountant's review report should not be dated earlier than the date on which the accountant has accumulated review evidence sufficient to provide a reasonable basis for concluding that the accountant has obtained limited assurance that there are no material modifications that should be made to the financial statements in order for the statements to be in conformity with the applicable financial reporting framework).

See Review Exhibit D, "Illustrative Review Reports," for examples of review reports.

.29 Each page of the financial statements reviewed by the accountant should include a reference, such as "See Independent Accountant's Review Report."

.30 When the accountant is unable to perform the inquiry and analytical procedures he or she considers necessary to obtain limited assurance that there are no material modifications that should be made to the financial statements in order for the statements to be in conformity with the applicable financial reporting framework, or the client does not provide the accountant with a representation letter, the review will be incomplete. A review that is incomplete does not provide an adequate basis for issuing a review report. In such a situation, the accountant should consider the matters discussed in paragraphs .56–.61 of section 80 in deciding whether it is appropriate to issue a compilation report on the financial statements.

AR §90.30

86   Statements on Standards for Accounting and Review Services

.31 The accountant may be asked to issue a review report on one financial statement, such as a balance sheet, and not on other related financial statements, such as the statements of income, retained earnings, and cash flows. The accountant may do so if the scope of his or her inquiry and analytical procedures has not been restricted.

.32 Financial statements prepared in accordance with an OCBOA are not considered appropriate in form unless the financial statements include

- a description of the OCBOA, including a summary of significant accounting policies and a description of the primary differences from GAAP. The effects of the differences need not be quantified.

- informative disclosures similar to those required by GAAP if the financial statements contain items that are the same as, or similar to, those in financial statements prepared in accordance with GAAP.

Emphasis of a Matter

.33 The accountant may emphasize, in any report on financial statements, a matter disclosed in the financial statements. Such explanatory information should be presented in a separate paragraph of the accountant's report. Emphasis paragraphs are never required; they may be added solely at the accountant's discretion.

Examples of matters that the accountant may wish to emphasize are

- uncertainties.
- that the entity is a component of a larger business enterprise.
- that the entity has had significant transactions with related parties.
- unusually important subsequent events.
- accounting matters, other than those involving a change or changes in accounting principles, affecting the comparability of the financial statements with those of the preceding period.

Departures From the Applicable Financial Reporting Framework

.34 An accountant who is engaged to review financial statements may become aware of a departure from the applicable financial reporting framework (including inadequate disclosure) that is material to the financial statements. If the financial statements are not revised, the accountant should consider whether modification of the standard report is adequate to disclose the departure.

.35 If the accountant concludes that modification of the standard report is appropriate, the departure should be disclosed in a separate paragraph of the report, including disclosure of the effects of the departure on the financial statements if such effects have been determined by management or are known as the result of the accountant's procedures. The accountant is not required to determine the effects of a departure if management has not done so, provided that the accountant states in the report that such determination has not been made.

See Review Exhibit D for examples of review reports that disclose departures from the applicable financial reporting framework.

AR §90.31

Review of Financial Statements

87

.36 If the accountant believes that modification of the standard report is not adequate to indicate the deficiencies in the financial statements as a whole, the accountant should withdraw from the review engagement and provide no further services with respect to those financial statements. The accountant may wish to consult with his or her legal counsel in those circumstances.

Restricting the Use of an Accountant's Review Report

General Use and Restricted Use Reports

.37 The term *general use* applies to accountants' reports that are not restricted to specified parties. Accountants' reports on financial statements prepared in conformity with an applicable financial reporting framework ordinarily are not restricted regarding use. However, nothing in this section precludes the accountant from restricting the use of any report.

.38 The term *restricted use* applies to accountants' reports intended only for one or more specified third parties. The need for restriction on the use of a report may result from a number of circumstances, including, but not limited to, the purpose of the report and the potential for the report to be misunderstood when taken out of the context in which it was intended to be used.

.39 The accountant should restrict the use of a report when the subject matter of the accountant's report or the presentation being reported on is based on measurement or disclosure criteria contained in contractual agreements[8] or regulatory provisions that are not in conformity with an applicable financial reporting framework.

Reporting on Subject Matter or Presentations Based on Measurement or Disclosure Criteria Contained in Contractual Agreements or Regulatory Provisions

.40 When reports are issued on subject matter or presentations based on measurement or disclosure criteria contained in contractual agreements or regulatory provisions that are not in conformity with an applicable financial reporting framework, the accountant should restrict the report because the basis, assumptions, or purpose of such presentations (contained in such agreements or regulatory provisions) are developed for, and directed only to, the parties to the agreement or regulatory agency responsible for the provisions and because the report, subject matter, or presentation may be misunderstood by those who are not adequately informed of the basis, assumptions, or purpose of the presentation.

Combined Reports Covering Both Restricted Use and General Use Subject Matter or Presentations

.41 If the accountant issues a single combined report covering both (*a*) subject matter or presentations that require a restriction on use to specified parties and (*b*) subject matter or presentations that ordinarily do not require such a restriction, the use of such a single combined report should be restricted to the specified parties.

Inclusion of a Separate Restricted Use Report in the Same Document With a General-Use Report

.42 When required by law or regulation, a separate restricted use report may be included in a document that also contains a general use report. The

---

[8] A *contractual agreement*, as discussed in this section, is an agreement between the client and one or more third parties other than the accountant.

AR §90.42

88　　Statements on Standards for Accounting and Review Services

inclusion of a separate restricted-use report in a document that contains a general use report does not affect the intended use of either report. The restricted use report remains restricted regarding use, and the general use report continues for general use.

Adding Other Specified Parties

.43 Subsequent to the completion of an engagement resulting in a restricted use report or in the course of such an engagement, the accountant may be asked to consider adding other parties as specified parties.

.44 If the accountant is reporting on subject matter or a presentation based on measurement or disclosure criteria contained in contractual agreements or regulatory provisions, as described in paragraph .40, the accountant may agree to add other parties as specified parties based on the accountant's consideration of factors such as the identity of the other parties, their knowledge of the basis of the measurement or disclosure criteria, and the intended use of the report. If the accountant agrees to add other parties as specified parties, the accountant should obtain affirmative acknowledgment, preferably in writing, from the other parties of their understanding of the nature of the engagement, the measurement or disclosure criteria used in the engagement, and the related report. If the other parties are added after the accountant has issued his or her report, the report may be reissued, or the accountant may provide other written acknowledgment that the other parties have been added as specified parties. If the report is reissued, the report date should not be changed. If the accountant provides written acknowledgment that the other parties have been added as specified parties, such written acknowledgment ordinarily should state that no procedures have been performed subsequent to the date of the report.

Limiting the Distribution of Reports

.45 Because of the reasons presented in paragraph .38, the accountant should consider informing his or her client that restricted use reports are not intended for distribution to nonspecified parties, regardless of whether they are included in a document containing a separate general use report.[9] This section does not preclude the accountant, in connection with establishing the terms of the engagement, from reaching an understanding with the client that the intended use of the report will be restricted, and from obtaining the client's agreement that the client and the specified parties will not distribute the report to parties other than those identified in the report. However, the accountant is not responsible for controlling a client's distribution of restricted use reports. Accordingly, a restricted use report should alert readers to the restriction on the use of the report by indicating that the report is not intended to be and should not be used by anyone other than the specified parties.

Report Language—Restricted Use

.46 An accountant's report that is restricted should contain a separate paragraph at the end of the report that includes the following elements:

    a.   A statement indicating that the report is intended solely for the information and use of the specified parties.

---

[9] In some cases, restricted use reports filed with regulatory agencies are required by law or regulation to be made available to the public as a matter of public record. Also, a regulatory agency as part of its oversight responsibility for an entity may require access to restricted use reports in which they are not named as a specified party.

AR §90.43

Review of Financial Statements

89

    b.   An identification of the specified parties to whom use is restricted. The report may list the specified parties or refer the reader to the specified parties listed elsewhere in the report.

    c.   A statement that the report is not intended to be and should not be used by anyone other than the specified parties.

An Entity's Ability to Continue as a Going Concern

.47 During the performance of review procedures, evidence or information may come to the accountant's attention indicating that there may be an uncertainty about the entity's ability to continue as a going concern for a reasonable period of time, not to exceed one year beyond the date of the financial statements being reviewed (hereinafter referred to as a *reasonable period of time*). In those circumstances, the accountant should request that management consider the possible effects of the going concern uncertainty on the financial statements, including the need for related disclosure.

.48 After management communicates to the accountant the results of its consideration of the possible effects on the financial statements, the accountant should consider the reasonableness of management's conclusions, including the adequacy of the related disclosures, if applicable.

.49 If the accountant determines that management's conclusions are unreasonable or the disclosure of the uncertainty regarding the entity's ability to continue as a going concern is not adequate, he or she should follow the guidance in paragraphs .34–.36 with respect to departures from the applicable financial reporting framework.

.50 The accountant may emphasize an uncertainty about an entity's ability to continue as a going concern, provided that the uncertainty is disclosed in the financial statements. In such circumstances, the accountant should follow the guidance in paragraph .33.

Subsequent Events

.51 Evidence or information that a subsequent event that has a material effect on the reviewed financial statements has occurred may come to the accountant's attention in the following ways:

    a.   During the performance of review procedures

    b.   Subsequent to the date of the accountant's review report but prior to the release of the report

In either case, the accountant should request that management consider the possible effects on the financial statements, including the adequacy of any related disclosure, if applicable.

.52 If the accountant determines that the subsequent event is not adequately accounted for in the financial statements or disclosed in the notes, he or she should follow the guidance in paragraphs .34–.36.

.53 Occasionally, a subsequent event has such a material impact on the entity that the accountant may wish to include in his or her review report an explanatory paragraph directing the reader's attention to the event and its effects. Such an emphasis of matter paragraph may be added at the accountant's discretion, provided that the matter is disclosed in the financial statements. See paragraph .33 for additional guidance with respect to emphasis of matter paragraphs.

AR §90.53

Subsequent Discovery of Facts Existing at the Date of the Report

.54 Subsequent to the date of the report on the financial statements that the accountant has reviewed, he or she may become aware that facts may have existed at that date that might have caused him or her to believe that information supplied by the entity was incorrect, incomplete, or otherwise unsatisfactory had the accountant then been aware of such facts. Because of the variety of conditions that might be encountered, some of the procedures contained in this section are necessarily set out only in general terms; the specific actions to be taken in a particular case may vary with the circumstances. The accountant would be well advised to consult with his or her legal counsel when he or she encounters the circumstances to which this section may apply because of legal implications that may be involved in actions contemplated herein.

.55 After the date of the accountant's review report, the accountant has no obligation to perform other review procedures with respect to the financial statements unless new information comes to his or her attention. However, when the accountant becomes aware of information that relates to financial statements previously reported on by him or her but that was not known to the accountant at the date of the report (and that is of such a nature and from such a source that the accountant would have investigated it had it come to his or her attention during the course of the review), the accountant should, as soon as practicable, undertake to determine whether the information is reliable and whether the facts existed at the date of the report. The accountant should discuss the matter with his or her client at whatever management levels the accountant deems appropriate and request cooperation in whatever investigation may be necessary. In addition to management, the accountant may deem it appropriate to discuss the matter with those charged with governance. If the nature and effect of the matter are such that (*a*) the accountant's report or the financial statements would have been affected if the information had been known to the accountant at the accountant's review report date and had not been reflected in the financial statements and (*b*) the accountant believes that persons currently using or likely to use the financial statements exist who would attach importance to the information, the accountant should perform the additional procedures deemed necessary to obtain limited assurance that there are no material modifications that should be made to the financial statements in order for the statements to be in conformity with the applicable financial reporting framework. Consideration should be given to, among other things, the time elapsed since the financial statements were issued.

.56 When the accountant has concluded that action should be taken to prevent further use of the accountant's report or the financial statements, the accountant should advise his or her client to make appropriate disclosure of the newly discovered facts and their impact on the financial statements to persons who are known to be currently using or who are likely to use the financial statements. When the client undertakes to make appropriate disclosure, the method used and the disclosure made will depend on the circumstances. For example

    a.   if the effect of the subsequently discovered information on the accountant's report or the financial statements can promptly be determined, disclosure should consist of issuing, as soon as practicable, revised financial statements and, when applicable, the accountant's report. The reasons for the revision usually should be described in a note to the financial statements and, when applicable, referred to in the accountant's report. Generally, only the

AR §90.54

Review of Financial Statements   **91**

most recently issued reviewed financial statements would need to be revised, even though the revision resulted from events that had occurred in prior years.

b.   when issuance of financial statements for a subsequent period is imminent, so that disclosure is not delayed, appropriate disclosure of the revision can be made in such statements instead of reissuing the earlier statements, pursuant to subparagraph (a).

c.   when the effect on the financial statements of the subsequently discovered information cannot be promptly determined, the issuance of revised financial statements would necessarily be delayed. In this circumstance, when it appears that the information will require a revision of the statements, appropriate disclosure would consist of notification by the client to persons who are known to be using or who are likely to use the financial statements that the statements should not be used; that revised financial statements will be issued; and, when applicable, that the accountant's report will be issued as soon as practicable.

.57 The accountant should take whatever steps he or she deems necessary to satisfy himself or herself that the client has made the disclosures specified in paragraph .56.

.58 If the client refuses to make the disclosures specified in paragraph .56, the accountant should notify the appropriate personnel at the highest levels within the entity, such as the manager (owner) or those charged with governance, of such refusal and of the fact that, in the absence of disclosure by the client, the accountant will take steps as outlined here to prevent further use of the financial statements and the accountant's report. The steps that can appropriately be taken will depend upon the degree of certainty of the accountant's knowledge that persons exist who are currently using or who will use the financial statements and the accountant's report and who would attach importance to the information. The steps that can be taken also will depend on the accountant's ability as a practical matter to communicate with these persons. Unless the accountant's attorney recommends a different course of action, the accountant should take the following steps to the extent applicable:

a.   Notification to the client that the accountant's report must no longer be associated with the financial statements.

b.   Notification to the regulatory agencies having jurisdiction over the client that the accountant's report should no longer be used.

c.   Notification to each person known to the accountant to be using the financial statements that the financial statements and the accountant's report should no longer be used. In many instances, it will not be practicable for the accountant to give appropriate individual notification to stakeholders whose identities ordinarily are unknown to him or her; notification to a regulatory agency having jurisdiction over the client will usually be the only practicable way for the accountant to provide appropriate disclosure. Such notification should be accompanied by a request that the agency take whatever steps it may deem appropriate to accomplish the necessary disclosure.

.59 The following guidelines should govern the content of any disclosure made by the accountant, in accordance with paragraph .58, to persons other than his or her client:

a.   The disclosure should include a description of the nature of the subsequently acquired information and its effect on the financial statements.

AR §90.59

92 Statements on Standards for Accounting and Review Services

    b. The information disclosed should be as precise and factual as possible and should not go beyond that which is reasonably necessary to accomplish the purpose mentioned in the preceding subparagraph (*a*). Comments concerning the conduct or motives of any person should be avoided.

If the client has not cooperated, the accountant's disclosure need not detail the specific information but can merely indicate that the client has not cooperated with the accountant's attempt to substantiate information that has come to the accountant's attention and that, if the information is true, the accountant believes that the review report must no longer be used or associated with the financial statements. No such disclosure should be made unless the accountant believes that the financial statements are likely to be misleading and that the accountant's review report should not be used.

Supplementary Information

.60 When the basic financial statements are accompanied by information presented for supplementary analysis purposes, the accountant should clearly indicate the degree of responsibility, if any, he or she is taking with respect to such information.

When the accountant has reviewed the basic financial statements, an explanation should be included in the review report or in a separate report on the other data. The report should state that the review has been made for the purpose of expressing a conclusion that there are no material modifications that should be made to the financial statements in order for them to be in conformity with the applicable financial reporting framework and that either

- the other data accompanying the financial statements are presented only for purposes of additional analysis and have been subjected to the inquiry and analytical procedures applied in the review of the basic financial statements, and the accountant did not become aware of any material modifications that should be made to such data, or

- the other data accompanying the financial statements are presented only for purposes of additional analysis and have not been subjected to the inquiry and analytical procedures applied in the review of the basic financial statements but were compiled from information that is the representation of management, without audit or review, and the accountant does not express an opinion or provide any assurance on such data.

Communicating to Management and Others

.61 When evidence or information comes to the accountant's attention during the performance of review procedures that fraud or an illegal act may have occurred, that matter should be brought to the attention of the appropriate level of management. The accountant need not report matters regarding illegal acts that are clearly inconsequential and may reach agreement in advance with the entity on the nature of such items to be communicated. When matters regarding fraud or an illegal act involve senior management, the accountant should report the matter to an individual or group at a higher level within the entity, such as the manager (owner) or those charged with governance. The communication may be oral or written. If the communication is oral, the accountant should document it. When matters regarding fraud or an illegal act involve an owner of the business, the accountant should consider resigning from the

AR §90.60

Review of Financial Statements

93

engagement. Additionally, the accountant should consider consulting with his or her legal counsel whenever any evidence or information comes to his or her attention during the performance of review procedures that fraud or an illegal act may have occurred, unless such illegal act is clearly inconsequential.

.62 The disclosure of any evidence or information that comes to the accountant's attention during the performance of review procedures that fraud or an illegal act may have occurred to parties other than the client's senior management (or those charged with governance, if applicable) ordinarily is not part of the accountant's responsibility and, ordinarily, would be precluded by the accountant's ethical or legal obligations of confidentiality. The accountant should recognize, however, that in the following circumstances, a duty to disclose to parties outside of the entity may exist:

    a.   To comply with certain legal and regulatory requirements

    b.   To a successor accountant when the successor decides to communicate with the predecessor accountant, in accordance with section 400, regarding acceptance of an engagement to compile or review the financial statements of a nonissuer

    c.   In response to a subpoena

Because potential conflicts between the accountant's ethical and legal obligations for confidentiality of client matters may be complex, the accountant may wish to consult with legal counsel before discussing matters covered by paragraph .61 with parties outside the client.

Change in Engagement From Audit to Review

.63 The accountant who has been engaged to audit the financial statements of a nonissuer in accordance with auditing standards generally accepted in the United States of America may, before the completion of the audit, be requested to change the engagement to a review of financial statements. A request to change the engagement may result from a change in circumstances affecting the entity's requirement for an audit, a misunderstanding regarding the nature of an audit or review, or a restriction.

.64 Before the accountant, who was engaged to perform an audit in accordance with auditing standards generally accepted in the United States of America, agrees to change the engagement to a review, at least the following should be considered:

    a.   The reason given for the client's request, particularly the implications of a restriction on the scope of the audit, whether imposed by the client or by circumstances

    b.   The additional audit effort required to complete the audit

    c.   The estimated additional cost to complete the audit

.65 A change in circumstances that affects the entity's requirement for an audit, or a misunderstanding concerning the nature of an audit or review would ordinarily be considered a reasonable basis for requesting a change in the engagement.

.66 In considering the implications of a restriction on the scope of the audit, the accountant should evaluate the possibility that information affected by the scope restriction may be incorrect, incomplete, or otherwise unsatisfactory. Nevertheless, when the accountant has been engaged to audit an entity's financial statements and has been prohibited by the client from corresponding with the entity's legal counsel, the accountant ordinarily would be precluded from issuing a review report on the financial statements.

AR §90.66

94 Statements on Standards for Accounting and Review Services

.67 In all circumstances, if the audit procedures are substantially complete or the cost to complete such procedures is relatively insignificant, the accountant should consider the propriety of accepting a change in the engagement.

.68 If the accountant concludes, based upon his or her professional judgment, that there is reasonable justification to change the engagement and if he or she complies with the standards applicable to a review engagement, the accountant should issue an appropriate review report. The report should not include reference to (*a*) the original engagement, (*b*) any audit procedures that may have been performed, or (*c*) scope limitations that resulted in the changed engagement.

Effective Date

.69 This section is effective for reviews of financial statements for periods ending on or after December 15, 2010.

AR §90.67

Review of Financial Statements   **95**

.70

Review Exhibit A—Illustrative Engagement Letter

[*Appropriate Salutation*]

This letter is to confirm our understanding of the terms and objectives of our engagement and the nature and limitations of the services we will provide.

We will perform the following services:

We will review the financial statements of XYZ Company as of and for the year ended December 31, 20XX, and issue an accountant's report thereon in accordance with Statements on Standards for Accounting and Review Services (SSARSs) issued by the American Institute of Certified Public Accountants (AICPA).

The objective of a review is to obtain limited assurance that there are no material modifications that should be made to the financial statements in order for the statements to be in conformity with [*the applicable financial reporting framework (for example, accounting principles generally accepted in the United States of America)*].

You are responsible for

a. the preparation and fair presentation of the financial statements in accordance with [*the applicable financial reporting framework (for example, accounting principles generally accepted in the United States of America)*].

b. designing, implementing, and maintaining internal control relevant to the preparation and fair presentation of the financial statements.

c. preventing and detecting fraud.

d. identifying and ensuring that the entity complies with the laws and regulations applicable to its activities.

e. making all financial records and related information available to us.

f. providing us, at the conclusion of the engagement, with a letter that confirms certain representations made during the review.

We are responsible for conducting the engagement in accordance with SSARSs issued by the AICPA.

A review includes primarily applying analytical procedures to your financial data and making inquiries of company management. A review is substantially less in scope that an audit, the objective of which is the expression of an opinion regarding the financial statements as a whole. A review does not contemplate obtaining an understanding of the entity's internal control; assessing fraud risk; testing accounting records by obtaining sufficient appropriate audit evidence through inspection, observation, confirmation, or the examination of source documents (for example, cancelled checks or bank images); or other procedures ordinarily performed in an audit. Accordingly, we will not express an opinion regarding the financial statements as a whole.

Our engagement cannot be relied upon to disclose errors, fraud, or illegal acts. However, we will inform the appropriate level of management of any material errors and of any evidence or information that comes to our attention during the performance of our review procedures that fraud may have occurred. In addition, we will report to you any evidence or information that comes to our

AR §90.70

96   Statements on Standards for Accounting and Review Services

attention during the performance of our review procedures regarding illegal acts that may have occurred, unless they are clearly inconsequential.

If, for any reason, we are unable to complete the review of your financial statements, we will not issue a report on such statements as a result of this engagement.

Our fees for these services...

We will be pleased to discuss this letter with you at any time. If the foregoing is in accordance with your understanding, please sign the copy of this letter in the space provided and return it to us.

Sincerely yours,

_____

[Signature of accountant]

Acknowledged:

XYZ Company

_____

President

_____

Date

AR §90.70

Review of Financial Statements

.71

Review Exhibit B—Illustrative Representation Letter

The following representation letter is included for illustrative purposes only. The accountant may decide, based on the circumstances of the review engagement or the industry in which the entity operates, that other matters should be specifically included in the letter or that some of the representations included in the illustrative letter are not necessary.

[Date][1]

To [the Accountant]

We are providing this letter in connection with your review of the [identification of financial statements] of [name of entity] as of [dates (for example, December 31, 20X1, and December 31, 20X2)] and for the [periods of review (for example, for the years then ended)] for the purpose of obtaining limited assurance that that there are no material modifications that should be made to the financial statements in order for the statements to be in conformity with [the applicable financial reporting framework (for example, accounting principles generally accepted in the United States of America)]. We confirm that we are responsible for the fair presentation of the financial statements in accordance with [the applicable financial reporting framework] and the selection and application of the accounting policies.

Certain representations in this letter are described as being limited to matters that are material. Items are considered material, regardless of size, if they involve an omission or misstatement of accounting information that, in the light of surrounding circumstances, makes it probable that the judgment of a reasonable person using the information would be changed or influenced by the omission or misstatement.[2]

We confirm, to the best of our knowledge and belief, (as of [the date of the accountant's review report]) the following representations made to you during your review:

1. The financial statements referred to previously are fairly presented in accordance with [the applicable financial reporting framework (for example, accounting principles generally accepted in the United States of America)].

2. We have made the following available to you

   a. financial records and related data.

   b. minutes of the meetings of stockholders, directors, and committees of directors, or summaries of actions of recent meetings for which minutes have not yet been prepared.

3. No material transactions exist that have not been properly recorded in the accounting records underlying the financial statements.

4. We acknowledge our responsibility for the preparation and fair presentation of the financial statements in accordance with [the applicable financial reporting framework (for example, accounting principles generally accepted in the United States of America)].

---

[1] This date should be the date that the client presents and signs the letter. In no event should the letter be presented and signed prior to the date of the accountant's review report.

[2] The qualitative discussion of materiality used in this letter is adapted from Financial Accounting Standards Board Statement of Financial Accounting Concepts No. 2, *Qualitative Characteristics of Accounting Information*.

AR §90.71

98 Statements on Standards for Accounting and Review Services

5. We acknowledge our responsibility for designing, implementing, and maintaining internal control relevant to the preparation and fair presentation of the financial statements.

6. We acknowledge our responsibility to prevent and detect fraud.

7. We have no knowledge of any fraud or suspected fraud affecting the entity involving management or others where the fraud could have a material effect on the financial statements, including any communications received from employees, former employees, or others.

8. We have no plans or intentions that may materially affect the carrying amounts or classification of assets and liabilities.

9. No material losses exist (such as from obsolete inventory or purchase or sales commitments) that have not been properly accrued or disclosed in the financial statements.

10. None of the following exist:

    a. Violations or possible violations of laws or regulations, whose effects should be considered for disclosure in the financial statements or as a basis for recording a loss contingency

    b. Unasserted claims or assessments that our lawyer has advised us are probable of assertion that must be disclosed in accordance with Financial Accounting Standards Board (FASB) *Accounting Standards Codification* (ASC) 450, *Contingencies*.[3]

    c. Other material liabilities or gain or loss contingencies that are required to be accrued or disclosed by FASB ASC 450.

11. The company has satisfactory title to all owned assets, and no liens or encumbrances on such assets exist, nor has any asset been pledged as collateral, except as disclosed to you and reported in the financial statements.

12. We have complied with all aspects of contractual agreements that would have a material effect on the financial statements in the event of noncompliance.

13. The following have been properly recorded or disclosed in the financial statements:

    a. Related party transactions, including sales, purchases, loans, transfers, leasing arrangements, and guarantees, and amounts receivable from or payable to related parties.

    b. Guarantees, whether written or oral, under which the company is contingently liable.

    c. Significant estimates and material concentrations known to management that are required to be disclosed in accordance with FASB ASC 275, *Risks and Uncertainties*. [*Significant estimates are estimates at the balance sheet date*

---

[3] If management has not consulted a lawyer regarding litigation, claims, and assessments, the representation might be worded as follows:

We are not aware of any pending or threatened litigation, claims, or assessments or unasserted claims or assessments that are required to be accrued or disclosed in the financial statements in accordance with Financial Accounting Standards Board *Accounting Standards Codification* 450, *Contingencies*, and we have not consulted a lawyer concerning litigation, claims, or assessments.

AR §90.71

Review of Financial Statements

that could change materially with the next year. Concentrations refer to volumes of business, revenues, available sources of supply, or markets or geographic areas for which events could occur that would significantly disrupt normal finances within the next year.]

[Add additional representations that are unique to the entity's business or industry. See the following for additional illustrative representations.]

14. We are in agreement with the adjusting journal entries you have recommended, and they have been posted to the company's accounts (if applicable).

15. To the best of our knowledge and belief, no events have occurred subsequent to the balance-sheet date and through the date of this letter that would require adjustment to or disclosure in the aforementioned financial statements.[4]

16. We have responded fully and truthfully to all inquiries made to us by you during your review.

[Name of Owner or Chief Executive Officer and Title]

[Name of Chief Financial Officer and Title, where applicable]

Representation letters ordinarily should be tailored to include additional appropriate representations from management relating to matters specific to the entity's business or industry. The following is a list of additional representations that may be appropriate in certain situations. This list is not intended to be all-inclusive. The accountant should consider the effects of pronouncements issued subsequent to the issuance of this section.

---

[4] If the accountant dual dates his or her report, the accountant should consider whether obtaining additional representations relating to the subsequent event is appropriate.

AR §90.71

100 Statements on Standards for Accounting and Review Services

General

Condition	Illustrative Examples
The effect of a new accounting principle is not known.	We have not completed the process of evaluating the impact that will result from adopting Financial Accounting Standards Board (FASB) *Accounting Standards Codification* (ASC) [*XXX,Title*], as discussed in note [X]. The company is therefore unable to disclose the impact that adopting FASB ASC *XXX* will have on its financial position and the results of operations when such statement is adopted.
Justification exists for a change in accounting principles.	We believe that [*describe the newly adopted accounting principle*] is preferable to [*describe the former accounting principle*] because [*describe management's justification for the change in accounting principles*].
Financial circumstances are strained, with disclosure of management's intentions and the entity's ability to continue as a going concern.	Note [X] to the financial statements discloses all of the matters of which we are aware that are relevant to the company's ability to continue as a going concern, including significant conditions and events, and management's plans.
The possibility exists that the value of specific significant long lived assets or certain identifiable intangibles may be impaired.	We have reviewed long lived assets and certain identifiable intangibles to be held and used for impairment whenever events or changes in circumstances have indicated that the carrying amount of its assets might not be recoverable and have appropriately recorded the adjustment.
The entity has a variable interest in another entity.	Variable interest entities (VIEs) and potential VIEs and transactions with VIEs and potential VIEs have been properly recorded and disclosed in the financial statements in accordance with accounting principles generally accepted in the United States of America.
	We have considered both implicit and explicit variable interests in (*a*) determining whether potential VIEs should be considered VIEs, (*b*) calculating expected losses and residual returns, and (*c*) determining which party, if any, is the primary beneficiary.
	We have provided you with lists of all identified variable interests in (*a*) VIEs, (*b*) potential VIEs that we considered but judged not to be VIEs, and (*c*) entities that were afforded the scope exceptions of FASB ASC 810, *Consolidation*.

(*continued*)

AR §90.71

Review of Financial Statements

101

General

Condition	Illustrative Examples
	We have advised you of all transactions with identified VIEs, potential VIEs, or entities afforded the scope exceptions of FASB ASC 810.

We have made available all relevant information about financial interests and contractual arrangements with related parties, de facto agents, and other entities, including but not limited to, their governing documents, equity and debt instruments, contracts, leases, guarantee arrangements, and other financial contracts and arrangements.

The information we provided about financial interests and contractual arrangements with related parties, de facto agents, and other entities includes information about all transactions, unwritten understandings, agreement modifications, and written and oral side agreements.

Our computations of expected losses and expected residual returns of entities that are VIEs and potential VIEs are based on the best information available and include all reasonably possible outcomes.

Regarding entities in which the company has variable interests (implicit and explicit), we have provided all information about events and changes in circumstances that could potentially cause reconsideration about whether the entities are VIEs or whether the company is the primary beneficiary or has a significant variable interest in the entity.

We have made and continue to make exhaustive efforts to obtain information about entities in which the company has an implicit or explicit interest, but that were excluded from complete analysis under FASB ASC 810 due to lack of essential information to determine one or more of the following:

- Whether the entity is a VIE
- Whether the company is the primary beneficiary
- The accounting required to consolidate the entity

The work of a specialist has been used by the entity.

We agree with the findings of specialists in evaluating the [*describe assertion*] and have adequately considered the qualifications of the specialist in determining the amounts and disclosures used in the financial statements and underlying accounting records. We did not give or cause any instructions to be given to specialists with respect to the values or amounts derived in an attempt to bias their work, and we are not otherwise aware of any matters that have had an impact on the independence or objectivity of the specialists.

AR §90.71

102 Statements on Standards for Accounting and Review Services

Assets

Condition	Illustrative Examples
Cash Disclosure is required of compensating balances or other arrangements involving restrictions on cash balances, lines of credit, or similar arrangements.	Arrangements with financial institutions involving compensating balances or other arrangements involving restrictions on cash balances, lines of credit, or similar arrangements have been properly disclosed.
Financial Instruments Management intends to and has the ability to hold to maturity debt securities classified as held-to-maturity.	Debt securities that have been classified as held-to-maturity have been so classified due to the company's intent to hold such securities to maturity and the company's ability to do so. All other debt securities have been classified as available-for-sale or trading.
Management considers the decline in value of debt or equity securities to be temporary.	We consider the decline in value of debt or equity securities classified as either available-for-sale or held-to-maturity to be temporary.
Management has determined the fair value of significant financial instruments that do not have readily determinable market values.	The methods and significant assumptions used to determine fair values of financial instruments are as follows: [*describe methods and significant assumptions used to determine fair values of financial instruments*]. The methods and significant assumptions used result in a measure of fair value appropriate for financial statement measurement and disclosure purposes.
Financial instruments with off-balance-sheet risk and financial instruments with concentrations of credit risk exist.	The following information about financial instruments with off-balance-sheet risk and financial instruments with concentrations of credit risk has been properly disclosed in the financial statements:

1. The extent, nature, and terms of financial instruments with off-balance-sheet risk

2. The amount of credit risk of financial instruments with off-balance-sheet risk and information about the collateral supporting such financial instruments

3. Significant concentrations of credit risk arising from all financial instruments and information about the collateral supporting such financial instruments

(continued)

AR §90.71

Review of Financial Statements

103

Assets

Condition	Illustrative Examples
Receivables Receivables have been recorded in the financial statements.	Receivables recorded in the financial statements represent valid claims against debtors for sales or other charges arising on or before the balance-sheet date and have been appropriately reduced to their estimated net realizable value.
Inventories Excess or obsolete inventories exist.	Provision has been made to reduce excess or obsolete inventories to their estimated net realizable value.
Investments Unusual considerations are involved in determining the application of equity accounting.	*[For investments in common stock that are either nonmarketable or of which the entity has a 20 percent or greater ownership interest, select the appropriate representation from the following:]* • The equity method is used to account for the company's investment in the common stock of [investee] because the company has the ability to exercise significant influence over the investee's operating and financial policies. • The cost method is used to account for the company's investment in the common stock of [investee] because the company does not have the ability to exercise significant influence over the investee's operating and financial policies.
Deferred Charges Material expenditures have been deferred.	We believe that all material expenditures that have been deferred to future periods will be recoverable.
Deferred Tax Assets A deferred tax asset exists at the balance sheet date.	The valuation allowance has been determined pursuant to the provisions of FASB ASC 740, *Income Taxes*, including the company's estimation of future taxable income, if necessary, and is adequate to reduce the total deferred tax asset to an amount that will more likely than not be realized. *[Complete with appropriate wording detailing how the entity determined the valuation allowance against the deferred tax asset.]* or A valuation allowance against deferred tax assets at the balance-sheet date is not considered necessary because it is more likely than not that the deferred tax asset will be fully realized.

AR §90.71

104 Statements on Standards for Accounting and Review Services

Liabilities

Condition	Illustrative Examples
Debt Short term debt could be refinanced on a long term basis and management intends to do so.	The company has excluded short-term obligations totaling $[amount] from current liabilities because it intends to refinance the obligations on a long-term basis. [*Complete with appropriate wording detailing how amounts will be refinanced as follows:*] • The company has issued a long term obligation [*debt security*] after the date of the balance sheet but prior to the issuance of the financial statements for the purpose of refinancing the short-term obligations on a long term basis. • The company has the ability to consummate the refinancing, by using the financing agreement referred to in note [X] to the financial statements.
Tax-exempt bonds have been issued.	Tax-exempt bonds issued have retained their tax-exempt status.
Taxes Management intends to reinvest undistributed earnings of a foreign subsidiary.	We intend to reinvest the undistributed earnings of [*name of foreign subsidiary*].
Contingencies Estimates and disclosures have been made of environmental remediation liabilities and related loss contingencies.	Provision has been made for any material loss that is probable from environmental remediation liabilities associated with [*name of site*]. We believe that such estimate is reasonable based on available information and that the liabilities and related loss contingencies and the expected outcome of uncertainties have been adequately described in the company's financial statements.
Agreements may exist to repurchase assets previously sold.	Agreements to repurchase assets previously sold have been properly disclosed.
Pension and Postretirement Benefits An actuary has been used to measure pension liabilities and costs.	We believe that the actuarial assumptions and methods used to measure pension liabilities and costs for financial accounting purposes are appropriate in the circumstances.

(continued)

AR §90.71

Review of Financial Statements

105

Liabilities

Condition	*Illustrative Examples*
Involvement with a multiemployer plan exists.	We are unable to determine the possibility of a withdrawal liability in a multiemployer benefit plan. or We have determined that there is the possibility of a withdrawal liability in a multiemployer plan in the amount of $[XX].
Postretirement benefits have been eliminated.	We do not intend to compensate for the elimination of postretirement benefits by granting an increase in pension benefits. or We plan to compensate for the elimination of postretirement benefits by granting an increase in pension benefits in the amount of $[XX].
Employee layoffs that would otherwise lead to a curtailment of a benefit plan are intended to be temporary.	Current employee layoffs are intended to be temporary.
Management intends to either continue to make or not make frequent amendments to its pension or other postretirement benefit plans, which may affect the amortization period of prior service cost, or has expressed a substantive commitment to increase benefit obligations.	We plan to continue to make frequent amendments to its pension or other postretirement benefit plans, which may affect the amortization period of prior service cost. or We do not plan to make frequent amendments to its pension or other postretirement benefit plans.

Equity

Condition	*Illustrative Example*
Capital stock repurchase options or agreements or capital stock reserved for options, warrants, conversions, or other requirements exist.	Capital stock repurchase options or agreements or capital stock reserved for options, warrants, conversions, or other requirements have been properly disclosed.

AR §90.71

106 Statements on Standards for Accounting and Review Services

Income Statement

Condition	Illustrative Examples
There may be a loss from sales commitments.	Provisions have been made for losses to be sustained in the fulfillment of or from inability to fulfill any sales commitments.
There may be losses from purchase commitments.	Provisions have been made for losses to be sustained as a result of purchase commitments for inventory quantities in excess of normal requirements or at prices in excess of prevailing market prices.
Nature of the product or industry indicates the possibility of undisclosed sales terms.	We have fully disclosed to you all sales terms, including all rights of return or price adjustments and all warranty provisions.

AR §90.71

Review of Financial Statements

.72

Review Exhibit C—Illustrative Updating Management Representation Letter

The following letter is presented for illustrative purposes only. It may be used in the circumstances described in paragraph .23. Management need not repeat all of the representations made in the previous representation letter.

If matters exist that should be disclosed to the accountant, they may be indicated by listing them following the representation. For example, if an event subsequent to the date of the accountant's review report is disclosed in the financial statements, the final paragraph could be modified as follows: "To the best of our knowledge and belief, except as discussed in note X to the financial statements, no events have occurred..."

[Date][1]

To [Accountant]

In connection with your review(s) of the [identification of financial statements] of [name of entity] as of [dates] and for the [periods of review] for the purpose of obtaining limited assurance that that there are no material modifications that should be made to the financial statements in order for the statements to be in conformity with [the applicable financial reporting framework (for example, accounting principles generally accepted in the United States of America)], you were previously provided with a representation letter under date of [date of previous representation letter]. No information has come to our attention that would cause us to believe that any of those previous representations should be modified.

To the best of our knowledge and belief, no events have occurred subsequent to [date of latest balance sheet reported on by the accountant or date of previous representation letter] and through the date of this letter that would require adjustment to or disclosure in the aforementioned financial statements.

_____

[Name of Owner or Chief Executive
Officer and Title]

_____

[Name of Chief Financial Officer
and Title, when applicable]

---

[1] The accountant has two methods available for dating the report when a subsequent event requiring disclosure occurs after the completion of the review but before issuance of the report on the related financial statements. The accountant may use dual dating (for example, "February 16, 20XX, except for note Y, as to which the date is March 1, 20XX,") or may date the report as of the later date.

AR §90.72

108 Statements on Standards for Accounting and Review Services

.73

Review Exhibit D—Illustrative Review Reports

Standard accountant's review report on financial statements prepared in accordance with accounting principles generally accepted in the United States of America

Independent Accountant's Review Report

[*Appropriate Salutation*]

I (We) have reviewed the accompanying balance sheet of XYZ Company as of December 31, 20XX, and the related statements of income, retained earnings, and cash flows for the year then ended. A review includes primarily applying analytical procedures to management's (owners') financial data and making inquiries of company management (owners). A review is substantially less in scope than an audit, the objective of which is the expression of an opinion regarding the financial statements as a whole. Accordingly, I (we) do not express such an opinion.

Management (owners) is (are) responsible for the preparation and fair presentation of the financial statements in accordance with accounting principles generally accepted in the United States of America and for designing, implementing, and maintaining internal control relevant to the preparation and fair presentation of the financial statements.

My (our) responsibility is to conduct the review in accordance with Statements on Standards for Accounting and Review Services issued by the American Institute of Certified Public Accountants. Those standards require me (us) to perform procedures to obtain limited assurance that there are no material modifications that should be made to the financial statements. I (We) believe that the results of my (our) procedures provide a reasonable basis for our report.

Based on my (our) review, I am (we are) not aware of any material modifications that should be made to the accompanying financial statements in order for them to be in conformity with accounting principles generally accepted in the United States of America.

[*Signature of accounting firm or accountant, as appropriate*]

[*Date*]

Standard accountant's review report on financial statements prepared in accordance with the income tax basis of accounting

Independent Accountant's Review Report

[*Appropriate Salutation*]

I (We) have reviewed the accompanying statement of assets, liabilities, and equity —income tax basis of XYZ Company as of December 31, 20XX, and the related statement of revenue and expenses—income tax basis for the year then ended. A review includes primarily applying analytical procedures to management's (owners') financial data and making inquiries of company management (owners). A review is substantially less in scope than an audit, the objective of which is the expression of an opinion regarding the financial statements as a whole. Accordingly, I (we) do not express such an opinion.

Management (owners) is (are) responsible for the preparation and fair presentation of the financial statements in accordance with the income tax basis for accounting and for designing, implementing, and maintaining

AR §90.73

Review of Financial Statements

109

internal control relevant to the preparation and fair presentation of the financial statements.

My (our) responsibility is to conduct the review in accordance with Statements on Standards for Accounting and Review Services issued by the American Institute of Certified Public Accountants. Those standards require me (us) to perform procedures to obtain limited assurance that there are no material modifications that should be made to the financial statements. I (We) believe that the results of my (our) procedures provides a reasonable basis for our report.

Based on my (our) review, I am (we are) not aware of any material modifications that should be made to the accompanying financial statements in order for them to be in conformity with the income tax basis of accounting, as described in note X.

[*Signature of accounting firm or accountant, as appropriate*]

[*Date*]

Accountant's review report disclosing a departure from accounting principles generally accepted in the United States of America

Independent Accountant's Review Report

[*Appropriate Salutation*]

I (We) have reviewed the accompanying balance sheet of XYZ Company as of December 31, 20XX, and the related statements of income, retained earnings, and cash flows for the year then ended. A review includes primarily applying analytical procedures to management's (owners') financial data and making inquiries of company management (owners). A review is substantially less in scope than an audit, the objective of which is the expression of an opinion regarding the financial statements as a whole. Accordingly, I (we) do not express such an opinion.

Management (owners) is (are) responsible for the preparation and fair presentation of the financial statements in accordance with accounting principles generally accepted in the United States of America and for designing, implementing, and maintaining internal control relevant to the preparation and fair presentation of the financial statements.

My (our) responsibility is to conduct the review in accordance with Statements on Standards for Accounting and Review Services issued by the American Institute of Certified Public Accountants. Those standards require me (us) to perform procedures to obtain limited assurance that there are no material modifications that should be made to the financial statements. I (We) believe that the results of my (our) procedures provide a reasonable basis for our report.

Based on my (our) review, with the exception of the matter(s) described in the following paragraph(s), I am (we are) not aware of any material modifications that should be made to the accompanying financial statements in order for them to be in conformity with accounting principles generally accepted in the United States of America.

As disclosed in note X to the financial statements, accounting principles generally accepted in the United States of America require that inventory cost consist of material, labor, and overhead. Management has informed (me) us that the inventory of finished goods and work in process is stated in the accompanying financial statements at material and labor cost only, and that the effects of this departure from accounting principles generally

AR §90.73

110 Statements on Standards for Accounting and Review Services

accepted in the United States of America on financial position, results of operations, and cash flows have not been determined.

or

As disclosed in note X to the financial statements, the company has adopted [*description of newly adopted method*], whereas it previously used [*description of previous method*]. Although the [*description of newly adopted method*] is in conformity with accounting principles as generally accepted in the United States of America, the company does not appear to have reasonable justification for making a change as required by Financial Accounting Standards Board *Accounting Standards Codification* 250, *Accounting Changes and Error Corrections.*

[*Signature of accounting firm or accountant, as appropriate*]

[*Date*]

AR §90.73

AR Section 9090

Review of Financial Statements: Accounting and Review Services Interpretations of Section 90

1. Reporting When There Are Significant Departures From the Applicable Financial Reporting Framework

.01 *Question*—When the financial statements include significant departures from the applicable financial reporting framework, may the accountant modify his or her standard report in accordance with paragraphs .34–.36 of section 90, *Review of Financial Statements*, to include a statement that the financial statements are not in conformity with the applicable financial reporting framework?

.02 *Interpretation*—No. Including such a statement in the accountant's review report would be tantamount to expressing an adverse opinion on the financial statements as a whole. Such an opinion can be expressed only in the context of an audit engagement. Furthermore, such a statement in a review report would confuse users because it would contradict the results of engagement as required by paragraph .28(f) of section 90.

.03 However, paragraph .33 of section 90 states that an accountant may emphasize, in any report on financial statements, a matter disclosed in the financial statements. The accountant may wish, therefore, to emphasize the limitations of the financial statements in a separate paragraph of his or her review report, depending on his or her assessment of the possible dollar magnitude of the effects of the departures, the significance of the affected items to the entity, the pervasiveness and overall impact of the misstatements, and whether disclosure has been made of the effects of the departures. Such separate paragraph, which would follow the other modifications of his or her report (see illustrations in Review Exhibit D), might read as follows (the illustration assumes that the accountant is reporting on financial statements in which there are significant departures from accounting principles generally accepted in the United States of America):

> Because the significance and pervasiveness of the matters previously discussed makes it difficult to assess their impact on the financial statements as a whole, users of these financial statements should recognize that they might reach different conclusions about the company's financial position, results of operations, and cash flows if they had access to revised financial statements prepared in conformity with accounting principles generally accepted in the United States of America.

.04 Inclusion of such a separate paragraph in the accountant's review report is not a substitute for disclosure of the specific departures or the effects of such departures when they have been determined by management or are known as a result of the accountant's procedures.

[Issue Date: August 1981; Revised: November 2002; Revised: May 2004; Revised: July 2005; Revised: December 2010 to conform to SSARS No. 19 (formerly Interpretation No. 7 to section 100).]

112 Statements on Standards for Accounting and Review Services

2. Reporting on Tax Returns

.05 *Question*—May an accountant comply with a request from a nonissuer to issue a review report on financial information contained in a tax return, as in Form 1040, *U.S. Individual Income Tax Return*, or Form 1120, *U.S. Corporation Income Tax Return*, or in an information return, as in Form 990, *Return of Organization Exempt from Income Tax*; Form 1065, *U.S. Partnership Return of Income*; or Form 5500, *Return of Employee Benefit Plan*?

.06 *Interpretation*—Yes. Although paragraph .01 of section 90 states that the section establishes standards and provides guidance on reviews of financial statements and financial information contained in a tax return is not included in the definition of financial statements, an accountant may decide to accept an engagement to issue a review report on such a return. In that case, the performance and reporting requirements of section 90 would apply.

[Issue Date: November 1982; Revised: February 2008;
Revised: December 2010 to conform to SSARS No. 19 (formerly Interpretation
No. 10 to section 100).]

3. Additional Procedures Performed in a Review Engagement

.07 *Question*—If an accountant performs procedures customarily performed in an audit but not in a review, is the accountant required to change the engagement to an audit?

.08 *Interpretation*—No. Paragraph .07 of section 90 states that review evidence obtained through the performance of analytical procedures and inquiry will ordinarily provide the accountant with a reasonable basis for obtaining limited assurance. However, paragraph .07 further states that the accountant should perform additional procedures if the accountant determines such procedures to be necessary to obtain limited assurance that the financial statements are not materially misstated.

.09 The wording of confirmation requests or other communications related to additional procedures performed in the course of a review engagement should not use phrases such as "as part of an *audit* of the financial statements" (emphasis supplied).

[Issue Date: March 1983; Revised: October 2000; Revised: November 2002;
Revised: May 2004; Revised: December 2010 to conform to SSARS No. 19
(formerly Interpretation No. 13 to section 100).]

4. Submitting Draft Financial Statements

.10 *Question*—Accountants frequently submit draft financial statements (*a*) because information needed to complete a review of the financial statements will not be available until a later date or (*b*) to provide the client with the opportunity to read and analyze the financial statements prior to their final issuance. Is it permissible for the accountant to submit draft financial statements to management without intending to comply with the reporting provisions of section 90?

.11 *Interpretation*—No. An accountant is precluded from submitting draft financial statements unless he or she intends to submit those financial statements in final form accompanied by an appropriate review report prescribed by section 90. However, as long as the accountant intends to issue a review report on the financial statements in final form and labels each page of draft financial statements with words such as "Draft," "Preliminary Draft," "Draft—Subject to Changes," or "Working Draft," the accountant is not required to comply with

AR §9090.05

Review of Financial Statements

113

the reporting provisions of section 90 with respect to those draft financial statements. In the rare circumstance in which the accountant intended to but never submitted final financial statements, the accountant may want to document the reasons why he or she was unable to submit financial statements in final form accompanied by an appropriate review report.

[Issue Date: September 1990; Revised: October 2000; Revised: December 2010 to conform to SSARS No. 19 (formerly Interpretation No. 17 to section 100).]

5. Reporting When Financial Statements Contain a Departure From Promulgated Accounting Principles That Prevents the Financial Statements From Being Misleading

.12 *Question*—Rule 203, *Accounting Principles* (ET sec. 203 par. .01), of the AICPA Code of Professional Conduct states

> A member shall not (1) express an opinion or state affirmatively that the financial statements or other financial data of any entity are presented in conformity with generally accepted accounting principles or (2) state that he or she is not aware of any material modifications that should be made to such statements or data in order for them to be in conformity with generally accepted accounting principles, if such statements or data contain any departure from an accounting principle promulgated by bodies designated by Council to establish such principles that has a material effect on the statements or data taken as a whole. If, however, the statements or data contain such a departure and the member can demonstrate that due to unusual circumstances the financial statements or data would otherwise have been misleading, the member can comply with the rule by describing the departure, its approximate effects, if practicable, and the reasons why compliance with the principle would result in a misleading statement.

Paragraphs .34–.36 of section 90 do not address the Rule 203 circumstances. When the circumstances contemplated by Rule 203 are present, how should the accountant report on the information described in the rule?

.13 *Interpretation*—When the circumstances contemplated by Rule 203 are present in a review engagement, the accountant's review report should include, in a separate paragraph or paragraphs, the information required by Rule 203. In such a case, the accountant would not modify the standard review report, except for the addition of the separate paragraph(s) that contains the information required by Rule 203, unless there are other reasons to do so that are not associated with the departure from a promulgated principle.

[Issue Date: February 1991; Revised: October 2000; Revised: November 2002; Revised: May 2004; Revised: July 2005; Revised: December 2010 to conform to SSARS No. 19 (formerly Interpretation No. 19 to section 100).]

6. Special-Purpose Financial Statements to Comply With Contractual Agreements or Regulatory Provisions

.14 *Question*—An accountant may be asked to review special purpose financial statements prepared to comply with a contractual agreement or regulatory provision that specifies a special basis of presentation. In most circumstances, these financial statements are intended solely for the use of the parties to the agreement, regulatory bodies, or other specified parties. How should the accountant modify the standard review report when reporting on these special-purpose financial statements?

AR §9090.14

114   Statements on Standards for Accounting and Review Services

.15 *Interpretation*—An accountant who is asked to review special-purpose financial statements prepared to comply with a contractual agreement or a regulatory provision that specifies a special basis of presentation may issue a review report on those financial statements in accordance with section 90 as described in this interpretation. This interpretation describes reporting on

    a.   special-purpose financial statements prepared in compliance with a contractual agreement or regulatory provision that does not constitute a complete presentation of the entity's assets, liabilities, revenues, and expenses, but is otherwise prepared in conformity with generally accepted accounting principles (GAAP) or an other comprehensive basis of accounting (OCBOA), or

    b.   a special-purpose financial presentation (may be a complete set of financial statements or a single financial statement) prepared on a basis of accounting prescribed in an agreement that does not result in a presentation in conformity with GAAP or an OCBOA.

Financial Statements Prepared on a Basis of Accounting Prescribed in a Contractual Agreement or Regulatory Provision That Results in an Incomplete Presentation but One That Is Otherwise in Conformity With GAAP or an OCBOA

.16 An entity may engage an accountant to review a special-purpose financial statement prepared in compliance with a contractual agreement or regulatory provision that does not constitute a complete presentation of the entity's assets, liabilities, revenues, or expenses, but is otherwise prepared in conformity with GAAP or an OCBOA. For example, a governmental agency may require a statement of gross income and certain expenses of an entity's real estate operation in which income and expenses are measured in conformity with accounting principles generally accepted in the United States of America, but expenses are defined to exclude certain items such as interest, depreciation, and income taxes. Such a statement may also present the excess of gross income over defined expenses. Also, a buy-sell agreement may specify a statement of gross assets and liabilities of the entity measured in conformity with GAAP, but limited to the assets to be sold and liabilities to be transferred pursuant to the agreement.

.17 The accountant's report on reviewed special-purpose financial statements prepared in accordance with a basis of accounting prescribed in a contractual agreement or regulatory provision but that is otherwise prepared in conformity with GAAP or an OCBOA should be modified to include a separate paragraph with the following information:

- An explanation of what the financial statement is intended to present and a reference to the note to the special-purpose financial statement that describes the basis of presentation.

- If the basis of presentation is in conformity with GAAP or an OCBOA, a statement that the presentation is not intended to be a complete presentation of the entity's assets, liabilities, revenues, and expenses.

- A separate paragraph at the end of the report stating that the report is intended solely for the information and use of those within the entity, the parties to the contract or agreement, the regulatory agency with which the report is being filed, or those with whom the entity is negotiating directly, and is not intended to be and should not be used by anyone other than these specified parties.

AR §9090.15

Review of Financial Statements 115

.18 The following is an illustrative example of a review report on special purpose financial statements:

I (we) have reviewed the accompanying statement of gross income and direct operating expenses of XYZ Company for the year ended December 31, 20X1. A review includes primarily applying analytical procedures to management (owners') financial data and making inquiries of company management (owners). A review is substantially less in scope than an audit, the objective of which is the expression of an opinion regarding the statement of gross income and direct operating expenses as a whole. Accordingly, I (we) do not express such an opinion.

Management (owners) is (are) responsible for the preparation and fair presentation of the statement of gross income and direct operating expenses in accordance with the regulatory provision described in Note A and for designing, implementing, and maintaining internal control relevant to the preparation and fair presentation of the statement of gross income and direct operating expenses.

My (our) responsibility is to conduct the review in accordance with Statements on Standards for Accounting and Review Services issued by the American Institute of Certified Public Accountants. Those standards require me (us) to perform procedures to obtain limited assurance that there are no material modifications that should be made to the statement of gross income and direct operating expenses. I (We) believe that the results of my (our) procedures provide a reasonable basis for our report.

The accompanying statement was prepared for the purpose of presenting gross income and direct operating expenses of XYZ Company pursuant to the regulatory provision described in Note A, and is not intended to be a complete presentation of XYZ Company's income and expenses.

Based on my (our) review, I am (we are) not aware of any material modifications that should be made to the accompanying statement of gross income and direct operating expenses in order for it to be in conformity with accounting principles generally accepted in the United States of America.

This report is intended solely for the information and use of [*the specified parties*] and is not intended to be and should not be used by anyone other than these specified parties.

Financial Statements Prepared on a Basis of Accounting Prescribed in an Agreement That Results in a Presentation That Is Not in Conformity With GAAP or an OCBOA

.19 An entity may engage an accountant to review a special-purpose financial statement prepared in conformity with a basis of accounting that departs from GAAP or an OCBOA. A loan agreement, for example, may require the borrower to prepare consolidated financial statements in which assets, such as inventory, are presented on a basis that is not in conformity with GAAP or an OCBOA. Also, an acquisition agreement may require the financial statements of the entity being acquired (or a segment of it) to be prepared in conformity with GAAP except for certain assets, such as receivables, inventories, and properties for which a valuation basis is specified in the agreement.

.20 Financial statements prepared under a basis of accounting as discussed in the preceding are not considered to be prepared in conformity with an OCBOA because the criteria used to prepare such financial statements do not meet the requirement of "having substantial support," even though the criteria are definite.

AR §9090.20

116   Statements on Standards for Accounting and Review Services

.21 The accountant's report on reviewed special-purpose financial statements prepared on a basis of accounting prescribed in an agreement that results in a presentation that is not in conformity with GAAP or an OCBOA should be modified to include a separate paragraph with the following information:

- An explanation of what the presentation is intended to present and a reference to the note to the special-purpose financial statements that describes the basis of presentation.

- A statement that the financial statement is not intended to be a presentation in conformity with GAAP or an OCBOA.

- A description and the source of significant interpretations, if any, made by the Company's management relating to the provisions of a relevant agreement.

- A separate paragraph at the end of the report stating that the report is intended solely for the information and use of those within the entity, the parties to the contract or agreement, the regulatory agency with which the report is being filed, or those with whom the entity is negotiating directly, and is not intended to be and should not be used by anyone other than these specified parties. For example, if the financial statements have been prepared for the specified purpose of obtaining bank financing, the report's use should be restricted to the various banks with whom the entity is negotiating the proposed financing.

.22 The following is an illustrative example of a review report on special-purpose financial statements:

I (we) have reviewed the accompanying special-purpose statement of assets and liabilities of XYZ Company as of December 31, 20X1. A review includes primarily applying analytical procedures to management (owners') financial data and making inquiries of company management (owners). A review is substantially less in scope than an audit, the objective of which is the expression of an opinion regarding the statement of assets and liabilities as a whole. Accordingly, I (we) do not express such an opinion.

Management (owners) is (are) responsible for the preparation and fair presentation of the statement of assets and liabilities in accordance with Section 4 of a loan agreement between DEF Bank and the Company as discussed in Note A and for designing, implementing, and maintaining internal control relevant to the preparation and fair presentation of the statement of assets and liabilities.

My (our) responsibility is to conduct the review in accordance with Statements on Standards for Accounting and Review Services issued by the American Institute of Certified Public Accountants. Those standards require me (us) to perform procedures to obtain limited assurance that there are no material modifications that should be made to the statement of assets and liabilities. I (We) believe that the results of my (our) procedures provide a reasonable basis for our report.

The accompanying special-purpose statement of assets and liabilities was prepared for the purpose of complying with Section 4 of a loan agreement between DEF Bank and the Company as discussed in Note A and is not intended to be a presentation in conformity with accounting principles generally accepted in the United States of America.

Based on my (our) review, I am (we are) not aware of any material modifications that should be made to the accompanying special-purpose statement of assets and liabilities in order for it to be in conformity with the basis of accounting described in Note A.

AR §9090.21

Review of Financial Statements 117

This report is intended solely for the information and use of the [*specified parties*]

[Issue Date: December 2006; Revised: December 2010 to conform to SSARS No. 19 (formerly Interpretation No. 28 to section 100).]

7. Reporting on an Uncertainty, Including an Uncertainty About an Entity's Ability to Continue as a Going Concern

.23 *Question*—How should an accountant modify the standard review report when, during the performance of review procedures, evidence or information comes to the accountant's attention that there may be an uncertainty about the entity's ability to continue as a going concern for a reasonable period of time, not to exceed one year beyond the date of the financial statements being compiled or reviewed?

.24 *Interpretation*—Continuation of an entity as a going concern is assumed in financial reporting in the absence of significant information to the contrary. The accountant should follow the guidance in paragraphs .47–.50 of section 90 with respect to his or her consideration of the entity's ability to continue as a going concern during the performance of review procedures.

.25 If the accountant concludes that management's disclosure of the uncertainty regarding the entity's ability to continue as a going concern is adequate but further decides to include an emphasis-of-matter paragraph with respect to the uncertainty in the accountant's review report, he or she may use the following language:

> As discussed in Note X, certain conditions indicate that the Company may be unable to continue as a going concern. The accompanying financial statements do not include any adjustments that might be necessary should the Company be unable to continue as a going concern.

.26 *Question*—If the accountant, while performing a review, becomes aware of a material uncertainty other than a going concern uncertainty (for example, an uncertainty regarding pending or threatened litigation), what should the accountant consider in deciding whether a report modification is necessary?

.27 *Interpretation*—If the accountant determines that the disclosure of the uncertainty is not in accordance with the applicable financial reporting framework, he or she should follow the guidance in paragraphs .34–.36 of section 90.

.28 If the accountant concludes that management's disclosure of the uncertainty is in accordance with the applicable financial reporting framework but further decides to include an emphasis-of-matter paragraph with respect to the uncertainty in the accountant's review report, he or she may use the following language (the following is assuming that the financial statements were prepared in accordance with accounting principles generally accepted in the United States of America):

> As discussed in Note X, the Company is currently named in a legal action. The Company has determined that it is not possible to predict the eventual outcome of the legal action but has determined that the resolution of the action will not result in an adverse judgment that would materially affect the financial statements. Accordingly, the accompanying financial statements do not include any adjustments related to the legal action under FASB ASC 450.

[Issue date: February 2007; Revised: February 2008; Amended: December 2008; Revised: June 2009; Revised: December 2010 to conform to SSARS No. 19 (formerly Interpretation No. 29 to section 100)]

AR §9090.28

118   Statements on Standards for Accounting and Review Services

8. Reviews of Financial Statements Prepared in Accordance With International Financial Reporting Standards

.29 *Question*—The International Accounting Standards Board (IASB) has been designated by the Council of the AICPA as the body to establish international financial reporting standards for both private and public entities pursuant to Rule 202, *Compliance With Standards* (ET sec. 202 par. .01), and Rule 203 of the AICPA Code of Professional Conduct as of May 18, 2008. As a result, how would an accountant apply the reporting guidance in section 90 when engaged to review financial statements presented in accordance with International Financial Reporting Standards (IFRSs) as issued by the IASB?

.30 *Interpretation*—A report illustration of how an accountant would apply the reporting guidance in section 90 when reporting on financial statements presented in accordance with IFRSs is as follows:

<u>Independent Accountant's Review Report</u>

[Appropriate Salutation]

I (We) have reviewed the accompanying balance sheets of XYZ Company as of December 31, 20X2 and 20X1, and the related statements of income, retained earnings, and cash flows for the year then ended. A review includes primarily applying analytical procedures to management's (owners') financial data and making inquiries of company management (owners). A review is substantially less in scope than an audit, the objective of which is the expression of an opinion regarding the financial statements as a whole. Accordingly, I (we) do not express such an opinion.

Management (owners) is (are) responsible for the preparation and fair presentation of the financial statements in accordance with International Financial Reporting Standards as issued by the International Accounting Standards Board and for designing, implementing, and maintaining internal control relevant to the preparation and fair presentation of the financial statements.

My (our) responsibility is to conduct the reviews in accordance with Statements on Standards for Accounting and Review Services issued by the American Institute of Certified Public Accountants. Those standards require me (us) to perform procedures to obtain limited assurance that there are no material modifications that should be made to the financial statements. I (We) believe that the results of my (our) procedures provide a reasonable basis for our report.

Based on my (our) reviews, I am (we are) not aware of any material modifications that should be made to the accompanying financial statements in order for them to be in conformity with International Financial Reporting Standards as issued by the International Accounting Standards Board.

[Signature of accounting firm or accountant, as appropriate]

[Date]

.31 *Question*—Unlike accounting principles generally accepted in the United States of America as issued by the Financial Accounting Standards Board (FASB), IFRSs require an entity to disclose comparative information in respect of the previous comparative period for all amounts presented in the current year's financial statements. When the accountant reviews financial statements that omit prior year information, should such omission be disclosed in the accountant's review report as a departure from IFRSs as issued by the IASB in accordance with paragraphs .34–.36 of section 90?

AR §9090.29

Review of Financial Statements

119

.32 *Interpretation*—Yes. Because IFRSs require an entity to disclose comparative information in respect of the previous comparative period for all amounts presented in the current year's financial statements, the failure to include such information in financial statements would be a departure from generally accepted accounting principles. An example of a paragraph that may be added to the accountant's review report is as follows:

> Comparative information with respect to the year ended December 31, 20XX-1 has not been presented. International Financial Reporting Standards [or *IFRSs for SMEs*] as issued by the International Accounting Standards Board require an entity to disclose comparative information in respect of the previous comparative period for all amounts presented in the current year's financial statements.

[Issue Date: May 2008; Revised: June 2010; Revised: August 2010; Revised: December 2010 (formerly Interpretation No. 30 to section 100).]

9. Reviews of Financial Statements Prepared in Accordance With a Financial Reporting Framework Generally Accepted in Another Country

.33 *Question*—An accountant may be engaged to review financial statements that have been prepared in conformity with a financial reporting framework generally accepted in another country (including financial statements prepared in accordance with a jurisdictional variation of IFRSs such that the entity's financial statements do not contain an explicit and unreserved statement of compliance with IFRSs as issued by the IASB). How should an accountant apply the reporting requirements in section 90 when reporting on those financial statements?

.34 *Interpretation*— If the financial statements are intended for use only outside of the United States of America, the accountant may report using the standard form of U.S. review report modified as appropriate to identify the applicable financial reporting framework; or alternatively, the accountant may report using the standard review report form and content of the other country. (See Interpretation No. 10 with respect to Considerations Related to Reviews Performed in Accordance with International Standard on Review Engagements [ISRE] 2400, *Engagements to Review Financial Statements*).

.35 The standard review report used in another country, even when it appears similar to that used in the United States of America, may convey a different meaning and entail a different responsibility on the part of the accountant due to custom or culture. Issuing a standard review report of another country may require an understanding of local laws. When issuing the accountant's standard review report of another country, the accountant is required to obtain an understanding of applicable legal responsibilities, in addition to the review standards and accounting principles generally accepted in the other country, as indicated in paragraph .13 of AR section 90. Therefore, depending on the nature and extent of the accountant's knowledge and experience, the accountant may wish to consult with persons having expertise in the reporting practices of the other country and associated legal responsibilities to obtain the understanding needed to issue that country's standard review report.

.36 If the accountant's report is intended for use in the United States of America, the reporting requirements described in paragraphs .27–.32 of section 90 would apply. Additionally, paragraph .38 of section 90 states that a need for restriction on the use of the report may result from a number of circumstances, including, but not limited to, the purpose of the report and the potential for the report to be misunderstood when taken out of context in which it was intended to be used. Because of the nature of the basis of presentation of the financial

AR §9090.36

120　　Statements on Standards for Accounting and Review Services

statements, there is a presumption that the report would be misunderstood or taken out of context in which it was intended to be used. In such instances, the accountant may use the following form of report:

Independent Accountant's Review Report

[*Appropriate Salutation*]

I (We) have reviewed the accompanying balance sheets of XYZ Company as of December 31, 20X2 and 20X1, and the related statements of income, retained earnings, and cash flows for the year then ended. A review includes primarily applying analytical procedures to management's (owners') financial data and making inquiries of company management (owners). A review is substantially less in scope than an audit, the objective of which is the expression of an opinion regarding the financial statements as a whole. Accordingly, I (we) do not express such an opinion.

Management (owners) is (are) responsible for the preparation and fair presentation of the financial statements in accordance with [*the financial reporting framework generally accepted in another country, including identification of the nationality of the framework*] and for designing, implementing, and maintaining internal control relevant to the preparation and fair presentation of the financial statements.

My (our) responsibility is to conduct the reviews in accordance with Statements on Standards for Accounting and Review Services issued by the American Institute of Certified Public Accountants. Those standards require me (us) to perform procedures to obtain limited assurance that there are no material modifications that should be made to the financial statements. I (We) believe that the results of my (our) procedures provide a reasonable basis for our report.

Based on my (our) reviews, I am (we are) not aware of any material modifications that should be made to the accompanying financial statements in order for them to be in conformity with [*the financial reporting framework generally accepted in another country, including identification of the nationality of the framework*].

This report is intended solely for the information and the use of [*specified parties*] and is not intended to be and should not be used by anyone other than the specified parties.

[*Signature of accounting firm or accountant, as appropriate*]

[*Date*]

.37 When the financial statements will be used both outside of the United States of America as well as in the United States of America, nothing precludes the accountant from issuing two reports—a report to be used only outside of the United States of America and another report to be used in the United States of America.

[Issue Date: May 2008; Revised: June 2010; Revised: August 2010; Revised: December 2010 (formerly Interpretation No. 30 to section 100).]

10. Considerations Related to Reviews Performed in Accordance with International Standard on Review Engagements 2400, *Engagements to Review Financial Statements*, Issued by the International Audit and Assurance Standards Board

.38 *Question*—May a U.S. accountant perform a review of historical financial statements of a U.S. entity[1] in accordance with ISRE 2400, *Engagements*

---

[1] A *U.S. entity* is an entity that is either organized or domiciled in the United States of America.

AR §9090.37

Review of Financial Statements

to Review Financial Statements issued by the International Audit and Assurance Standards Board? The financial statements may have been prepared in accordance with IFRS or accounting principles generally accepted in the United States of America.

.39 *Interpretation*—An accountant performing a review of historical financial statements of a U.S. entity is required to follow the review standards as promulgated by the AICPA's Accounting and Review Services Committee. However, those standards do not prohibit an accountant from indicating that the review also was conducted in accordance with another set of review standards. In an engagement to review the historical financial statements in accordance with ISRE 2400, the accountant may perform the review in accordance with Statements on Standards for Accounting and Review Services (SSARSs) as well as ISRE 2400. Such a review report may read as follows:

> I (We) have reviewed the accompanying balance sheets of XYZ Company as of December 31, 20X2 and 20X1, and the related statements of income, retained earnings, and cash flows for the years then ended. A review includes primarily applying analytical procedures to management (owners') financial data and making inquiries of company management (owners). A review is substantially less in scope than an audit, the objective of which is the expression of an opinion regarding the financial statements as a whole. Accordingly, I (we) do not express such an opinion.
>
> Management (owners) is (are) responsible for the preparation and fair presentation of the financial statements in accordance with International Financial Reporting Standards as issued by the International Accounting Standards Board and for designing, implementing, and maintaining internal control relevant to the preparation and fair presentation of the financial statements.
>
> My (our) responsibility is to conduct the reviews in accordance with Statements on Standards for Accounting and Review Services issued by the American Institute of Certified Public Accountants and in accordance with International Standard on Review Engagements (ISRE 2400) issued by the International Audit & Assurance Standards Board. Those standards require me (us) to perform procedures to obtain limited assurance that there are no material modifications that should be made to the financial statements. I (We) believe that the results of my (our) procedures provide a reasonable basis for our report.
>
> Based on my (our) reviews, I am (we are) not aware of any material modifications that should be made to the accompanying financial statements in order for them to be in conformity with or International Financial Reporting Standards as issued by the International Accounting Standards Board.

.40 If the report is for use only outside of the United States of America, the accountant is still required to apply SSARSs, except for requirements related to report form and content.

[Issue Date: May 2008; Revised: June 2010; Revised: August 2010; Revised: December 2010 (formerly Interpretation No. 30 to section 100).]

11. Required Supplementary Information That Accompanies Reviewed Financial Statements

.41 *Question*—Paragraph .60 of section 90 addresses situations when the basic financial statements are accompanied by information presented for supplementary analysis purposes. Certain information presented for supplementary analysis purposes may be required by a body designated by the AICPA

122 Statements on Standards for Accounting and Review Services

Council to establish GAAP pursuant to Rule 202 and Rule 203[2] (hereinafter referred to as "required supplementary information"). Examples of required supplementary information that may accompany reviewed financial statements include the following:

- With respect to common interest realty associations, estimates of current or future costs of major repairs and replacements of common property that will be required in the future as required by FASB *Accounting Standards Codification* 972-235-50-3

- Management's discussion and analysis and budgetary comparison statements as required by Governmental Accounting Standards Board Statement No. 34, *Basic Financial Statements—and Management's Discussion and Analysis—for State and Local Governments*

Is the accountant required to apply procedures to required supplementary information that accompanies reviewed financial statements?

.42 *Interpretation*—No. SSARSs do not require the accountant to apply procedures to any information presented for supplementary analysis purposes, including required supplementary information.

.43 *Question*—Paragraph .60 of section 90 states that when the basic financial statements are accompanied by information presented for supplementary analysis purposes, the accountant should indicate the degree of responsibility, if any, he or she is taking with respect to such information. How may an accountant modify the accountant's review report to refer to the required supplementary information and explain the circumstances regarding its presentation?

.44 *Interpretation*—The accountant may modify the accountant's review report by including a separate paragraph that refers to the required supplementary information and explains the circumstances regarding its presentation. That separate paragraph would be presented after the paragraph that reports the results of the engagement and may read as follows:

The Required Supplementary Information Is Included

[*Identify the applicable financial reporting framework (for example, accounting principles generally accepted in the United States of America)*] require that [*identify the required supplementary information*] on page XX be presented to supplement the basic financial statements. Such information, although not a part of the basic financial statements, is required by [*identify the designated accounting standard setter*] who considers it to be an essential part of financial reporting and for placing the basic financial statements in an appropriate operational, economic, or historical context. Such information was not audited, reviewed, or compiled by me (us) and, accordingly, I (we) do not express an opinion or provide any assurance on it.

All Required Supplementary Information Omitted

Management has omitted [*describe the missing required supplementary information*] that [*identify the applicable financial reporting framework (for example, accounting principles generally accepted in the United States of America)*] require to be presented to supplement the basic financial statements. Such missing information, although not a part of the basic financial statements, is required by [*identify the designated accounting standard setter*] who considers

---

[2] The bodies designated by the AICPA Council to establish professional standards with respect to financial accounting and reporting principles pursuant to these rules are the Financial Accounting Standards Board, the Governmental Accounting Standards Board, the Federal Accounting Standards Advisory Board, and the International Accounting Standards Board.

AR §9090.42

Review of Financial Statements 123

it to be an essential part of financial reporting and for placing the basic financial statements in an appropriate operational, economic, or historical context. The results of our review of the basic financial statements are not affected by this missing information.

Some Required Supplementary Information Is Omitted and Some Is Presented in Accordance With the Prescribed Guidelines Regarding the Required Supplementary Information

[*Identify the applicable financial reporting framework (for example, accounting principles generally accepted in the United States of America)*] require that [*identify the included supplementary information*] be presented to supplement the basic financial statements. Such information, although not a part of the basic financial statements, is required by [*identify designated accounting standard setter*] who considers it to be an essential part of financial reporting for placing the basic financial statements in an appropriate operational, economic, or historical context. Such information was not audited, reviewed, or compiled by me (us) and, accordingly, I (we) do not express an opinion or provide any assurance on it.

Management has omitted [*describe the missing required supplementary information*] that [*identify the applicable financial reporting framework*] require to be presented to supplement the basic financial statements. Such missing information, although not a part of the basic financial statements, is required by [*identify designated accounting standard* setter] who considers it to be an essential part of financial reporting for placing the basic financial statements in an appropriate operational, economic, or historical context. The results of our review of the basic financial statements are not affected by this missing information.

[Issue Date: October 2011.]

AR §9090.44

AR Section 100

Compilation and Review of Financial Statements

Superseded, December 2010, by the issuance of SSARS No. 19.

Compilation of Specified Elements

AR Section 110

Compilation of Specified Elements, Accounts, or Items of a Financial Statement

Issue date, unless otherwise indicated: July 2005

Source: SSARS No. 13; SSARS No. 17

.01 Statements on Standards for Accounting and Review Services (SSARSs) provide guidance concerning the standards and procedures applicable when an accountant is engaged to report on compiled financial statements or submits financial statements to his or her client or to third parties. By definition, presentations of specified elements, accounts, or items of a financial statement are not financial statements. This statement expands SSARSs to apply when an accountant is engaged to report or issues a report on one or more compiled specified elements, accounts, or items of a financial statement. If, however, the specified element, account, or item of a financial statement is included as supplementary information, the accountant should refer to paragraph .53 of section 80, *Compilation of Financial Statements.* [Paragraph revised, December 2010, to reflect conforming changes necessary due to the issuance of SSARS No. 19.]

.02 A compilation of one or more specified elements, accounts, or items of a financial statement is limited to assisting management (owners) in presenting financial information without undertaking to obtain or provide any assurance that there are no material modifications that should be made to that information. [Paragraph revised, December 2010, to reflect conforming changes necessary due to the issuance of SSARS No. 19.]

.03 Examples of specified elements, accounts, or items of a financial statement that an accountant may compile include schedules of rentals, royalties, profit participation, or provision for income taxes.

Conditions for Compiling Specified Elements, Accounts, or Items of a Financial Statement

.04 Nothing in this statement is intended to preclude an accountant from assisting management (owners) in presenting one or more specified elements, accounts, or items of a financial statement and submitting such specified elements, accounts, or items of a financial statement to the client or to third parties without the issuance of a compilation report, unless the accountant has been engaged to report on such compiled specified elements, accounts, or items of a financial statement. If an accountant assists management (owners) in presenting a schedule of one or more specified elements, accounts, or items of a financial statement,[1] the accountant should consider how such a presentation of specified elements, accounts, or items will be used. The accountant should consider the potential of being associated with the schedule and the likelihood that the user may inappropriately infer, through that association, an unintended level

---

[1] [Footnote deleted, December 2010, to reflect conforming changes necessary due to the issuance of Statement on Standards for Accounting and Review Services (SSARS) No. 19.]

AR §110.04

128 Statements on Standards for Accounting and Review Services

of reliance on the information. If the accountant believes that he or she will be associated with the information, the accountant should consider issuing a compilation report so a user will not infer an unintended level of reliance on the information. [Paragraph revised, December 2010, to reflect conforming changes necessary due to the issuance of SSARS No. 19.]

.05 An engagement to report on one or more compiled specified elements, accounts, or items of a financial statement may be undertaken as a separate engagement or in conjunction with a compilation, review, or audit of financial statements. [Paragraph revised, December 2010, to reflect conforming changes necessary due to the issuance of SSARS No. 19.]

Understanding With the Entity

.06 When an accountant is engaged to report on one or more compiled specified elements, accounts, or items of a financial statement, the accountant should establish an understanding with management regarding the services to be performed and should document the understanding through a written communication with management. Such an understanding reduces the risks that either the accountant or management may misinterpret the needs or expectations of the other party. For example, it reduces the risk that management may inappropriately rely on the accountant to protect the entity against certain risks or perform certain functions that are management's responsibility. The accountant should ensure that the understanding includes the objectives of the engagement, management's responsibilities, the accountant's responsibilities, and the limitations of the engagement. In some cases, the accountant may establish such understanding with those charged with governance. An understanding with management and, if applicable, those charged with governance, regarding a compilation of specified elements, accounts, or items of a financial statement should include the following matters:

- The objective of a compilation of specified elements, accounts, or items of a financial statement is to assist management in presenting such financial information.

- The accountant utilizes information that is the representation of management (owners) without undertaking to obtain any assurance that there are no material modifications that should be made to the specified element, account, or item of a financial statement in order for the specified element, account, or item to be in conformity with the applicable financial reporting framework.

- Management is responsible for the preparation and fair presentation of the specified element, account, or item of a financial statement in accordance with the applicable financial reporting framework.

- Management is responsible for designing, implementing, and maintaining internal control relevant to the preparation and fair presentation of the specified element, account, or item of a financial statement.

- Management is responsible for the prevention and detection of fraud.

- Management is responsible for identifying and ensuring that the entity complies with the laws and regulations applicable to its activities.

AR §110.05

Compilation of Specified Elements

129

- Management is responsible for making all financial records and related information available to the accountant.

- The accountant is responsible for conducting the engagement in accordance with SSARSs issued by the AICPA.

- A compilation differs significantly from a review or an audit of specified elements, accounts, or items of a financial statement. A compilation does not contemplate performing inquiry, analytical procedures, or other procedures performed in a review. Additionally, a compilation does not contemplate obtaining an understanding of the entity's internal control; assessing fraud risk; testing accounting records by obtaining sufficient appropriate audit evidence through inspection, observation, confirmation, or the examination of source documents (for example, cancelled checks or bank images); or other procedures ordinarily performed in an audit. Accordingly, the accountant will not express an opinion or provide any assurance regarding the specified element, account, or item of a financial statement.

- The engagement cannot be relied upon to disclose errors, fraud,[2] or illegal acts.[3]

- The accountant will inform the appropriate level of management of any material errors and of any evidence or information that comes to the accountant's attention during the performance of compilation procedures[4] that fraud or an illegal act may have occurred.[5] The accountant need not report any matters regarding illegal acts that may have occurred that are clearly inconsequential and may reach agreement in advance with the entity on the nature of any such matters to be communicated.

- The effect of any independence impairments on the expected form of the accountant's compilation report, if applicable.

[Paragraph revised, December 2010, to reflect conforming changes necessary due to the issuance of SSARS No. 19.]

.07 When the accountant is engaged to report on one or more compiled specified elements, accounts, or items of a financial statement and evidence or information comes to his or her attention during the engagement that fraud or an illegal act may have occurred, the accountant should adhere to the communication requirements contained in paragraphs .54–.55 of section 80. [Paragraph revised, December 2010, to reflect conforming changes necessary due to the issuance of SSARS No. 19.]

---

[2] For purposes of this statement, *fraud* is an intentional act that results in a misstatement in compiled specified elements, accounts, or items of a financial statement.

[3] For purposes of this statement, illegal acts are violations of laws or government regulations, excluding fraud.

[4] Performance requirements with respect to an engagement to compile one or more specified elements, accounts, or items of a financial statement are contained in paragraphs .08 and .09.

[5] Whether the act is, in fact, fraudulent or illegal is a determination that is normally beyond the accountant's professional competence. An accountant, in reporting on one or more specified elements, accounts, or items of a financial statement, presents himself or herself as one who is proficient in accounting and compilation services. The accountant's training, experience, and understanding of the client and its industry may provide a basis for recognition that some client acts coming to his or her attention may be fraudulent or illegal. However, the determination about whether a particular act is fraudulent or illegal would generally be based on the advice of an informed expert qualified to practice law or may have to await final determination by a court of law.

AR §110.07

130 Statements on Standards for Accounting and Review Services

Performance Requirements

.08 When the accountant is engaged to report on one or more compiled specified elements, accounts, or items of a financial statement, he or she should adhere to the compilation performance requirements contained in paragraphs .06–.13 of section 80. [Paragraph revised, December 2010, to reflect conforming changes necessary due to the issuance of SSARS No. 19.]

.09 Before issuance of a compilation report on one or more specified elements, accounts, or items of a financial statement, the accountant should read such compiled specified elements, accounts, or items of a financial statement and consider whether the information appears to be appropriate in form and free of obvious material errors. In this context, the term *error* refers to mistakes in the compilation of the specified elements, accounts, or items of a financial statement, including arithmetical or clerical mistakes, and mistakes in the application of accounting principles, including inadequate disclosures. [Paragraph revised, December 2010, to reflect conforming changes necessary due to the issuance of SSARS No. 19.]

Documentation Requirements

.10 When the accountant is engaged to report on one or more compiled specified elements, accounts, or items of a financial statement, he or she should adhere to the documentation requirements contained in paragraphs .14–.15 of section 80. [Paragraph added, December 2010, to reflect conforming changes necessary due to the issuance of SSARS No. 19.]

Reporting Requirements

.11 The accountant's objective in reporting on one or more compiled specified elements, accounts, or items of a financial statement is to prevent misunderstanding of the degree of responsibility the accountant is assuming when his or her name is associated with the elements, accounts, or items of a financial statement. When the accountant issues a compilation report on one or more specified elements, accounts, or items of a financial statement, the basic elements of the report are as follows:

    a.   *Title.* The accountant's compilation report should have a title that clearly indicates that it is the accountant's compilation report. The accountant may indicate that he or she is independent in the title, if applicable. Appropriate titles would be "Accountant's Compilation Report" or "Independent Accountant's Compilation Report."

    b.   *Addressee.* The accountant's report should be addressed as appropriate in the circumstances of the engagement.

    c.   *Introductory paragraph.* The introductory paragraph in the accountant's report should

        i. identify the entity whose elements, accounts, or items of a financial statement have been compiled;

        ii. state that the specified element(s), account(s), or item(s) have been compiled;

        iii. identify the specified element(s), account(s), or item(s) that have been compiled;

        iv. specify the date or period covered by the specified element(s), account(s), or items;

AR §110.08

Compilation of Specified Elements 131

     v. include a statement that the accountant has not audited or reviewed the specified element(s), account(s), or item(s) and, accordingly, does not express an opinion or provide any assurance about whether the specified element(s), account(s), or item(s) are in accordance with the applicable financial reporting framework; and

    vi. if the compilation was performed in conjunction with a compilation of the entity's financial statements, the paragraph should so state and indicate the date of the accountant's compilation report on those financial statements. Furthermore, any departure from the standard report on those statements should also be disclosed if considered relevant to the presentation of the specified element(s), account(s), or item(s).

d. *Management's responsibility for the specified element(s), account(s), or item(s) and for internal control over financial reporting.* A statement that management (owners) is (are) responsible for the preparation and fair presentation of the specified element(s), account(s), or item(s) in accordance with the applicable financial reporting framework and for designing, implementing, and maintaining internal control relevant to the preparation and fair presentation of the specified element(s), account(s), or item(s).

e. *Accountant's responsibility.* A statement that the accountant's responsibility is to conduct the compilation in accordance with SSARSs issued by the AICPA.

f. A statement that the objective of a compilation is to assist management in presenting financial information in the form of specified element(s), account(s), or item(s) of a financial statement without undertaking to obtain or provide any assurance that there are no material modifications that should be made to the specified element(s), account(s), or item(s) of a financial statement.

g. *Signature of the accountant.* The manual or printed signature of the accounting firm or the accountant, as appropriate.

h. *Date of the accountant's report.* The date of the compilation report (the date of completion of the compilation should be used as the date of the accountant's report).

Procedures that the accountant might have performed as part of the compilation engagement should not be described in the report.

See exhibit B, "Illustrative Accountant's Compilation Reports on Specified Elements, Accounts, or Items of a Financial Statement," for illustrative compilation reports.

[Paragraph renumbered and revised, December 2010, to reflect conforming changes necessary due to the issuance of SSARS No. 19.]

    .12   Each page of the specified elements, accounts, or items of a financial statement compiled by the accountant should include a reference, such as "See accountant's compilation report" or "See independent accountant's compilation report." [Paragraph renumbered and revised, December 2010, to reflect conforming changes necessary due to the issuance of SSARS No. 19.]

    [.13]   [Paragraph renumbered and deleted, December 2010, to reflect conforming changes necessary due to the issuance of SSARS No. 19.]

AR §110[.13]

132　Statements on Standards for Accounting and Review Services

Reporting When the Accountant Is Not Independent

.14　When the accountant is issuing a report with respect to a compilation of specified element(s), account(s), or item(s) of a financial statement for an entity, with respect to which the accountant is not independent, the accountant's report should be modified. In making a judgment about whether he or she is independent, the accountant should be guided by the AICPA Code of Professional Conduct. The accountant should indicate his or her lack of independence in a final paragraph of the accountant's compilation report. An example of such a disclosure would be[6]

> I am (we are) not independent with respect to XYZ Company.

The accountant is not precluded from disclosing a description about the reason(s) that his or her independence is impaired. The following are examples of descriptions the accountant may use:

    a.　I am (We are) not independent with respect to XYZ Company as of and for the year ended December 31, 20XX, because I (a member of the engagement team) had a direct financial interest in XYZ Company.

    b.　I am (We are) not independent with respect to XYZ Company as of and for the year ended December 31, 20XX, because an individual of my immediate family (an immediate family member of one of the members of the engagement team) was employed by XYZ Company.

    c.　I am (We are) not independent with respect to XYZ Company as of and for the year ended December 31, 20XX, because I (we) performed certain accounting services (the accountant may include a specific description of those services) that impaired my (our) independence.

If the accountant elects to disclose a description about the reasons his or her independence is impaired, the accountant should ensure that all reasons are included in the description.

[Paragraph renumbered and revised, December 2010, to reflect conforming changes necessary due to the issuance of SSARS No. 19.]

.15　This section is effective for engagements entered into after December 15, 2005. Early application is permitted. [Paragraph renumbered and revised, December 2010, to reflect conforming changes necessary due to the issuance of SSARS No. 19.]

---

[6]　[Footnote deleted, December 2010, to reflect conforming changes necessary due to the issuance of SSARS No. 19.]

AR §110.14

Compilation of Specified Elements **133**

.16

Exhibit A

Illustrative Engagement Letter for a Compilation of Specified Elements, Accounts, or Items of a Financial Statement

[*Appropriate Salutation*]

This letter is to confirm our understanding of the terms and objectives of our engagement and the nature and limitations of the services we will provide.

We will perform the following services:

We will compile, from information you provide, [*identify specified element, account, or item of the financial statement, schedule of accounts receivable or schedule of depreciation – income tax basis*] of XYZ Company as of December 31, 20XX, and issue an accountant's report thereon in accordance with Statements on Standards for Accounting and Review Services issued by the American Institute of Certified Public Accountants.

The objective of a compilation is to assist you in presenting financial information in the form of [*identify specified element, account, or item of the financial statement*]. We will utilize information that is your representation without undertaking to obtain or provide any assurance that there are no material modifications that should be made to the [*identify specified element, account, or item of the financial statement*] in order for [*identify specified element, account, or item of the financial statement*] to be in conformity with [*the applicable financial accounting framework (for example, accounting principles generally accepted in the United States of America)*].

You are responsible for

  a. the preparation and fair presentation of [*identify specified element, account, or item of the financial statement*] in accordance with [*the applicable financial reporting framework (for example, accounting principles generally accepted in the United States of America)*].

  b. designing, implementing, and maintaining internal control relevant to the preparation and fair presentation of [*identify specified element, account, or item of the financial statement*].

  c. preventing and detecting fraud.

  d. identifying and ensuring that the entity complies with the laws and regulations applicable to its activities.

  e. making all financial records and related information available to us.

We are responsible for conducting the engagement in accordance with SSARSs issued by the AICPA.

A compilation differs significantly from a review or an audit of financial information. A compilation does not contemplate performing inquiry, analytical procedures, or other procedures performed in a review. Additionally, a compilation does not contemplate obtaining an understanding of the entity's internal control; assessing fraud risk; testing accounting records by obtaining sufficient appropriate audit evidence through inspection, observation, confirmation, the

AR §110.16

134 Statements on Standards for Accounting and Review Services

examination of source documents (for example, cancelled checks or bank images); or other procedures ordinarily performed in an audit. Accordingly, we will not express an opinion or provide any assurance regarding the [*identify specified element, account, or item of the financial statement*] being compiled.

Our engagement cannot be relied upon to disclose errors, fraud, or illegal acts. However, we will inform the appropriate level of management of any material errors, and of any evidence or information that comes to our attention during the performance of our compilation procedures that fraud may have occurred. In addition, we will report to you any evidence or information that comes to our attention during the performance of our compilation procedures regarding illegal acts that may have occurred, unless they are clearly inconsequential.

If, during the period covered by the engagement letter, the accountant's independence is or will be impaired, insert the following:

> We are not independent with respect to XYZ Company. We will disclose that we are not independent in our compilation report.

If, for any reason, we are unable to complete the compilation of your [*identify specified element, account, or item of the financial statement*], we will not issue a report on such schedule as a result of this engagement.

Our fees for these services . . . .

We will be pleased to discuss this letter with you at any time.

If the foregoing is in accordance with your understanding, please sign the copy of this letter in the space provided and return it to us.[*]

Sincerely yours,

_____

[*Signature of accountant*]

Acknowledged:

XYZ Company

_____

President

_____

Date

[As amended, effective for compilations and reviews of financial statements for periods ending on or after December 15, 2008, by SSARS No. 17. Renumbered and revised, December 2010, to reflect conforming changes necessary due to the issuance of SSARS No. 19.]

---

[*] [Footnote deleted, December 2010, to reflect conforming changes necessary due to the issuance of SSARS No. 19.]

AR §110.16

Compilation of Specified Elements

135

Exhibit B

Illustrative Compilation Reports on Specified Elements, Accounts, or Items of a Financial Statement

Standard Compilation Report on a Schedule of Accounts Receivable Prepared in Accordance With Accounting Principles Generally Accepted in the United States of America

Accountant's Compilation Report

[*Appropriate Salutation*]

I (we) have compiled the accompanying schedule of accounts receivable of XYZ Company as of December 31, 20XX. I (we) have not audited or reviewed the accompanying schedule of accounts receivable and, accordingly, do not express an opinion or provide any assurance about whether the schedule of accounts receivable is in accordance with accounting principles generally accepted in the United States of America.

Management (owners) is (are) responsible for the preparation and fair presentation of the schedule of accounts receivable in accordance with accounting principles generally accepted in the United States of America and for designing, implementing, and maintaining internal control relevant to the preparation and fair presentation of the schedule of accounts receivable.

My (our) responsibility is to conduct the compilation in accordance with Statements on Standards for Accounting and Review Services issued by the American Institute of Certified Public Accountants. The objective of a compilation is to assist management in presenting financial information in the form of a schedule of accounts receivable without undertaking to obtain or provide any assurance that there are no material modifications that should be made to the schedule of accounts receivable.

[*Signature of accounting firm or accountant, as appropriate*]

[*Date*]

Standard Compilation Report on a Schedule of Depreciation Prepared in Accordance With the Basis of Accounting the Entity Uses for Federal Income Tax Purposes

Accountant's Compilation Report

[*Appropriate Salutation*]

I (we) have compiled the accompanying schedule of depreciation of XYZ Company as of December 31, 20XX. I (we) have not audited or reviewed the accompanying schedule of depreciation and, accordingly, do not express an opinion or provide any assurance about whether the schedule of depreciation is in accordance with the basis of accounting the Company uses for federal income tax purposes.

Management (owners) is (are) responsible for the preparation and fair presentation of the schedule of depreciation in accordance with the basis of accounting the Company uses for federal income tax purposes and for designing, implementing, and maintaining internal control relevant to the preparation and fair presentation of the schedule of depreciation.

AR §110.17

136   Statements on Standards for Accounting and Review Services

My (our) responsibility is to conduct the compilation in accordance with Statements on Standards for Accounting and Review Services issued by the American Institute of Certified Public Accountants. The objective of a compilation is to assist management in presenting financial information in the form of a schedule of depreciation without undertaking to obtain or provide any assurance that there are no material modifications that should be made to the schedule of depreciation.

[*Signature of accounting firm or accountant, as appropriate*]

[*Date*]

[Added, December 2010, to reflect presentation style and conforming changes necessary due to the issuance of SSARS No. 19.]

AR §110.17

AR Section 120
Compilation of Pro Forma Financial Information

Issue date, unless otherwise indicated: July 2005

Source: SSARS No. 14; SSARS No. 17

.01 Statements on Standards for Accounting and Review Services (SSARSs) provide guidance concerning the standards and procedures applicable when an accountant is engaged to report on compiled financial statements or submits financial statements to his or her client or third parties. By definition, presentations of pro forma financial information are not financial statements. This statement expands SSARSs to apply when an accountant is engaged to report or issues a report on compiled pro forma financial information. If, however, the pro forma financial information is included as supplementary information, the accountant should refer to paragraph .53 of section 80, *Compilation of Financial Statements*. [Paragraph revised, December 2010, to reflect conforming changes necessary due to the issuance of SSARS No. 19.]

.02 A compilation of pro forma financial information is limited to assisting management (owners) in presenting financial information without undertaking to obtain or provide any assurance that there are no material modifications that should be made to that information. [Paragraph revised, December 2010, to reflect conforming changes necessary due to the issuance of SSARS No. 19.]

.03 The objective of pro forma financial information is to show what the significant effects on historical financial information might have been had a consummated or proposed transaction (or event) occurred at an earlier date. Pro forma financial information is commonly used to show the effects of transactions such as the following:

- Business combination

- Change in capitalization

- Disposition of a significant portion of the business

- Change in the form of business organization or status as an autonomous entity

- Proposed sale of securities and the application of the proceeds

.04 This objective is achieved primarily by applying pro forma adjustments to historical financial information. Pro forma adjustments should be based on management's assumptions and give effect to all significant effects directly attributable to the transaction (or event).

.05 Pro forma financial information should be labeled as such to distinguish it from historical financial information. This presentation should describe the transaction (or event) that is reflected in the pro forma financial information, the source of the historical financial information on which it is based, the significant assumptions used in developing the pro forma adjustments, and any significant uncertainties about those assumptions. The presentation should

AR §120.05

138 Statements on Standards for Accounting and Review Services

also indicate that the pro forma financial information should be read in conjunction with the related historical financial information and that the pro forma financial information is not necessarily indicative of the results (such as financial position and results of operations, as applicable) that would have been attained had the transaction (or event) actually taken place earlier.

Conditions for Compiling Pro Forma Financial Information

.06 Nothing in this statement is intended to preclude an accountant from assisting management (owners) in presenting pro forma financial information and submitting such pro forma financial information to the client or to third parties without the issuance of a compilation report, unless the accountant has been engaged to report on such compiled pro forma financial information. If an accountant assists management (owners) in presenting pro forma financial information,[1] the accountant should consider how such a presentation of pro forma financial information will be used. The accountant should consider the potential of being associated with pro forma financial information and the likelihood that the user may inappropriately infer, through that association, an unintended level of reliance on the information. If the accountant believes that he or she will be associated with the information, the accountant should consider issuing a compilation report so a user will not infer an unintended level of reliance on the information. [Paragraph revised, December 2010, to reflect conforming changes necessary due to the issuance of SSARS No. 19.]

.07 An engagement to report on compiled pro forma financial information may be undertaken as a separate engagement or in conjunction with a compilation of financial statements. The accountant may agree to compile pro forma financial information only if the document that contains the pro forma financial information includes (or incorporates by reference) the historical financial statements of the entity on which the pro forma financial information is based. Historical interim financial information may be presented in condensed form. In the case of a business combination, the document should include (or incorporate by reference) the appropriate historical financial information for the significant constituent parts of the combined entity. [Paragraph revised, December 2010, to reflect conforming changes necessary due to the issuance of SSARS No. 19.]

.08 Additionally, the historical financial statements of the entity (or, in the case of a business combination, of each significant constituent part of the combined entity) on which the pro forma financial information is based must have been compiled, reviewed, or audited. The accountant's compilation or review report or the auditor's report on the historical financial statements should be included (or incorporated by reference) in the document containing the pro forma financial information.

Understanding With the Entity

.09 When an accountant is engaged to report on compiled pro forma financial information, the accountant should establish an understanding with

---

[1] [Footnote deleted, December 2010, to reflect conforming changes necessary due to the issuance of Statement on Standards for Accounting and Review Services (SSARS) No. 19.]

AR §120.06

Compilation of Pro Forma Financial Information 139

management regarding the services to be performed and should document the understanding through a written communication with management. Such an understanding reduces the risks that either the accountant or management may misinterpret the needs or expectations of the other party. For example, it reduces the risk that management may inappropriately rely on the accountant to protect the entity against certain risks or perform certain functions that are management's responsibility. The accountant should ensure that the understanding includes the objectives of the engagement, management's responsibilities, the accountant's responsibilities, and the limitations of the engagement. In some cases, the accountant may establish such understanding with those charged with governance. An understanding with management and, if applicable, those charged with governance regarding a compilation of pro forma financial information should include the following matters:

- The objective of a compilation of pro forma information is to assist management in presenting such financial information.

- The accountant utilizes information that is the representation of management (owners) without undertaking to obtain any assurance that there are no material modifications that should be made to the pro forma financial information in order for the pro forma financial information to be in conformity with the applicable financial reporting framework.

- Management is responsible for the preparation and fair presentation of the pro forma financial information in accordance with the applicable financial reporting framework.

- Management is responsible for designing, implementing, and maintaining internal control relevant to the preparation and fair presentation of the pro forma financial information.

- Management is responsible for the prevention and detection of fraud.

- Management is responsible for identifying and ensuring that the entity complies with the laws and regulations applicable to its activities.

- Management is responsible for making all financial records and related information available to the accountant.

- The accountant is responsible for conducting the engagement in accordance with SSARSs issued by the AICPA.

- A compilation differs significantly from a review or an audit of pro forma financial information. A compilation does not contemplate performing inquiry, analytical procedures, or other procedures performed in a review. Additionally, a compilation does not contemplate obtaining an understanding of the entity's internal control; assessing fraud risk; testing accounting records by obtaining sufficient appropriate audit evidence through inspection, observation, confirmation, or the examination of source documents (for example, cancelled checks or bank images); or other procedures ordinarily performed in an audit. Accordingly, the accountant will not express an opinion or provide any assurance regarding the pro forma financial information.

AR §120.09

140   Statements on Standards for Accounting and Review Services

- The engagement cannot be relied upon to disclose errors, fraud,[2] or illegal acts.[3]

- The accountant will inform the appropriate level of management of any material errors and of any evidence or information that comes to the accountant's attention during the performance of compilation procedures[4] that fraud or an illegal act may have occurred.[5] The accountant need not report any matters regarding illegal acts that may have occurred that are clearly inconsequential and may reach agreement in advance with the entity on the nature of any such matters to be communicated.

- The effect of any independence impairments on the expected form of the accountant's compilation report, if applicable.

[Paragraph revised, December 2010, to reflect conforming changes necessary due to the issuance of SSARS No. 19.]

.10 When the accountant is engaged to report on compiled pro forma financial information and evidence or information comes to his or her attention during the engagement that fraud or an illegal act may have occurred, the accountant should adhere to the communication requirements contained in paragraphs .54–.55 of section 80. [Paragraph revised, December 2010, to reflect conforming changes necessary due to the issuance of SSARS No. 19.]

Performance Requirements

.11 When the accountant is engaged to report on compiled pro forma financial information, he or she should adhere to the compilation performance requirements contained in paragraphs .06–.13 of section 80. [Paragraph revised, December 2010, to reflect conforming changes necessary due to the issuance of SSARS No. 19.]

.12 Before issuance of a compilation report on pro forma financial information, the accountant should read such compiled pro forma financial information, including the summary of significant assumptions,[6] and consider whether the information appears to be appropriate in form and free of obvious material errors. In this context, the term *error* refers to mistakes in the compilation of the pro forma financial information, including arithmetical or clerical mistakes, and mistakes in the application of accounting principles, including inadequate

---

[2] For purposes of this statement, *fraud* is an intentional act that results in a misstatement in compiled pro forma financial information.

[3] For purposes of this statement, *illegal* acts are violations of laws or government regulations, excluding fraud.

[4] Performance requirements with respect to an engagement to compile pro forma financial information are contained in paragraphs .11–.12.

[5] Whether the act is, in fact, fraudulent or illegal is a determination that is normally beyond the accountant's professional competence. An accountant, in reporting on pro forma financial information, presents himself or herself as one who is proficient in accounting and compilation services. The accountant's training, experience, and understanding of the client and its industry may provide a basis for recognition that some client acts coming to his or her attention may be fraudulent or illegal. However, the determination about whether a particular act is fraudulent or illegal would generally be based on the advice of an informed expert qualified to practice law or may have to await final determination by a court of law.

[6] The accountant may not report on compiled pro forma financial information if the summary of significant assumptions is not presented. Nothing in this statement should be interpreted to preclude the accountant from reporting on compiled pro forma financial information when management elects to omit substantially all disclosures. In that situation, the accountant should follow the guidance in paragraph .20 of section 80, *Compilation of Financial Statements*. [Footnote revised, December 2010, to reflect conforming changes necessary due to the issuance of SSARS No. 19.]

AR §120.10

Compilation of Pro Forma Financial Information   **141**

disclosures. [Paragraph revised, December 2010, to reflect conforming changes necessary due to the issuance of SSARS No. 19.]

Documentation Requirements

.13 When the accountant is engaged to report on compiled pro forma financial information, he or she should adhere to the documentation requirements contained in paragraphs .14–.15 of section 80. [Paragraph added, December 2010, to reflect conforming changes necessary due to the issuance of SSARS No. 19.]

Reporting Requirements

.14 The accountant's objective in reporting on compiled pro forma financial information is to prevent misunderstanding of the degree of responsibility the accountant is assuming when his or her name is associated with the pro forma financial information. When the accountant issues a compilation report on pro forma financial information, the basic elements of the report are as follows:

 a.   *Title.* The accountant's compilation report should have a title that clearly indicates that it is the accountant's compilation report. The accountant may indicate that he or she is independent in the title, if applicable. Appropriate titles would be "Accountant's Compilation Report" or "Independent Accountant's Compilation Report."

 b.   *Addressee.* The accountant's report should be addressed as appropriate in the circumstances of the engagement.

 c.   *Introductory paragraph.* The introductory paragraph in the accountant's report should

     i.   identify the entity whose pro forma financial information has been compiled.

     ii.   state that the pro forma financial information has been compiled.

     iii.   identify the pro forma financial information that has been compiled.

     iv.   specify the date or period covered by the pro forma financial information.

     v.   reference the financial statements from which the historical financial information is derived and include a statement on whether such financial statements were compiled, reviewed, or audited. (The report on pro forma financial information should refer to any modifications in the accountant's or auditor's report on historical financial statements.)

     vi.   include a statement that the accountant has not audited or reviewed the pro forma financial information and, accordingly, does not express an opinion or provide any assurance about whether pro forma financial information is in accordance with the applicable financial reporting framework.

     vii.   if the compilation was performed in conjunction with a compilation of the entity's financial statements, the paragraph should so state and indicate the date of the accountant's compilation report on those financial statements. Furthermore, any departure from the standard report on

AR §120.14

142   Statements on Standards for Accounting and Review Services

those statements should also be disclosed if considered relevant to the presentation of the pro forma financial information.

d. *Management's responsibility for the pro forma financial information and for internal control over financial reporting.* A statement that management (owners) is (are) responsible for the preparation and fair presentation of the pro forma financial information in accordance with the applicable financial reporting framework and for designing, implementing, and maintaining internal control relevant to the preparation and fair presentation of the pro forma financial information.

e. *Accountant's responsibility.* A statement that the accountant's responsibility is to conduct the compilation in accordance with SSARSs issued by the AICPA.

f. A statement that the objective of a compilation is to assist management in presenting financial information in the form of pro forma financial information without undertaking to obtain or provide any assurance that there are no material modifications that should be made to the pro forma financial information.

g. A separate paragraph explaining the objective of pro forma financial information and its limitations.

h. *Signature of the accountant.* The manual or printed signature of the accounting firm or the accountant, as appropriate.

i. *Date of the accountant's report.* The date of the compilation report (the date of completion of the compilation should be used as the date of the accountant's report).

Procedures that the accountant might have performed as part of the compilation engagement should not be described in the report.

See exhibit B, "Illustrative Accountant's Compilation Report on Pro Forma Financial Information," for an illustrative compilation report.

[Paragraph renumbered and revised, December 2010, to reflect conforming changes necessary due to the issuance of SSARS No. 19.]

.15 Each page of the pro forma financial information compiled by the accountant should include a reference, such as "See accountant's compilation report" or "See independent accountant's compilation report." [Paragraph renumbered and revised, December 2010, to reflect conforming changes necessary due to the issuance of SSARS No. 19.]

[.16] [Paragraph renumbered and deleted, December 2010, to reflect conforming changes necessary due to the issuance of SSARS No. 19.][7–8]

Reporting When the Accountant Is Not Independent

.17 When the accountant is issuing a report with respect to a compilation of pro forma financial information for an entity, with respect to which the accountant is not independent, the accountant's report should be modified. In making a judgment about whether he or she is independent, the accountant should be guided by the AICPA Code of Professional Conduct. The accountant

---

[7–8] [Footnotes deleted, December 2010, to reflect conforming changes necessary due to the issuance of SSARS No. 19.]

AR §120.15

Compilation of Pro Forma Financial Information

143

should indicate his or her lack of independence in a final paragraph of the accountant's compilation report. An example of such a disclosure would be[9] If the accountant is not independent, he or she should specifically disclose the lack of independence. However, the reason for the lack of independence should not be described. When the accountant is not independent, the following should be included as the last paragraph of the report:

I am (we are) not independent with respect to XYZ Company.

The accountant is not precluded from disclosing a description about the reason(s) that his or her independence is impaired. The following are examples of descriptions the accountant may use:

a. I am (We are) not independent with respect to XYZ Company as of and for the year ended December 31, 20XX, because I (a member of the engagement team) had a direct financial interest in XYZ Company.

b. I am (We are) not independent with respect to XYZ Company as of and for the year ended December 31, 20XX, because an individual of my immediate family (an immediate family member of one of the members of the engagement team) was employed by XYZ Company.

c. I am (We are) not independent with respect to XYZ Company as of and for the year ended December 31, 20XX, because I (we) performed certain accounting services (the accountant may include a specific description of those services) that impaired my (our) independence.

If the accountant elects to disclose a description about the reasons his or her independence is impaired, the accountant should ensure that all reasons are included in the description.

[Paragraph renumbered and revised, December 2010, to reflect conforming changes necessary due to the issuance of SSARS No. 19.]

.18 This section is effective for engagements entered into after December 15, 2005. Early application is permitted. [Paragraph renumbered, December 2010, to reflect conforming changes necessary due to the issuance of SSARS No. 19.]

---

[9] [Footnote deleted, December 2010, to reflect conforming changes necessary due to the issuance of SSARS No. 19.]

AR §120.18

144   **Statements on Standards for Accounting and Review Services**

.19

Exhibit A

Illustrative Engagement Letter for a Compilation of Pro Forma Financial Information

[*Appropriate Salutation*]

This letter is to confirm our understanding of the terms and objectives of our engagement and the nature and limitations of the services we will provide.

We will perform the following services:

We will compile, from information you provide, the pro forma financial information of XYZ Company as of December 31, 20XX, and issue an accountant's report thereon in accordance with Statements on Standards for Accounting and Review Services issued by the American Institute of Certified Public Accountants.

The objective of a compilation is to assist you in presenting financial information in the form of pro forma financial information. We will utilize information that is your representation without undertaking to obtain or provide any assurance that there are no material modifications that should be made to the pro forma financial information in order for the pro forma financial information to be in conformity with [*the applicable financial accounting framework (for example, accounting principles generally accepted in the United States of America)*].

You are responsible for

- a. the preparation and fair presentation of the pro forma financial information in accordance with [*the applicable financial reporting framework (for example, accounting principles generally accepted in the United States of America)*].

- b. designing, implementing, and maintaining internal control relevant to the preparation and fair presentation of the pro forma financial information.

- c. preventing and detecting fraud.

- d. identifying and ensuring that the entity complies with the laws and regulations applicable to its activities.

- e. making all financial records and related information available to us.

We are responsible for conducting the engagement in accordance with SSARSs issued by the AICPA.

A compilation differs significantly from a review or an audit of financial information. A compilation does not contemplate performing inquiry, analytical procedures, or other procedures performed in a review. Additionally, a compilation does not contemplate obtaining an understanding of the entity's internal control; assessing fraud risk; testing accounting records by obtaining sufficient appropriate audit evidence through inspection, observation, confirmation, the examination of source documents (for example, cancelled checks or bank images); or other procedures ordinarily performed in an audit. Accordingly, we will not express an opinion or provide any assurance regarding the pro forma financial information being compiled.

Our engagement cannot be relied upon to disclose errors, fraud, or illegal acts. However, we will inform the appropriate level of management of any material

AR §120.19

Compilation of Pro Forma Financial Information   **145**

errors, and of any evidence or information that comes to our attention during the performance of our compilation procedures, that fraud may have occurred. In addition, we will report to you any evidence or information that comes to our attention during the performance of our compilation procedures regarding illegal acts that may have occurred, unless they are clearly inconsequential.

If, during the period covered by the engagement letter, the accountant's independence is or will be impaired, insert the following:

> We are not independent with respect to XYZ Company. We will disclose that we are not independent in our compilation report.

If, for any reason, we are unable to complete the compilation of your pro forma financial information, we will not issue a report on such schedule as a result of this engagement.

Our fees for these services . . . .

We will be pleased to discuss this letter with you at any time.

If the foregoing is in accordance with your understanding, please sign the copy of this letter in the space provided and return it to us.[*]

Sincerely yours,

_____

[*Signature of accountant*]

Acknowledged:

XYZ Company

_____

President

_____

Date

[As amended, effective for compilations and reviews of financial statements for periods ending on or after December 15, 2008, by SSARS No. 17. Renumbered and revised, December 2010, to reflect conforming changes necessary due to the issuance of SSARS No. 19.]

---

[*] [Footnote deleted, December 2010, to reflect conforming changes necessary due to the issuance of SSARS No. 19.]

AR §120.19

146 Statements on Standards for Accounting and Review Services

.20

Exhibit B

Illustrative Compilation Report on Pro Forma Financial Information

Compilation report on pro forma financial information reflecting a business combination prepared in accordance with accounting principles generally accepted in the United States of America

Accountant's Compilation Report

[Appropriate Salutation]

I (we) have compiled the accompanying pro forma financial information of XYZ Company as of December 31, 20XX, reflecting the business combination of the Company and ABC Company. The historical condensed financial statements are derived from the historical unaudited financial statements of XYZ Company, which were compiled by me (us), and of ABC Company, which were compiled by another (other) accountant(s).[1] I (we) have not audited or reviewed the accompanying pro forma financial information and, accordingly, do not express an opinion or provide any assurance about whether the pro forma financial information is in accordance with accounting principles generally accepted in the United States of America.

Management (owners) is (are) responsible for the preparation and fair presentation of the pro forma financial information in accordance with accounting principles generally accepted in the United States of America and for designing, implementing, and maintaining internal control relevant to the preparation and fair presentation of the pro forma financial information.

My (our) responsibility is to conduct the compilation in accordance with Statements on Standards for Accounting and Review Services issued by the American Institute of Certified Public Accountants. The objective of a compilation is to assist management in presenting financial information in the form of pro forma financial information without undertaking to obtain or provide any assurance that there are no material modifications that should be made to the pro forma financial information.

The objective of this pro forma financial information is to show what the significant effects on the historical financial information might have been had the transaction (or event) occurred at an earlier date. However, the pro forma financial information is not necessarily indicative of the results of operations or related effects on financial position that would have been attained had the transaction (or event) actually occurred earlier.

Paragraph the accountant may add after the previous paragraph when management has elected to omit substantially all disclosures, but the pro forma financial

---

[1] When one set of historical financial statements is audited or reviewed and the other is audited, reviewed, or compiled, wording similar to the following would be appropriate:

The historical condensed financial statements are derived from the historical financial statements of XYZ Company, which were compiled by me (us), and of ABC Company, which were reviewed by another (other) accountant(s), appearing elsewhere herein (or incorporated by reference).

If either accountant's review report or auditor's report includes an explanatory paragraph or is modified, that fact should be referred to within the report.

AR §120.20

Compilation of Pro Forma Financial Information

information is otherwise in conformity with accounting principles generally accepted in the United States of America.

[*Signature of accounting firm or accountant, as appropriate*]

[*Date*]

[Added, December 2010, to reflect the presentation style and conforming changes necessary due to the issuance of SSARS No. 19.]

AR §120.20

Reporting on Comparative Financial Statements   **149**

AR Section 200
Reporting on Comparative Financial Statements

Issue date, unless
otherwise indicated:
October 1979

Source: SSARS No. 2;
SSARS No. 3; SSARS No. 4;
SSARS No. 5; SSARS No. 7;
SSARS No. 11; SSARS No. 12;
SSARS No. 15; SSARS No. 17

.01 This section establishes standards for reporting on comparative financial statements[1] of a nonissuer when financial statements of one or more periods presented have been compiled and reported on or reviewed in accordance with section 80, *Compilation of Financial Statements*, or section 90, *Review of Financial Statements*, respectively. [2] [Paragraph revised, October 2000, to reflect conforming changes necessary due to the issuance of Statement on Standards for Accounting and Review Services (SSARS) No. 8. Paragraph amended, effective for compilations and reviews of financial statements for periods ending after December 15, 2008, by SSARS No. 17. Paragraph revised December 2010 to reflect conforming changes necessary due to the issuance of SSARS No. 19.]

.02 When comparative financial statements are presented, the accountant should issue an appropriate report(s) covering each period presented in accordance with the provisions of this section. Exhibit A, "Illustrative Compilation Reports on Comparative Financial Statements," and exhibit B, "Illustrative Review Reports on Comparative Financial Statements," provide illustrative reports on comparative financial statements, including how the title of the report may be modified when the level of service between the years is different. [3]

.03 Client-prepared financial statements of some periods that have not been audited, reviewed, or compiled may be presented on separate pages of a document that also contains financial statements of other periods on which the accountant has reported if they are accompanied by an indication by the client that the accountant has not audited, reviewed, or compiled those financial statements and that the accountant assumes no responsibility for them. Whenever the accountant becomes aware that financial statements of other periods that have not been audited, reviewed, or compiled have been presented in columnar form in a document with financial statements on which he or she has

---

[1] [Footnote deleted, December 2010, to reflect conforming changes necessary due to the issuance of Statement on Standards for Accounting and Review Services (SSARS) No. 19.]

[2] The terms *nonissuer* and *financial statements* are defined in paragraph .04 of section 60, *Framework for Performing and Reporting on Compilation and Review Engagements*. [As amended, effective for compilations and reviews of financial statements for periods ending after December 15, 2008, by Statement on Standards for Accounting and Review Services (SSARS) No. 17. Footnote revised, December 2010, to reflect conforming changes necessary due to the issuance of SSARS No. 19.]

[3] [Footnote deleted to reflect the conforming changes necessary due to the issuance of SSARS No. 8.]

AR §200.03

150 Statements on Standards for Accounting and Review Services

reported and that his or her name has been used or his or her report included in the document, he or she should advise his or her client that the use of his or her name or report is inappropriate and should consider what other actions might be appropriate, including consultation with his or her attorney.

.04 An accountant may modify his or her report with respect to one or more financial statements for one or more periods while issuing an unmodified report on the other financial statements presented.

.05 Compiled financial statements that omit substantially all of the disclosures required by an applicable financial reporting framework[4] are not comparable to financial statements that include such disclosures. Accordingly, the accountant should not issue a report on comparative financial statements when statements for one or more, but not all, of the periods presented omit substantially all of the disclosures required by an applicable financial reporting framework. (See paragraphs .30–.31 for guidance on reporting on financial statements that previously did not omit substantially all of the disclosures required by an applicable financial reporting framework.) [Paragraph amended by the issuance of SSARS No. 15, July 2007. Paragraph revised, December 2010, to reflect conforming changes necessary due to the issuance of SSARS No. 19.]

.06 Each page of the comparative financial statements compiled or reviewed by the accountant should include a reference such as "See Accountant's Compilation Report" or "See Independent Accountant's Review Report." [Paragraph revised, December 2010, to reflect conforming changes necessary due to the issuance of SSARS No. 19.]

Definitions

.07 The following definitions apply for purposes of this section:

Comparative financial statements. Financial statements of two or more periods presented in columnar form.

Continuing accountant. An accountant who has been engaged to audit, review, or compile and report on the financial statements of the current period and one or more consecutive periods immediately prior to the current period.

Updated report. A report issued by a continuing accountant that takes into consideration information that he or she becomes aware of during his or her current engagement and that re-expresses his or her previous conclusions or, depending on the circumstances, expresses different conclusions on the financial statements of a prior period as of the date of his or her current report.[5]

Reissued report. A report issued subsequent to the date of the original report that bears the same date as the original report. A reissued report may need to be revised for the effects of specific events; in these circumstances, the report should be dual-dated with the original date and a separate date that applies to the effects of such events.

---

[4] [Footnote deleted, December 2010, to reflect conforming changes necessary due to the issuance of SSARS No. 19]

[5] See paragraph .17 of section 80, *Compilation of Financial Statements*, and paragraph .28 of section 90, *Review of Financial Statements*. [Footnote revised, November 2002, to reflect conforming changes necessary due to the issuance of Statement on Standards for Accounting and Review Services No. 9. Footnote revised, May 2004, to reflect the conforming changes necessary due to the issuance of Statement on Standards for Accounting and Review Services No. 10. Footnote revised, December 2010, to reflect conforming changes necessary due to the issuance of SSARS No. 19.]

AR §200.04

Reporting on Comparative Financial Statements **151**

Continuing Accountant's Standard Report

.08 A continuing accountant who performs the same or a higher level of service with respect to the financial statements of the current period should update his or her report on the financial statements of a prior period presented with those of the current period.[6] A continuing accountant who performs a lower level of service with respect to the financial statements of the current period should either (a) include as a separate paragraph of his or her report a description of the responsibility assumed for the financial statements of the prior period (see paragraphs .11–.12) or (b) reissue his or her report on the financial statements of the prior period.

.09 [Paragraph deleted, December 2010, to reflect presentation style and conforming changes necessary due to the issuance of SSARS No. 19.]

.10 [Paragraph deleted, December 2010, to reflect presentation style and conforming changes necessary due to the issuance of SSARS No. 19.]

.11 A continuing accountant who performs a compilation of the current-period financial statements and has previously reviewed one or more prior-period financial statements should report as indicated in either (a) or (b) that follow:

   a. Issue a compilation report on the current-period financial statements that includes a description of the responsibility assumed for the financial statements of the prior period. The description should include the original date of the accountant's report and should also state that he or she has not performed any procedures in connection with that review engagement after that date.

   b. Combine his or her compilation report on the financial statements of the current period with his or her reissued review report on the financial statements of the prior period or present them separately. The combined report should state that the accountant has not performed any procedures in connection with that review engagement after the date of his or her review report.

.12 See exhibit A and exhibit B for examples of a continuing accountant's standard report on comparative financial statements when

- the same level of service has been performed for both periods.

- the financial statements of the current period have been reviewed and those of the prior period have been compiled.

- the financial statements of the current period have been compiled and those of the prior period have been reviewed.

[Paragraph revised, December 2010, to reflect presentation style and conforming changes necessary due to the issuance of SSARS No. 19.]

Continuing Accountant's Changed Reference to a Departure From the Applicable Financial Reporting Framework

.13 During his or her current engagement, the accountant should be aware that circumstances or events may affect the prior-period financial statements

---

[6] For purposes of this section, a *review* is a higher level of service and a *compilation* is a lower level of service. When one of the periods is audited, see paragraphs .28–.29.

AR §200.13

152 Statements on Standards for Accounting and Review Services

presented, including the adequacy of informative disclosures. The accountant should consider the effects on his or her report on the prior-period financial statements of circumstances or events coming to his or her attention.

.14 When the accountant's report on the financial statements of the prior period contains a changed reference to a departure from the applicable financial reporting framework,[7] his or her report should include a separate explanatory paragraph indicating

    a.   the date of the accountant's previous report.

    b.   the circumstances or events that caused the reference to be changed.

    c.   when applicable, that the financial statements of the prior period have been changed.

[Paragraph revised, December 2010, to reflect presentation style and conforming changes necessary due to the issuance of SSARS No. 19.]

.15 See exhibit A and exhibit B for examples of reports which include an explanatory paragraph when an accountant's report contains a changed reference to a departure from accounting principles generally accepted in the United States of America. [Paragraph revised, December 2010, to reflect presentation style and conforming changes necessary due to the issuance of SSARS No. 19.]

Predecessor's Compilation or Review Report

.16 A predecessor may reissue his or her report at the client's request if he or she is able to make satisfactory arrangements with his or her former client and if he or she complies with the provisions of paragraphs .20–.24. However, a predecessor is not required to reissue his or her compilation or review report on the financial statements of a prior period. If he or she does not reissue his or her compilation or review report on the financial statements of a prior period, a successor should either (*a*) make reference to the report of the predecessor in accordance with the provisions of paragraphs .17–.19 or (*b*) perform a compilation, review, or audit of the financial statements of the prior period and report on them accordingly.[8]

Predecessor's Compilation or Review Report Not Presented

.17 When the financial statements of a prior period have been compiled or reviewed by a predecessor whose report is not presented and the successor has not compiled or reviewed those financial statements, the successor should make reference in an additional paragraph(s) of his or her report on the current-period financial statements to the predecessor's report on the prior-period financial statements. This reference should include the following matters:

    a.   A statement that the financial statements of the prior period were compiled or reviewed by another accountant (other accountants).[9]

    b.   The date of his or her (their) report.

---

[7] A changed reference includes the removal of a prior reference or the inclusion of a new reference.

[8] [Footnote deleted by the issuance of SSARS No. 4, December 1981.]

[9] The successor accountant should not name the predecessor accountant in his or her report unless the predecessor accountant if the predecessor accountant's practice was acquired by, or merged with, that of the successor accountant. [Footnote amended, effective May 2004, by SSARS No. 11. Footnote revised, December 2010, to reflect conforming changes necessary due to the issuance of SSARS No. 19.]

AR §200.14

Reporting on Comparative Financial Statements

153

    c. If the financial statements of the prior period were compiled, a statement that the other accountant(s) did not audit or review the financial statements and, accordingly, did not express an opinion or provide any assurance about whether the financial statements are in accordance with the applicable financial reporting framework.

    d. If the financial statements of the prior period were reviewed, a statement that, based on his or her review, the other accountant(s) are not aware of any material modifications that should be made to the financial statements in order for them to be in conformity with the applicable financial reporting framework, other than those modifications, if any, indicated in the report.

    e. A description or a quotation of any modifications of the standard report and of any paragraphs emphasizing a matter regarding the financial statements.

[Paragraph revised, December 2010, to reflect conforming changes necessary due to the issuance of SSARS No. 19.]

.18 See exhibit A and exhibit B for examples of reports when the predecessor compiled or reviewed the financial statements of the prior period, respectively. [Paragraph revised, December 2010, to reflect presentation style and conforming changes necessary due to the issuance of SSARS No. 19.]

[.19] [Paragraph deleted, December 2010, to reflect presentation style and conforming changes necessary due to the issuance of SSARS No. 19.]

Predecessor's Compilation or Review Report Reissued

.20 Before reissuing a compilation or review report on the financial statements of a prior period, a predecessor should consider whether his or her report is still appropriate. In making this determination, the predecessor should consider (a) the current form and manner of presentation of the prior-period financial statements, (b) subsequent events not previously known, and (c) changes in the financial statements that require the addition or deletion of modifications to the standard report.

.21 A predecessor should perform the following procedures before reissuing his or her compilation or review report on the financial statements of a prior period:

    a. Read the financial statements of the current period and the successor's report.

    b. Compare the prior-period financial statements with those previously issued and with those of the current period.

    c. Obtain a letter from the successor that indicates whether he or she is aware of any matter that, in his or her opinion, might have a material effect on the financial statements, including disclosures, reported on by the predecessor. The predecessor should not refer in his or her reissued report to this letter or to the report of the successor.

.22 If a predecessor becomes aware of information, including information about events or transactions occurring subsequent to the date of his or her previous report, that he or she believes may affect the prior-period financial statements or his or her report on them, he or she should (a) make inquiries or perform analytical procedures similar to those he or she would have performed if he or she had been aware of such information at the date of his or her report on the prior-period financial statements and (b) perform any other

AR §200.22

154   Statements on Standards for Accounting and Review Services

procedures he or she considers necessary in the circumstances. For example, the predecessor may wish to discuss this information with the successor or to review the engagement documentation of the successor as it relates to the matters affecting the prior-period financial statements. If the predecessor decides, based on the information obtained, that his or her report on the prior-period financial statements should be revised, he or she should follow the guidance in paragraphs .14–.15 and .23–.24. [Paragraph revised, December 2010, to reflect conforming changes necessary due to the issuance of SSARS No. 19.]

.23   A predecessor's knowledge of the current affairs of his or her former client is obviously limited in the absence of a continuing relationship. Consequently, when reissuing his or her report on the prior-period financial statements, a predecessor should use the date of his or her previous report to avoid any implication that he or she has performed procedures after that date other than those described in paragraphs .20–.22. If the predecessor revises his or her report or if the financial statements are restated, he or she should dual-date his or her report (for example, "March 1, 20X1, except for note X, as to which the date is March 15, 20X2"). The predecessor's responsibility for events occurring subsequent to the completion of his or her engagement is limited to the specific event referred to in the note or otherwise disclosed. He or she should also obtain a written statement from the former client setting forth the information currently acquired and its effect on the prior-period financial statements and, if applicable, expressing an understanding of its effect on the predecessor's reissued report.

.24   If a predecessor is unable to complete the procedures described in paragraphs .20–.23, he or she should not reissue his or her report and may wish to consult with his or her attorney regarding the appropriate course of action.

Restated Prior-Period Financial Statements

.25   When prior-period financial statements have been restated,[10] the predecessor accountant would normally reissue his or her report following the guidance in paragraph .22. If the predecessor decides not to reissue his or her report, the successor accountant may be engaged to report on the financial statements for the prior year. If the predecessor accountant does not reissue his or her report and the successor accountant is not engaged to report on the prior year financial statements, the successor accountant should indicate in the introductory paragraph of his or her compilation or review report that a predecessor accountant reported on the financial statements of the prior period before restatement. In addition, if the successor accountant is engaged to compile or review the restatement adjustment(s), he or she may also indicate in the accountant's report that he or she compiled or reviewed the adjustment(s) that was (were) applied to restate prior-year financial statements. [Paragraph amended, effective for compilations and reviews of financial statements for periods ending after December 15, 2005, by SSARS No. 12.]

.26   See exhibit A and exhibit B for examples of reports when the predecessor accountant's report is not presented and the successor accountant is

---

[10] See paragraphs .10–.11 of section 400, *Communications Between Predecessor and Successor Accountants*, for guidance regarding communication to the predecessor accountant with respect to information that leads the successor accountant to believe that the financial statements reported on by the predecessor accountant may require revision. [Footnote added, effective for compilations and reviews of financial statements for periods ending after December 15, 2005, by SSARS No. 12.]

AR §200.23

Reporting on Comparative Financial Statements

engaged to compile or review the restatement adjustment(s), respectively.[11] [Paragraph amended, effective for compilations and reviews of financial statements for periods ending after December 15, 2005, by SSARS No. 12. Paragraph revised, December 2010, to reflect presentation style and conforming changes necessary due to the issuance of SSARS No. 19.]

[.27] [Paragraph deleted, December 2010, to reflect presentation style and conforming changes necessary due to the issuance of SSARS No. 19.][12]

Reporting When One Period Is Audited

[.28] [Paragraph deleted, December 2010, to remove reference to auditing literature.]

.29 When the current-period financial statements of a nonissuer have been compiled or reviewed and those of the prior period have been audited, the accountant should issue an appropriate compilation or review report on the current-period financial statements and either (*a*) the report on the prior period should be reissued or (*b*) the report on the current period should include as a separate paragraph an appropriate description of the responsibility assumed for the financial statements of the prior period. In the latter case, the separate paragraph should indicate (*a*) that the financial statements of the prior period were audited previously, (*b*) the date of the previous report, (*c*) the type of opinion expressed previously, (*d*) if the opinion was other than unqualified, the substantive reasons therefor, and (*e*) that no auditing procedures were performed after the date of the previous report. See exhibit A and exhibit B for examples of compilation and review reports, respectively, when the prior year financial statements were audited. [Paragraph renumbered by the issuance of SSARS No. 12, July 2005. Paragraph amended, effective for compilations and reviews of financial statements for periods ending after December 15, 2008, by SSARS No. 17. Paragraph revised, December 2010, to reflect the presentation style and conforming changes necessary due to the issuance of SSARS No. 19.]

Reporting on Financial Statements That Previously Did Not Omit Substantially All Disclosures

.30 An accountant who has compiled, reviewed, or audited financial statements that did not omit substantially all of the disclosures required by an applicable financial reporting framework may subsequently be requested to compile statements for the same period that do omit substantially all of those disclosures when they are to be presented in comparative financial statements. In these circumstances the accountant may report on comparative compiled financial statements that omit such disclosures if he or she includes in his or her report an additional paragraph indicating the nature of the previous service rendered with respect to those financial statements and the date of his or her previous report. [Paragraph renumbered by the issuance of Statement on SSARS No. 12, July 2005. Paragraph revised, December 2010, to reflect conforming changes necessary due to the issuance of SSARS No. 19.]

.31 See exhibit A for an example of a report appropriate when prior-period financial statements that omit substantially all disclosures have been compiled

---

[11] [Footnote deleted, December 2010, to reflect conforming changes necessary due to the issuance of SSARS No. 19.]

[12] [Footnote deleted, December 2010, to reflect conforming changes necessary due to the issuance of SSARS No. 19.]

AR §200.31

156   Statements on Standards for Accounting and Review Services

from previously reviewed financial statements for the same period. [Paragraph amended, effective for periods ending after December 15, 1993, by SSARS No. 7. Paragraph renumbered by the issuance of SSARS No. 12, July 2005. Paragraph revised, December 2010, to reflect the presentation style and conforming changes necessary due to the issuance of SSARS No. 19.]

[.32–.33] [Paragraphs deleted, December 2010, to reflect conforming changes necessary due to the issuance of SSARS No. 19.][13–14]

Transition

[.34–.36] [Paragraphs deleted to reflect conforming changes necessary due to the issuance of SSARS No. 8. Paragraphs renumbered by the issuance of SSARS No. 12, July 2005.]

Effective Date

.37 This section will be effective for reports on comparative financial statements for periods ending on or after November 30, 1979. However, earlier application is encouraged for periods ending on or after July 1, 1979. [Paragraph renumbered by the issuance of SSARS No. 12, July 2005.]

[13–14] [Footnotes deleted, December 2010, to reflect conforming changes necessary due to the issuance of SSARS No. 19.]

AR §200[.32]

Reporting on Comparative Financial Statements

.38

Exhibit A

Illustrative Compilation Reports on Comparative Financial Statements

Compilation Report on Comparative Financial Statements When a Compilation Has Been Performed for Both Periods

Accountant's Compilation Report

[Appropriate Salutation]

I (we) have compiled the accompanying balance sheets of XYZ Company as of December 31, 20X2 and 20X1, and the related statements of income, retained earnings, and cash flows for the years then ended. I (we) have not audited or reviewed the accompanying financial statements and, accordingly, do not express an opinion or provide any assurance about whether the financial statements are in accordance with accounting principles generally accepted in the United States of America.

Management (owners) is (are) responsible for the preparation and fair presentation of the financial statements in accordance with accounting principles generally accepted in the United States of America and for designing, implementing, and maintaining internal control relevant to the preparation and fair presentation of the financial statements.

My (our) responsibility is to conduct the compilations in accordance with Statements on Standards for Accounting and Review Services issued by the American Institute of Certified Public Accountants. The objective of a compilation is to assist management in presenting financial information in the form of financial statements without undertaking to obtain or provide any assurance that there are no material modifications that should be made to the financial statements.

[Signature of accounting firm or accountant, as appropriate]

[Date]

Compilation Report When the Financial Statements of the Current Year Have Been Compiled and Those of The Prior Year Have Been Reviewed

Accountant's Compilation Report[1]

[Appropriate Salutation]

I (we) have compiled the accompanying balance sheet of XYZ Company as of December 31, 20X2, and the related statements of income, retained earnings, and cash flows for the year then ended. I (we) have not audited or reviewed the 20X2 financial statements and, accordingly, do not express an opinion or provide any assurance about whether the financial statements are in accordance with accounting principles generally accepted in the United States of America.

Management (owners) is (are) responsible for the preparation and fair presentation of the financial statements in accordance with accounting principles

---

[1] Alternatively, an accountant may use a title that does not describe the level of service such as "Accountant's Report" or "Report of Certified Public Accountants" because the report refers to different levels of service.

AR §200.38

158   Statements on Standards for Accounting and Review Services

generally accepted in the United States of America and for designing, implementing, and maintaining internal control relevant to the preparation and fair presentation of the financial statements.

My (our) responsibility is to conduct the compilations in accordance with Statements on Standards for Accounting and Review Services issued by the American Institute of Certified Public Accountants. The objective of a compilation is to assist management in presenting financial information in the form of financial statements without undertaking to obtain or provide any assurance that there are no material modifications that should be made to the financial statements.

The accompanying 20X1 financial statements were previously reviewed by me (us) and I (we) stated that I was (we were) not aware of any material modifications that should be made to those financial statements in order for them to be in conformity with accounting principles generally accepted in the United States of America in my (our) report dated March 31, 20X2, but I (we) have not performed any procedures in connection with that review engagement since that date.

[Signature of accounting firm or accountant, as appropriate]

[Date]

Compilation Report on Comparative Financial Statements When the Accountant's Report Includes a Changed Reference to a Departure From Accounting Principles Generally Accepted in the United States of America

<u>**Accountant's Compilation Report**</u>

[Appropriate Salutation]

I (we) have compiled the accompanying balance sheets of XYZ Company as of December 31, 20X2 and 20X1, and the related statements of income, retained earnings, and cash flows for the years then ended. I (we) have not audited or reviewed the accompanying financial statements and, accordingly, do not express an opinion or provide any assurance about whether the financial statements are in accordance with accounting principles generally accepted in the United States of America.

Management (owners) is (are) responsible for the preparation and fair presentation of the financial statements in accordance with accounting principles generally accepted in the United States of America and for designing, implementing, and maintaining internal control relevant to the preparation and fair presentation of the financial statements.

My (our) responsibility is to conduct the compilations in accordance with Statements on Standards for Accounting and Review Services issued by the American Institute of Certified Public Accountants. The objective of a compilation is to assist management in presenting financial information in the form of financial statements without undertaking to obtain or provide any assurance that there are no material modifications that should be made to the financial statements.

In my (our) report dated March 1, 20X2 with respect to the 20X1 financial statements, we referred to a departure from accounting principles generally accepted in the United States of America because the company carried its land at appraised values. As described in Note X, the Company has changed its method of accounting for land and restated its 20X1 financial statements to conform with accounting principles generally accepted in the United States of America.

[Signature of accounting firm or accountant, as appropriate]

[Date]

AR §200.38

Reporting on Comparative Financial Statements   **159**

Compilation Report on Comparative Financial Statements When the Prior Period Financial Statements Were Compiled By a Predecessor Accountant and the Predecessor's Report Is Not Presented

Accountant's Compilation Report

[*Appropriate Salutation*]

I (we) have compiled the accompanying balance sheet of XYZ Company as of December 31, 20X2, and the related statements of income, retained earnings, and cash flows for the year then ended. I (we) have not audited or reviewed the accompanying financial statements and, accordingly, do not express an opinion or provide any assurance about whether the financial statements are in accordance with accounting principles generally accepted in the United States of America. The financial statements of XYZ Company as of December 31, 20X1, were compiled by other accountants whose report dated February 1, 20X2 stated that they have not audited or reviewed the 20X1 financial statements and, accordingly, do not express an opinion or provide any assurance about whether the financial statements are in accordance with accounting principles generally accepted in the United States of America.

Management (owners) is (are) responsible for the preparation and fair presentation of the financial statements in accordance with accounting principles generally accepted in the United States of America and for designing, implementing, and maintaining internal control relevant to the preparation and fair presentation of the financial statements.

My (our) responsibility is to conduct the 20X2 compilations in accordance with Statements on Standards for Accounting and Review Services issued by the American Institute of Certified Public Accountants. The objective of a compilation is to assist management in presenting financial information in the form of financial statements without undertaking to obtain or provide any assurance that there are no material modifications that should be made to the financial statements.

[*Signature of accounting firm or accountant, as appropriate*]

[*Date*]

Compilation Report on Comparative Financial Statements When the Predecessor Accountant's Report Is Not Presented, and the Successor Accountant Is Engaged to Compile the Restatement Adjustment(s)

Accountant's Compilation Report

[*Appropriate Salutation*]

I (we) have compiled the accompanying balance sheet of XYZ Company as of December 31, 20X2, and the related statements of income, retained earnings, and cash flows for the year then ended. I (we) have not audited or reviewed the accompanying financial statements and, accordingly, do not express an opinion or provide any assurance about whether the financial statements are in accordance with accounting principles generally accepted in the United States of America. The financial statements prior to adjustment of XYZ Company as of and for the year ended December 31, 20X1, were compiled by other accountants whose report dated February 1, 20X2, stated that they have not audited or reviewed the 20X1 financial statements and, accordingly, do not express an opinion or provide any assurance about whether the financial statements are in accordance with accounting principles generally accepted in the United States of America.

Management (owners) is (are) responsible for the preparation and fair presentation of the financial statements in accordance with accounting principles

AR §200.38

160   **Statements on Standards for Accounting and Review Services**

generally accepted in the United States of America and for designing, implementing, and maintaining internal control relevant to the preparation and fair presentation of the financial statements.

My (our) responsibility is to conduct the compilations in accordance with Statements on Standards for Accounting and Review Services issued by the American Institute of Certified Public Accountants. The objective of a compilation is to assist management in presenting financial information in the form of financial statements without undertaking to obtain or provide any assurance that there are no material modifications that should be made to the financial statements.

I (We) also compiled the adjustments described in Note X that were applied to restate the 20X1 financial statements. I (we) have not audited or reviewed the adjustments described in Note X that were applied to restate the 20X1 financial statements and, accordingly, do not express an opinion or provide any assurance about whether the adjustments described in Note X that were applied to restate the 20X1 financial statements are in accordance with accounting principles generally accepted in the United States of America.

[Signature of accounting firm or accountant, as appropriate]

[Date]

Compilation Report on Comparative Financial Statements When the Prior Period Financial Statements Were Audited
Accountant's Compilation Report[2]

[Appropriate Salutation]

I (we) have compiled the accompanying balance sheet of XYZ Company as of December 31, 20X2, and the related statements of income, retained earnings, and cash flows for the year then ended. I (we) have not audited or reviewed the accompanying financial statements and, accordingly, do not express an opinion or provide any assurance about whether the financial statements are in accordance with accounting principles generally accepted in the United States of America.

Management (owners) is (are) responsible for the preparation and fair presentation of the financial statements in accordance with accounting principles generally accepted in the United States of America and for designing, implementing, and maintaining internal control relevant to the preparation and fair presentation of the financial statements.

My (our) responsibility is to conduct the compilations in accordance with Statements on Standards for Accounting and Review Services issued by the American Institute of Certified Public Accountants. The objective of a compilation is to assist management in presenting financial information in the form of financial statements without undertaking to obtain or provide any assurance that there are no material modifications that should be made to the financial statements.

The 20X1 financial statements were audited by me (us) (other accountants) and I (we) (they) expressed an unqualified opinion on them in my (our) (their) report dated March 1, 20X2, but I (we) (they) have not performed any auditing procedures since that date.

[Signature of accounting firm or accountant, as appropriate]

[Date]

---

[2] Alternatively, an accountant may use a title that does not describe the level of service such as "Accountant's Report" or "Report of Certified Public Accountants" because the report refers to different levels of service.

AR §200.38

Reporting on Comparative Financial Statements 161

Compilation Report on Comparative Financial Statements When Prior Period Financial Statements That Omit Substantially All Disclosures Have Been Compiled From Previously Reviewed Financial Statements of the Same Period

Accountant's Compilation Report

[Appropriate Salutation]

I (we) have compiled the accompanying balance sheets of XYZ Company as of December 31, 20X2 and 20X1, and the related statements of income, retained earnings, and cash flows for the years then ended. I (we) have not audited or reviewed the accompanying financial statements and, accordingly, do not express an opinion or provide any assurance about whether the financial statements are in accordance with accounting principles generally accepted in the United States of America.

Management (owners) is (are) responsible for the preparation and fair presentation of the financial statements in accordance with accounting principles generally accepted in the United States of America and for designing, implementing, and maintaining internal control relevant to the preparation and fair presentation of the financial statements.

My (our) responsibility is to conduct the compilations in accordance with Statements on Standards for Accounting and Review Services issued by the American Institute of Certified Public Accountants. The objective of a compilation is to assist management in presenting financial information in the form of financial statements without undertaking to obtain or provide any assurance that there are no material modifications that should be made to the financial statements.

Management has elected to omit substantially all of the disclosures required by accounting principles generally accepted in the United States of America. If the omitted disclosures were included in the financial statements, they might influence the user's conclusions about the company's financial position, results of operations, and cash flows. Accordingly, the financial statements are not designed for those who are not informed about such matters.

The 20X1 financial statements were compiled by me (us) from financial statements that did not omit substantially all of the disclosures required by accounting principles generally accepted in the United States of America and that I (we) previously reviewed as indicated in my (our) report dated March 1, 20X2.

[Signature of accounting firm or accountant, as appropriate]

[Date]

[Added, December 2010, to reflect presentation style and conforming changes necessary due to the issuance of SSARS No. 19.]

AR §200.38

162 Statements on Standards for Accounting and Review Services

.39

Exhibit B

Illustrative Review Reports on Comparative Financial Statements

Review Report on Comparative Financial Statements When a Review Has Been Performed for Both Periods

Independent Accountant's Review Report

[*Appropriate Salutation*]

I (We) have reviewed the accompanying balance sheets of XYZ Company as of December 31, 20X2 and 20X1, and the related statements of income, retained earnings, and cash flows for the years then ended. A review includes primarily applying analytical procedures to management's (owners') financial data and making inquiries of company management (owners). A review is substantially less in scope than an audit, the objective of which is the expression of an opinion regarding the financial statements as a whole. Accordingly, I (we) do not express such an opinion.

Management (owners) is (are) responsible for the preparation and fair presentation of the financial statements in accordance with accounting principles generally accepted in the United States of America and for designing, implementing, and maintaining internal control relevant to the preparation and fair presentation of the financial statements.

My (our) responsibility is to conduct the reviews in accordance with Statements on Standards for Accounting and Review Services issued by the American Institute of Certified Public Accountants. Those standards require me (us) to perform procedures to obtain limited assurance that there are no material modifications that should be made to the financial statements. I (We) believe that the results of my (our) procedures provide a reasonable basis for our report.

Based on my (our) reviews, I am (we are) not aware of any material modifications that should be made to the accompanying financial statements in order for them to be in conformity with accounting principles generally accepted in the United States of America.

[*Signature of accounting firm or accountant, as appropriate*]

[*Date*]

Review Report on Comparative Financial Statements When the Financial Statements of the Current Period Have Been Reviewed and Those of The Prior Period Have Been Compiled

Independent Accountant's Review Report[1]

[*Appropriate Salutation*]

I (We) have reviewed the accompanying balance sheet of XYZ Company as of December 31, 20X2, and the related statements of income, retained earnings, and cash flows for the year then ended. A review includes primarily applying analytical procedures to management's (owners') financial data and making

---

[1] Alternatively, an accountant may use a title that does not describe the level of service such as "Accountant's Report" or "Report of Certified Public Accountants" because the report refers to different levels of service.

AR §200.39

Reporting on Comparative Financial Statements 163

inquiries of company management (owners). A review is substantially less in scope than an audit, the objective of which is the expression of an opinion regarding the financial statements as a whole. Accordingly, I (we) do not express such an opinion.

Management (owners) is (are) responsible for the preparation and fair presentation of the financial statements in accordance with accounting principles generally accepted in the United States of America and for designing, implementing, and maintaining internal control relevant to the preparation and fair presentation of the financial statements.

My (our) responsibility is to conduct the reviews in accordance with Statements on Standards for Accounting and Review Services issued by the American Institute of Certified Public Accountants. Those standards require me (us) to perform procedures to obtain limited assurance that there are no material modifications that should be made to the financial statements. I (We) believe that the results of my (our) procedures provide a reasonable basis for our report.

Based on my (our) reviews, I am (we are) not aware of any material modifications that should be made to the 20X2 financial statements in order for them to be in conformity with accounting principles generally accepted in the United States of America.

The accompanying 20X1 financial statements of XYZ Company were compiled by me (us). The objective of a compilation is to assist management in presenting financial information in the form of financial statements without undertaking to obtain or provide any assurance that there are no material modifications that should be made to the financial statements. Accordingly, I (we) do not express an opinion or provide any assurance about whether the financial statements are in accordance with accounting principles generally accepted in the United States of America.

[*Signature of accounting firm or accountant, as appropriate*]

[*Date*]

Review Report on Comparative Financial Statements When the Accountant's Report Includes a Changed Reference to a Departure From Accounting Principles Generally Accepted in the United States Of America

Independent Accountant's Review Report

[*Appropriate Salutation*]

I (We) have reviewed the accompanying balance sheets of XYZ Company as of December 31, 20X2 and 20X1, and the related statements of income, retained earnings, and cash flows for the years then ended. A review includes primarily applying analytical procedures to management's (owners') financial data and making inquiries of company management (owners). A review is substantially less in scope than an audit, the objective of which is the expression of an opinion regarding the financial statements as a whole. Accordingly, I (we) do not express such an opinion.

Management (owners) is (are) responsible for the preparation and fair presentation of the financial statements in accordance with accounting principles generally accepted in the United States of America and for designing, implementing, and maintaining internal control relevant to the preparation and fair presentation of the financial statements.

My (our) responsibility is to conduct the reviews in accordance with Statements on Standards for Accounting and Review Services issued by the American Institute of Certified Public Accountants. Those standards require me (us) to perform

AR §200.39

164   Statements on Standards for Accounting and Review Services

procedures to obtain limited assurance that there are no material modifications that should be made to the financial statements. I (We) believe that the results of my (our) procedures provide a reasonable basis for our report.

In my (our) report dated March 1, 20X2, with respect to the 20X1 financial statements, we referred to a departure from accounting principles generally accepted in the United States of America because the company carried its land at appraised values. As described in Note X, the Company has changed its method of accounting for land and restated its 20X1 financial statements to conform with accounting principles generally accepted in the United States of America. Accordingly, my (our) present statement on the 20X1 financial statements, as presented herein, that I am (we are) not aware of any material modifications that should be made to the accompanying financial statements is different from that expressed in our previous report.

Based on my (our) reviews, I am (we are) not aware of any material modifications that should be made to the accompanying financial statements in order for them to be in conformity with accounting principles generally accepted in the United States of America.

[*Signature of accounting firm or accountant, as appropriate*]

[*Date*]

Review Report on Comparative Financial Statements When the Prior Period Financial Statements Were Reviewed by a Predecessor Accountant, and the Predecessor's Report Is Not Presented

Independent Accountant's Review Report

[*Appropriate Salutation*]

I (We) have reviewed the accompanying balance sheet of XYZ Company as of December 31, 20X2, and the related statements of income, retained earnings, and cash flows for the year then ended. A review includes primarily applying analytical procedures to management's (owners') financial data and making inquiries of company management (owners). A review is substantially less in scope than an audit, the objective of which is the expression of an opinion regarding the financial statements as a whole. Accordingly, I (we) do not express such an opinion. The financial statements of XYZ Company as of December 31, 20X1, were reviewed by other accountants whose report dated February 1, 20X2, stated that based on their procedures, they are not aware of any material modifications that should be made to the financial statements in order for them to be in conformity with accounting principles generally accepted in the United States of America.

Management (owners) is (are) responsible for the preparation and fair presentation of the financial statements in accordance with accounting principles generally accepted in the United States of America and for designing, implementing, and maintaining internal control relevant to the preparation and fair presentation of the financial statements.

My (our) responsibility is to conduct the review in accordance with Statements on Standards for Accounting and Review Services issued by the American Institute of Certified Public Accountants. Those standards require me (us) to perform procedures to obtain limited assurance that there are no material modifications that should be made to the financial statements. I (We) believe that the results of my (our) procedures provide a reasonable basis for our report.

Based on my (our) review, I am (we are) not aware of any material modifications that should be made to the 20X2 financial statements in order for them to be in

AR §200.39

Reporting on Comparative Financial Statements

165

conformity with accounting principles generally accepted in the United States of America.

[Signature of accounting firm or accountant, as appropriate]

[Date]

Review Report on Comparative Financial Statements When the Predecessor Accountant'S Report Is Not Presented, and the Successor Accountant Is Engaged to Review the Restatement Adjustments

Independent Accountant's Review Report

[Appropriate Salutation]

I (We) have reviewed the accompanying balance sheet of XYZ Company as of December 31, 20X2, and the related statements of income, retained earnings, and cash flows for the year then ended. A review includes primarily applying analytical procedures to management's (owners') financial data and making inquiries of company management (owners). A review is substantially less in scope than an audit, the objective of which is the expression of an opinion regarding the financial statements as a whole. Accordingly, I (we) do not express such an opinion. The financial statements of XYZ Company as of December 31, 20X1 prior to adjustment were reviewed by other accountants whose report dated February 1, 20X2, stated that based on their procedures, they are not aware of any material modifications that should be made to the financial statements in order for them to be in conformity with accounting principles generally accepted in the United States of America.

Management (owners) is (are) responsible for the preparation and fair presentation of the financial statements in accordance with accounting principles generally accepted in the United States of America and for designing, implementing, and maintaining internal control relevant to the preparation and fair presentation of the financial statements.

My (our) responsibility is to conduct the review in accordance with Statements on Standards for Accounting and Review Services issued by the American Institute of Certified Public Accountants. Those standards require me (us) to perform procedures to obtain limited assurance that there are no material modifications that should be made to the financial statements. I (We) believe that the results of my (our) procedures provide a reasonable basis for our report.

Based on my (our) review, I am (we are) not aware of any material modifications that should be made to the 20X2 financial statements in order for them to be in conformity with accounting principles generally accepted in the United States of America.

I (We) also reviewed the adjustments described in Note X that were applied to restate the 20X1 financial statements. Based on my (our) review, I am (we are) not aware of any material modifications that should be made to the adjustments described in Note X that were applied to restate the 20X1 financial statements in order for them to be in conformity with accounting principles generally accepted in the United States of America.

[Signature of accounting firm or accountant, as appropriate]

[Date]

AR §200.39

166 Statements on Standards for Accounting and Review Services

Review Report on Comparative Financial Statements When the Prior Period Financial Statements Were Audited
Independent Accountant's Review Report[2]

[*Appropriate Salutation*]

I (We) have reviewed the accompanying balance sheet of XYZ Company as of December 31, 20X2, and the related statements of income, retained earnings, and cash flows for the year then ended. A review includes primarily applying analytical procedures to management's (owners') financial data and making inquiries of company management (owners). A review is substantially less in scope than an audit, the objective of which is the expression of an opinion regarding the financial statements as a whole. Accordingly, I (we) do not express such an opinion.

Management (owners) is (are) responsible for the preparation and fair presentation of the financial statements in accordance with accounting principles generally accepted in the United States of America and for designing, implementing, and maintaining internal control relevant to the preparation and fair presentation of the financial statements.

My (our) responsibility is to conduct the review in accordance with Statements on Standards for Accounting and Review Services issued by the American Institute of Certified Public Accountants. Those standards require me (us) to perform procedures to obtain limited assurance that there are no material modifications that should be made to the financial statements. I (We) believe that the results of my (our) procedures provide a reasonable basis for our report.

Based on my (our) review, I am (we are) not aware of any material modifications that should be made to the 20X2 financial statements in order for them to be in conformity with accounting principles generally accepted in the United States of America.

The 20X1 financial statements were audited by me (us) (other accountants) and I (we) (they) expressed an unqualified opinion on them in my (our) (their) report dated March 1, 20X2, but I (we) (they) have not performed any auditing procedures since that date.

[Added, December 2010, to reflect presentation style and conforming changes necessary due to the issuance of SSARS No. 19.]

---

[2] Alternatively, an accountant may use a title that does not describe the level of service such as "Accountant's Report" or "Report of Certified Public Accountants" because the report refers to different levels of service.

AR §200.39

Reporting on Comparative Financial Statements **167**

AR Section 9200

Reporting on Comparative Financial Statements: Accounting and Review Services Interpretations of Section 200

1. Reporting on Financial Statements That Previously Did Not Omit Substantially All Disclosures

.01 *Question*—Paragraph 30 of SSARS No. 2 [section 200.30], *Reporting on Comparative Financial Statements*, states that an accountant who has compiled, reviewed, or audited financial statements that do not omit substantially all of the disclosures required by generally accepted accounting principles may subsequently compile financial statements for the same period that do omit substantially all of those disclosures when they are to be presented in comparative financial statements. In these circumstances, SSARS No. 2 [section 200] requires the accountant's compilation report to include an additional paragraph indicating (*a*) the nature of the service rendered with respect to the financial statements that previously did not omit substantially all disclosures and (*b*) the date of his previous report.

.02 When the accountant has previously audited such financial statements, he may have issued a qualified opinion (see paragraphs 38 and 39 of SAS No. 58 [AU section 508.38–.39], *Reports on Audited Financial Statements*) or an adverse opinion (see paragraphs 67 to 69 of SAS No. 58) [AU section 508.67–.69], or he may have disclaimed an opinion (see paragraphs 70 to 72 of SAS No. 58 [AU section 508.70–.72]). What effect, if any, should this have on the accountant's report on the comparative compiled financial statements? Also, when the accountant has previously compiled or reviewed such financial statements, what effect should a modification to his compilation or review report (see paragraphs 51 to 53 of SSARS No. 1 [section 100.51–.53]) have on the accountant's report on the comparative compiled financial statements?

.03 *Interpretation*—If financial statements that omit substantially all disclosures are compiled from financial statements that the accountant has previously audited, his report on the comparative compiled financial statements should indicate whether he expressed a qualified or adverse opinion, or disclaimed an opinion, on the audited financial statements, and the substantive reasons therefor. Similarly, if the accountant issued a modified compilation or review report or a report containing any paragraphs emphasizing a matter regarding the financial statements (see paragraphs 51 to 53 of SSARS No. 1 [section 100.51–.53]) on financial statements that previously did not omit substantially all disclosures, the accountant's reference to that report in his report on the comparative compiled financial statements should include a description or a quotation of any modifications of the standard report and of any paragraphs emphasizing a matter regarding the financial statements.

.04 Statements on standards for accounting and review services do not require an accountant to modify the standard compilation or review report for an uncertainty or an inconsistency in the application of generally accepted accounting principles. When the accountant's report on comparative compiled financial statements that omit substantially all of the disclosures required by generally

AR §9200.04

168   Statements on Standards for Accounting and Review Services

accepted accounting principles includes a reference to a previous audit report that includes an explanatory paragraph describing an uncertainty, users may assume, in the absence of an indication to the contrary, that the uncertainty has been resolved. Thus, in such circumstances, the accountant should consider the desirability of emphasizing the uncertainty in a separate paragraph of that portion of his report that relates to the financial statements for the current period.

[Issue Date: November, 1980; Revised: November, 2002; Revised: May, 2004; Revised: July, 2005.]

AR §9200.04

AR Section 300

Compilation Reports on Financial Statements Included in Certain Prescribed Forms

Issue date, unless
otherwise indicated:
December 1981

Source: SSARS No. 3; SSARS No. 5;
SSARS No. 7; SSARS No. 15; SSARS No. 17

.01 The requirements of section 80, *Compilation of Financial Statements*, and section 200, *Reporting on Comparative Financial Statements*, are applicable when the unaudited financial statements of a nonissuer are included in a prescribed form. This section provides reporting guidance when the accountant is engaged to compile financial statements included in a prescribed form and the prescribed form or related instructions call for departure from the applicable financial reporting framework by specifying a measurement principle not in conformity with the applicable financial reporting framework or by failing to request the disclosures or presentation required by applicable financial reporting framework.[1] This section also provides additional guidance applicable to reports on financial statements included in a prescribed form.[2] [Paragraph amended, effective for compilations and reviews of financial statements for periods ending after December 15, 2008, by Statement on Standards for Accounting and Review Services (SSARS) No. 17. Paragraph revised, December 2010, to reflect conforming changes necessary due to the issuance of SSARS No. 19.]

.02 For purposes of this section, a *prescribed form* is any standard preprinted form designed or adopted by the body to which it is to be submitted, for example, forms used by industry trade associations, credit agencies, banks, and governmental and regulatory bodies other than those concerned with the sale or trading of securities. A form designed or adopted by the entity whose financial statements are to be compiled is not considered to be a prescribed form. The terms *applicable financial reporting framework*, *financial statements*, and *nonissuer* are defined in paragraph .04 of section 60, *Framework for Performing and Reporting on Compilation and Review Engagements*. [Paragraph amended, effective for compilations and reviews of financial statements for periods ending after December 15, 2008, by SSARS No. 17. Paragraph revised, December 2010, to reflect conforming changes necessary due to the issuance of SSARS No. 19.]

.03 There is a presumption that the information required by a prescribed form is sufficient to meet the needs of the body that designed or adopted the

---

[1] See paragraphs .04 and .37–.39 of section 60, *Framework for Performing and Reporting on Compilation and Review Engagements*, for guidance with respect to applicable financial reporting frameworks. [Footnote amended, effective for compilations and reviews of financial statements for periods ending on or after December 15, 2007, by the issuance of Statements on Standards for Accounting and Review Services (SSARS) No. 15. Footnote revised, December 2010, to reflect conforming changes necessary due to the issuance of SSARS No. 19.]

[2] [Footnote deleted to reflect the incorporation of material into relevant sections of the Statements on Standards for Accounting and Review Services.]

AR §300.03

170 Statements on Standards for Accounting and Review Services

form and that there is no need for that body to be advised of departures from the applicable financial reporting framework required by the prescribed form or related instructions. See the exhibit, "Illustrative Compilation Reports When the Financial Statements Are Included in a Prescribed Form That Calls for a Departure From Accounting Principles Generally Accepted in the United States of America," for an illustrative example of a standard compilation report that may be used when the compiled financial statements are included in a prescribed form that calls for a departure from accounting principles generally accepted in the United States of America. [Paragraph amended, effective for periods ending after December 15, 1993, by SSARS No. 7. Paragraph amended, effective for compilations and reviews of financial statements for periods ending after December 15, 2008, by SSARS No. 17. Paragraph revised, December 2010, to reflect presentation style and conforming changes necessary due to the issuance of SSARS No. 19.]

.04 If the accountant becomes aware of a departure from an applicable financial reporting framework other than departures that may be called for by the prescribed form or related instructions (see paragraph .01), he or she should follow the guidance in paragraphs .27–.29 of section 80 regarding such departures. If the accountant becomes aware of a departure from the requirements of the prescribed form or related instructions, he or she should consider that departure as the equivalent of a departure from an applicable financial reporting framework in determining its effect on his or her report. See the exhibit for an illustration of a report containing a departure from the prescribed form or related instructions. [Paragraph revised, November 2002, to reflect conforming changes necessary due to the issuance of SSARS No. 9. Paragraph revised, May 2004, to reflect conforming changes necessary due to the issuance of SSARS No. 10. Paragraph revised, July 2005, to reflect conforming changes necessary due to the issuance of SSARS No. 12. Paragraph revised, December 2010, to reflect presentation style and conforming changes necessary due to the issuance of SSARS No. 19.]

.05 The accountant should not sign a preprinted report form that does not conform to the guidance in this section or section 80, whichever is applicable. In such circumstances, the accountant should append an appropriate report to the prescribed form. [Paragraph revised, December 2010, to reflect conforming changes necessary due to the issuance of SSARS No. 19.]

AR §300.04

.06

Exhibit

Illustrative Compilation Reports on Financial Statements Included in Certain Prescribed Forms

Standard Compilation Report When the Compiled Financial Statements Are Included in a Prescribed Form That Calls for a Presentation Departure From Accounting Principles Generally Accepted in the United States of America

Accountant's Compilation Report

[*Appropriate Salutation*]

I (we) have compiled the (identification of financial statements, including period covered and the name of entity) included in the accompanying prescribed form. I (we) have not audited or reviewed the financial statements included in the accompanying prescribed form and, accordingly, do not express an opinion or provide any assurance about whether the financial statements are in accordance with accounting principles generally accepted in the United States of America.

Management (owners) is (are) responsible for the preparation and fair presentation of the financial statements included in the form prescribed by (name of body) in accordance with accounting principles generally accepted in the United States of America and for designing, implementing, and maintaining internal control relevant to the preparation and fair presentation of the financial statements.

My (our) responsibility is to conduct the compilation in accordance with Statements on Standards for Accounting and Review Services issued by the American Institute of Certified Public Accountants. The objective of a compilation is to assist management in presenting financial information in the form of financial statements without undertaking to obtain or provide any assurance that there are no material modifications that should be made to the financial statements.

The financial statements included in the accompanying prescribed form are presented in accordance with the requirements of [*name of body*], and are not intended to be a presentation in accordance with accounting principles generally accepted in the United States of America.

This report is intended solely for the information and use of [*the specified parties*] and is not intended to be and should not be used by anyone other than these specified parties.

[*Signature of accounting firm or accountant, as appropriate*]

[*Date*]

AR §300.06

172   Statements on Standards for Accounting and Review Services

Compilation Report When the Compiled Financial Statements Are Prepared in Accordance With a Special Purpose Framework Prescribed by Contract or Regulation and That Framework Prescribes a Format for the Financial Information[3]

Accountant's Compilation Report

[*Appropriate Salutation*]

I (we) have compiled the [*identification of financial statements, including period covered and the name of entity*] included in the accompanying prescribed form. I (we) have not audited or reviewed the financial statements included in the accompanying prescribed form and, accordingly, do not express an opinion or provide any assurance about whether the financial statements are in accordance with the basis of accounting prescribed by [*describe contract or regulation*].

Management (owners) is (are) responsible for the preparation and fair presentation of the financial statements included in the form in accordance with the basis of accounting prescribed by [*describe contract or regulation*] and for designing, implementing, and maintaining internal control relevant to the preparation and fair presentation of the financial statements.

My (our) responsibility is to conduct the compilation in accordance with Statements on Standards for Accounting and Review Services issued by the American Institute of Certified Public Accountants. The objective of a compilation is to assist management in presenting financial information in the form of financial statements without undertaking to obtain or provide any assurance that there are no material modifications that should be made to the financial statements.

The financial statements included in the accompanying prescribed form are presented in accordance with the requirements of [*describe contract or regulation*], and are not intended to be a complete presentation of [*name of entity's*] assets and liabilities.

This report is intended solely for the information and use of [*the specified parties*] and is not intended to be and should not be used by anyone other than these specified parties.

[*Signature of accounting firm or accountant, as appropriate*]

[*Date*]

[Added, December 2010, to reflect presentation style and conforming changes necessary due to the issuance of SSARS No. 19.]

---

[3] See Interpretation No. 11, "Special-Purpose Financial Statements to Comply With Contractual Agreements or Regulatory Provisions," of section 80, *Compilation of Financial Statements* (sec. 9080 par. .32–.40).

AR §300.06

AR Section 9300

Compilation Reports on Financial Statements Included in Certain Prescribed Forms: Accounting and Review Services Interpretations of Section 300

1. Omission of Disclosures in Financial Statements Included in Certain Prescribed Forms

.01 *Question*—The accountant may have reviewed financial statements including disclosures required by generally accepted accounting principles and be asked to compile financial statements included in a prescribed form which does not request such disclosures. If the measurement principles to be used do not cause the compiled financial statements in the prescribed form to be materially different from the reviewed statements, can the accountant's compilation report on the prescribed form refer to the accountant's report on the reviewed financial statements?

.02 *Interpretation*—Yes. The footnote to paragraph 2 of SSARS No. 1 [section 100.02] (as amended) permits an accountant who has reviewed the financial statements of a nonissuer to issue a compilation report on financial statements for the same period that are included in a prescribed form that calls for a departure from generally accepted accounting principles. When the difference between the previously reviewed financial statements and the financial statements included in the prescribed form is limited to the omission of disclosures not requested by the form, the accountant may wish to refer to his review report in his report on the compiled financial statements included in the prescribed form. This might be accomplished by adding a sentence such as the following to the second paragraph of the report illustrated in paragraph 3 of SSARS No. 3 [section 300.03] or as a separate paragraph: "These financial statements were compiled by me (us) from financial statements for the same period which I (we) previously reviewed, as indicated in my (our) report dated_____."* The reference to a previous review report should include a description or a quotation of any modifications of the standard review report previously issued and of any paragraphs emphasizing a matter regarding the financial statements.

.03 If the measurement principles used in the compiled financial statements in the prescribed form cause such financial statements to be materially different from the previously reviewed financial statements, no reference should be made to the review engagement.

[Issue Date: May, 1982. Revised: February, 2008.]

---

* The report included in paragraph 3 of SSARS No. 3 [section 300.03] is an alternate form of report. If the accountant elects to use the standard compilation report included in SSARS No. 1, paragraph 18 [section 100.20] this sentence may be added to that report.

Communications Between Predecessor and Successor Accountants 175

AR Section 400

Communications Between Predecessor and Successor Accountants

Issue date, unless
otherwise indicated:
December 1981

Source: SSARS No. 4; SSARS No. 7;
SSARS No. 9; SSARS No. 15; SSARS No. 17

.01 This section provides guidance on communications between a predecessor and successor accountant when the successor accountant decides to communicate with the predecessor accountant regarding acceptance of an engagement to compile or review the financial statements of a nonissuer.[1] This section also provides guidance on inquiries a successor accountant may wish to make of a predecessor, and the predecessor's responses, to facilitate the conduct of the successor's compilation or review engagement. It also requires a successor accountant who becomes aware of information that leads him or her to believe the financial statements reported on by the predecessor accountant may require revision to request that the client communicate this information to the predecessor accountant. [Paragraph amended, effective for periods ending after December 15, 1993, by Statement on Standards for Accounting and Review Services (SSARS) No. 7. Paragraph amended, effective November 2002, by SSARS No. 9.]

.02 The following definitions apply for purposes of this section:

Successor accountant. An accountant who has been invited to make a proposal for an engagement to compile or review financial statements and is considering accepting the engagement or an accountant who has accepted such an engagement.

Predecessor accountant. An accountant who (a) has reported on the most recent compiled or reviewed financial statements or was engaged to perform, but did not complete, a compilation or review of the financial statements, and (b) has resigned, declined to stand for reappointment, or been notified that his or her services have been or may be terminated.

[Paragraph amended, effective November 2002, by SSARS No. 9.]

Inquiries Regarding Acceptance of an Engagement

.03 A successor accountant is not required to communicate with a predecessor accountant in connection with acceptance of a compilation or review engagement, but he or she may believe it is beneficial to obtain information that will assist in determining whether to accept the engagement. The successor accountant may consider making inquiries of the predecessor accountant when

---

[1] [Footnote deleted, November 2002, by the issuance of Statement on Standards for Accounting and Review Services (SSARS) No. 9.]

AR §400.03

176   Statements on Standards for Accounting and Review Services

circumstances such as the following exist:[2]

a. The information obtained about the prospective client and its management and principals is limited or appears to require special attention.

b. The change in accountants takes place substantially after the end of the accounting period for which statements are to be compiled or reviewed.

c. There have been frequent changes in accountants.

The successor accountant should bear in mind that the predecessor accountant and the client may have disagreed about accounting principles, procedures applied by the predecessor accountant, or similarly significant matters. [Paragraph amended, effective November 2002, by SSARS No. 9.]

.04 The successor accountant should request permission from the prospective client to make any inquiries of the predecessor accountant. Except as permitted by the AICPA Code of Professional Conduct, an accountant is precluded from disclosing any confidential information obtained in the course of an engagement unless the client specifically consents. Accordingly, if the successor accountant decides to communicate with the predecessor, the successor accountant should request the client to (a) permit the successor accountant to make inquiries of the predecessor accountant and (b) authorize the predecessor accountant to respond fully to those inquiries.[3] If the prospective client refuses to permit the predecessor accountant to respond or limits the response, the successor accountant should inquire about the reasons and consider the implications of that refusal in connection with acceptance of the engagement. [Paragraph amended, effective November 2002, by SSARS No. 9.]

.05 When the successor accountant decides to communicate with the predecessor accountant, the inquiries may be oral or written. The inquiries should be specific and reasonable regarding matters that will assist the successor accountant in determining whether to accept the engagement. Matters subject to inquiry would include (a) information that might bear on the integrity of management (owners), (b) disagreements with management (owners) about accounting principles or the necessity for the performance of certain procedures or similarly significant matters, (c) the cooperation of management (owners) in providing additional or revised information, if necessary, (d) the predecessor's knowledge of any fraud or illegal acts perpetrated within the client, and (e) the predecessor's understanding of the reason for the change of accountants. [Paragraph amended, effective November 2002, by SSARS No. 9.]

.06 The predecessor accountant should respond promptly and fully to the inquiries, on the basis of known facts. However, if the predecessor accountant decides, due to unusual circumstances[4] such as impending, threatened, or potential litigation; disciplinary proceedings; or other unusual circumstances, not to respond fully to the inquiries, the predecessor accountant should indicate that the response is limited. The successor accountant should consider the implications of a limited response in connection with acceptance of the engagement. [Paragraph amended, effective November 2002, by SSARS No. 9.]

---

[2] [Footnote deleted, November 1992, by the issuance of SSARS No. 7.]

[3] The successor accountant is not precluded from making these inquiries before making a proposal for the engagement.

[4] Unpaid fees, as discussed in paragraph .08, are not considered to be an unusual circumstance for purposes of this paragraph; however, see paragraph .08.

AR §400.04

Other Inquiries

[.07] [Paragraph deleted, November 2002, by the issuance of SSARS No. 9.]

.08 The successor accountant also may wish to review the predecessor's engagement documentation (terms such as *working papers* or *workpapers* are also sometimes used).[5] In these circumstances, the successor accountant should request the client to authorize the predecessor accountant to allow access. It is customary in such circumstances for the predecessor accountant to make himself or herself available to the successor accountant for consultation and to make available for review certain engagement documentation. The predecessor accountant should determine which documentation is to be made available for review and which may be copied. Ordinarily, the predecessor accountant should provide the successor accountant access to documentation relating to matters of continuing accounting significance and those relating to contingencies. Valid business reasons (including but not limited to unpaid fees), however, may lead the predecessor to decide not to allow access to the documentation.[6] The predecessor accountant may decide to reach an understanding with the successor accountant about the use of the documentation.[7] Further, when more than one accountant is considering acceptance of an engagement, the predecessor accountant should not be expected to make himself or herself or his or her documentation available until the client has designated one of those accountants as the successor accountant. [Paragraph amended, effective November 2002, by SSARS No. 9. Paragraph revised, December 2010, to reflect conforming changes necessary due to the issuance of SSARS No. 19.]

Successor Accountant's Use of Communications

.09 The successor accountant should not make reference to the report or work of a predecessor accountant in his or her own report, except as specifically permitted by section 200 with respect to the financial statements of a prior period. [Paragraph amended, effective November 2002, by SSARS No. 9. Paragraph amended, effective for compilations and reviews of financial statements for periods ending on or after December 15, 2007, by SSARS No. 15.]

Financial Statements Reported on by Predecessor Accountant

.10 If, during the engagement, the successor accountant becomes aware of information that leads him or her to believe that financial statements reported on by the predecessor accountant may require revision, the successor accountant should request the client to communicate this information to the predecessor accountant. Paragraphs .47–.52 of section 80, *Compilation of Financial Statements*, and paragraphs .54–.59 of section 90, *Review of Financial*

---

[5] [Footnote deleted, December 2010, to reflect conforming changes necessary due to the issuance of SSARS No. 19].

[6] See Interpretation No. 501-1, "Response to requests by clients and former clients for records," under Rule 501, *Acts Discreditable* (ET sec. 501 par. .02), for guidance on what constitutes an accountant's working papers. [Footnote added, April 30, 1982, by the Accounting and Review Services Committee.]

[7] Before permitting access to the documentation, the predecessor accountant may wish to obtain a written communication from the successor accountant regarding the use of the documentation. The exhibit contains an illustrative successor accountant acknowledgment letter. [Footnote added, effective November 2002, by SSARS No. 9. Footnote revised, December 2010, to reflect conforming changes necessary due to the issuance of SSARS No. 19.]

AR §400.10

178   Statements on Standards for Accounting and Review Services

Statements, provide guidance to the predecessor accountant in determining an appropriate course of action with respect to compilation and review engagements, respectively. [Paragraph amended, effective November 2002, by SSARS No. 9. Paragraph revised, May 2004, to reflect conforming changes necessary due to the issuance of SSARS No. 10. Paragraph revised, July 2005, to reflect conforming changes necessary due to the issuance of SSARS No. 12. Paragraph revised, December 2010, to reflect conforming changes necessary due to the issuance of SSARS No. 19.]

.11 If the client refuses to communicate with the predecessor accountant or if the successor accountant is not satisfied with the predecessor accountant's course of action, the successor accountant should evaluate (*a*) possible implications for the current engagement and (*b*) whether to resign from the engagement. Furthermore, the successor accountant may decide to consult with legal counsel in determining an appropriate course of further action. [Paragraph added, effective November 2002, by SSARS No. 9.]

AR §400.11

Communications Between Predecessor and Successor Accountants **179**

.12

Exhibit

Illustrative Successor Accountant Acknowledgment Letter

Paragraph .08 footnote 7 states, "Before permitting access to the documentation, the predecessor accountant may wish to obtain a written communication from the successor accountant regarding the use of the documentation." The following letter is presented for illustrative purposes only and is not required by professional standards.

[Date]

[Successor Accountant]

[Address]

We have previously [reviewed or compiled], in accordance with Statements on Standards for Accounting and Review Services the December 31, 20X1, financial statements of ABC Enterprises (ABC). In connection with your [review or compilation] of ABC's 20X2 financial statements, you have requested access to our documentation prepared in connection with that engagement. ABC has authorized our firm to allow you to review that documentation.

Our [review or compilation], and the documentation prepared in connection therewith, of ABC's financial statements was not planned or conducted in contemplation of your [review or compilation]. Therefore, items of possible interest to you may not have been specifically addressed. Our use of professional judgment for the purpose of this engagement means that matters may have existed that would have been assessed differently by you. We make no representation about the sufficiency or appropriateness of the information in our documentation for your purposes.

We understand that the purpose of your review of our documentation is to obtain information about ABC and our 20X1 [compilation or review] procedures to assist you in planning your 20X2 [compilation or review] of the financial statements of ABC. For that purpose only, we will provide you access to our documentation that relate to that objective.

Upon request, we will provide copies of the documentation that provide factual information about ABC. You agree to subject any such copies, or information otherwise derived from our documentation, to your normal policy for retention of documentation and protection of confidential client information. Furthermore, in the event of a third-party request for access to your documentation prepared in connection with your (reviews or compilations) of ABC, you agree to obtain our permission before voluntarily allowing any such access to our documentation or information otherwise derived from our documentation, and to obtain on our behalf any releases that you obtain from such third party. You agree to advise us promptly and provide us a copy of any subpoena, summons, or other court order for access to your documentation that include copies of our documentation or information otherwise derived therefrom.

Please confirm your agreement with the foregoing by signing and dating a copy of this letter and returning it to us.

Very truly yours,

[Predecessor Accountant]

By: _____

Accepted:

[Successor Accountant]

By: _____ Date: _____

AR §400.12

180 Statements on Standards for Accounting and Review Services

Even with the client's consent, access to the predecessor accountant's documentation may still be limited. Experience has shown that the predecessor accountant may be willing to grant broader access if given additional assurance concerning the use of the documentation. Accordingly, the successor accountant might consider agreeing to the following limitations on the review of the predecessor accountant's documentation in order to obtain broader access:

- The successor accountant will not comment, orally or in writing, to anyone as a result of the review about whether the predecessor accountant's engagement was performed in accordance with Statements on Standards for Accounting and Review Services.

- The successor accountant will not provide expert testimony or litigation services or otherwise accept an engagement to comment on issues relating to the quality of the predecessor accountant's engagement.

The following paragraph illustrates the above:

> Because your review of our documentation is undertaken solely for the purpose described above and may not entail a review of all our documentation, you agree that (1) the information obtained from the review will not be used by you for any other purpose, (2) you will not comment, orally or in writing, to anyone as a result of that review about whether our engagement was performed in accordance with Statements on Standards for Accounting and Review Services, (3) you will not provide expert testimony or litigation services or otherwise accept an engagement to comment on issues relating to the quality of our engagement.

[Added, effective November 2002, by SSARS No. 9. Revised, September 2005, to reflect conforming changes necessary due to the Accounting and Review Services Committee. Revised, December 2010, to reflect conforming changes necessary due to the issuance of SSARS No. 19.]

AR §400.12

AR Section 9400

Communications Between Predecessor and Successor Accountants: Accounting and Review Services Interpretations of Section 400

1. Reports on the Application of Accounting Principles

.01 *Question*—SSARS No. 4, *Communications Between Predecessor and Successor Accountants* [section 400], provides guidance on communication between a successor accountant and a predecessor accountant. The guidance provided concerns only the situation in which one accountant succeeds another in a compilation or review engagement.

.02 In other situations, an accountant in public practice may be requested by an entity that has not engaged that accountant to report on its financial statements to provide advice about the application of accounting principles or about the type of report to be issued on its financial statements (compilation, review, or audit report). Such requests are often made to obtain a second opinion about these matters from another accountant. What guidance should be followed by the accountant who is requested to provide advice on these matters?

.03 *Interpretation*—SAS No. 50, *Reports on the Application of Accounting Principles* [AU section 625], as amended, applies to any accountant in public practice asked to provide written advice on the application of accounting principles to specified transactions involving facts and circumstances of a specific entity, or the type of opinion that may be rendered on a specific entity's financial statements.

.04 SAS No. 50 [AU section 625] also applies to oral advice that the reporting accountant concludes is intended to be used by a principal to the transaction as an important factor considered in reaching a decision on the application of accounting principles to a specific transaction, or the type of opinion that may be rendered on a specific entity's financial statements.

.05 Paragraph 9 of SAS No. 50 [AU section 625.09] states that the reporting accountant who is requested to provide such written or oral advice by an entity should consult with that entity's accountant, if any, to ascertain all the available facts relevant to forming a professional judgment. The reporting accountant should follow the performance and reporting guidance in SAS No. 50 [AU section 625] for such engagements.

[Issue Date: August, 1987; Revised: November, 2002.]

AR §9400.05

AR Section 500

Reporting on Compiled Financial Statements

Deleted, November 1992, by the issuance of SSARS No. 7.

AR Section 600

Reporting on Personal Financial Statements Included in Written Personal Financial Plans

Issue date, unless
otherwise indicated:
September 1986

Source: SSARS No. 6

.01 This section provides an exemption from section 80, *Compilation of Financial Statements*, for personal financial statements that are included in written personal financial plans prepared by an accountant, and specifies the form of written report required under the exemption.[1] However, this statement does not preclude an accountant from complying with section 80 in such engagements. [Paragraph revised, December 2010, to reflect conforming changes necessary due to the issuance of Statement on Standards for Accounting and Review Services (SSARS) No. 19.]

.02 Because the purpose of such financial statements is solely to assist in developing the client's personal financial plan, they frequently omit disclosures required by an applicable financial reporting framework. [Paragraph revised, December 2010, to reflect conforming changes necessary due to the issuance of SSARS No. 19.]

.03 An accountant may submit a written personal financial plan containing unaudited personal financial statements to a client without complying with the requirements of section 80 when all of the following conditions exist:

    a. The accountant establishes an understanding with the client and documents the understanding through a written communication with the client that the financial statements

        i. will be used solely to assist the client and the client's advisers to develop the client's personal financial goals and objectives.

        ii. will not be used to obtain credit or for any purposes other than developing these goals and objectives.

    b. Nothing comes to the accountant's attention during the engagement that would cause the accountant to believe that the financial statements will be used to obtain credit or for any purposes other than developing the client's financial goals and objectives.

[Paragraph revised, December 2010, to reflect conforming changes necessary due to the issuance of SSARS No. 19.]

.04 An accountant using the exemption provided by this section should issue a written report stating that the unaudited financial statements

---

[1] For purposes of this statement, personal financial statements are those financial statements of an individual that meet the definition of *financial statements* in paragraph .04 of section 60, *Framework for Performing and Reporting on Compilation and Review Engagements*. [Footnote revised, December 2010, to reflect conforming changes necessary due to the issuance of Statement on Standards for Accounting and Review Services (SSARS) No. 19]

AR §600.04

186 Statements on Standards for Accounting and Review Services

    a.   are designed solely to help develop the financial plan.

    b.   may be incomplete or contain other departures from the applicable financial reporting framework and should not be used to obtain credit or for any purposes other than developing the personal financial plan.

    c.   have not been audited, reviewed, or compiled.

.05 See the exhibit, "Illustrative Report When the Accountant Submits a Written Financial Plan Containing Unaudited Personal Financial Statements That the Accountant Did Not Compile," for an illustration. [Paragraph revised, December 2010, to reflect conforming changes necessary due to the issuance of SSARS No. 19.]

.06 Each of the personal financial statements should include a reference to the accountant's report.

Effective Date

.07 This section is effective on September 30, 1986.

AR §600.05

.08

Exhibit

Illustrative Report When the Accountant Submits a Written Financial Plan Containing Unaudited Personal Financial Statements That the Accountant Did Not Compile

Accountant's Report

The accompanying Statement of Financial Condition of X, as of December 31, 20XX, was prepared solely to help you develop your personal financial plan. Accordingly, it may be incomplete or contain other departures from accounting principles generally accepted in the United States of America and should not be used to obtain credit or for any purposes other than developing your financial plan. We have not audited, reviewed, or compiled the statement.

[Added, December 2010, to reflect the presentation style and conforming changes necessary due to the issuance of SSARS No. 19.]

AR Section 9600

Reporting on Personal Financial Statements Included in Written Personal Financial Plans: Accounting and Review Services Interpretation of Section 600

1. Submitting a Personal Financial Plan to a Client's Advisers

.01 *Question*—Paragraph 3 of Statements on Standards for Accounting and Review Services (SSARS) No. 6, *Reporting on Personal Financial Statements Included in Written Personal Financial Plans* [section 600.03], states that an accountant may submit a written personal financial plan containing unaudited personal financial statements to a client without complying with the requirements of SSARS No. 1, *Compilation and Review of Financial Statements* [section 100] when, among other conditions, the accountant establishes an understanding with the client that the financial statements will be used solely to assist the client and the client's advisers to develop the client's personal financial goals and objectives. Does developing the client's personal financial goals and objectives encompass implementing the personal financial plan by the client or the client's advisers?

.02 *Interpretation*—Yes. Developing a client's personal financial goals and objectives includes implementing the personal financial plan by the client or the client's advisers because implementing the plan may be considered the culmination of the process of developing personal financial goals and objectives. Therefore, an accountant may submit a written personal financial plan containing unaudited personal financial statements to a client, to be used by the client or the client's advisers to implement the personal financial plan, without complying with the requirements of SSARS No. 1 [section 100], provided the conditions in paragraph 3 of SSARS No. 6 [section 600.03] exist.

.03 Examples of implementation of a personal financial plan by the client's advisers include use of the plan by:

- an insurance broker who will identify specific insurance products.
- an investment adviser who will provide specific recommendations about the investment portfolio.
- an attorney who will draft a will or trust documents.

[Issue Date: May 1991.]

AR

EXHIBITS

TABLE OF CONTENTS

	Page
Exhibit A—Analytical Procedures in a Review Engagement	193
Exhibit B—Going Concern Considerations	199
Exhibit C	203

AR Exhibit A
Analytical Procedures in a Review Engagement

Notice to Readers

The purpose of the documentation guidance contained in this exhibit is to illustrate how an accountant might document expectations in a review engagement. The examples are presented for illustrative purposes only and should not be considered to represent either minimum or maximum documentation requirements.

This exhibit is an other compilation and review publication as defined in AR section 50, *Standards for Accounting and Review Services*. Other compilation and review publications have no authoritative status; however, they may help the accountant understand and apply Statements on Standards for Accounting and Review Services (SSARS). If an accountant applies the guidance included in an other compilation and review publication, the accountant should be satisfied that, in his or her judgment, it is both appropriate and relevant to the circumstances of the subject engagement. This publication was reviewed by the AICPA Audit and Attest Standards staff and published by the AICPA and is presumed to be appropriate.

Expectations

Forming an expectation is an integral phase of the analytical procedure process. Expectations are the accountant's predictions of recorded amounts or ratios developed from recorded amounts. In performing analytical procedures, the accountant develops the expectation in such a way that a material difference between the expectation and the recorded amount or ratio is indicative of a possible misstatement and, therefore, the accountant should obtain explanations for the difference (for example, an unusual event occurred). Expectations are developed by identifying plausible relationships (for example, store square footage and retail sales) that are reasonably expected to exist based on the accountant's understanding of the client and the industry in which the client operates. The accountant selects from a variety of data sources to form expectations. For example, the accountant may use prior-period information (adjusted for expected changes), management's budgets or forecasts, industry data, or nonfinancial data. Additionally, information that is developed when an accountant compiles interim financial statements can be utilized by the accountant in developing expectations associated with the review of financial statements.

An accountant cannot, under any circumstances, perform effective analytical procedures without first developing expectations related to the results of those analytical procedures. Expectations developed by the accountant in performing analytical procedures in connection with a review of financial statements ordinarily are less encompassing than those developed in an audit.

Exhibit A

194

Exhibit A

Pursuant to paragraph .45 of AR section 100, *Compilation and Review of Financial Statements*, the accountant should document expectations and factors considered in the development of those expectations where significant expectations are not otherwise readily determinable from the documentation of the work performed.

The following are examples of how an accountant can document expectations. These examples are not intended to be all inclusive.

Example 1—Expected Increase in Revenue

An accountant is engaged to review the financial statements of a company that manufactures components that are utilized by other companies in customizing vehicles for use by the United States military. Because of various conflicts occurring in the world and the United States' role in those conflicts, the accountant reasonably expects sales to increase. Using his or her knowledge of the client, the client's business, and the industry in which the client operates, the accountant expects a 10 percent to 15 percent increase in sales. Further, the accountant concludes that receivables should increase and that loans payable and interest expense would also increase because the client would need to borrow money to fund the additional production.

Sample documentation

Teemickmag Military Supply Company
Analytical Procedures
For the year ended December 31, 20XX

Expectations

The following are factors that should affect the relationship between current and prior year amounts:

- Increase in military spending by the government due to world events should result in an increase in sales. Expected increase is between 10 percent and 15 percent. The accountant expects a similar increase in accounts receivable.

- Because of an increase in production of military vehicles, the company had to borrow additional funds. Therefore, expected increase in loans payable and interest expense is between 10 percent and 15 percent.

- No significant change in either days sales in inventory or inventory turnover is expected. Although a build-up in inventory is expected, that build-up is not expected to correspond with the increase in sales because the vehicles are expected to be sold near the date of completion. Any change greater than 5 percent will be subjected to additional inquiries.

Balance sheets and income statements are available for the current year and the two years prior to the current year.

Trend analysis

	Current Year	Prior Year	Change	% Change
Sales	$2,500,000	$2,175,000	$325,000	14.94%
Cost of goods sold	1,780,000	1,566,000	214,000	13.67%
Gross margin	720,000	609,000		
Gross margin as a % of sales	28.80%	28.00%		
Selling expenses	230,000	184,000	46,000	25.00%
Interest expense	48,000	42,000	6,000	14.29%

Exhibit A

Analytical Procedures in a Review Engagement

195

Balance sheet ratio analysis

	Current Year	Prior Year	Two Years Prior
Accounts receivable, net	$1,100,000	$843,000	$703,000
Inventory	1,000,000	832,000	694,000
Loans payable	498,000	437,000	418,000

Days sales in receivables

Days sales in receivables = Accounts receivable, net at end of period / (Net sales/365)

Current year days sales in receivables = $1,100,000 / ($2,500,000 / 365) = 161 days

Prior year days sales in receivables = $843,000 / ($2,175,000 / 365) = 141 days

The increase of 20 days sales in receivables (161 days – 141 days) represents a 14 percent increase. Because this increase is within the expected range, no further inquiry is necessary.

Days sales in inventory

Days sales in inventory = Inventory at the end of period / (Total cost of goods sold / 365)

Current year days sales in inventory = $1,000,000 / ($1,780,000 / 365) = 205 days

Prior year days sales in inventory = $832,000 / ($1,566,000 / 365) = 194 days

The increase of 11 days sales in inventory (205 days – 194 days) represents a 6 percent increase. Because this increase is greater than expected, the accountant should inquire of the client and document the reason for the unexpected increase.

Inventory turnover

Inventory turnover = Cost of goods sold / Average inventory

Current year inventory turnover = $1,780,000 / ([$1,100,000 + 832,000] / 2) = 1.84 times

Prior year inventory turnover = $ 1,566,000 / ([$832,000 + 694,000] / 2) = 2.05 times

The inventory turnover decreased 10 percent; therefore, because this decrease is greater than expected, the accountant should inquire of the client and document the reason for the unexpected decrease.

The preceding documentation would be adequate. Further, after performing the trend analysis, the accountant concludes that sales, costs of goods sold, and interest expense are all "reasonable" given the expectations associated with these amounts. In addition, with respect to balance sheet accounts, the increase in loans payable is also reasonable (14 percent increase) when considered with the corresponding increase in interest expense and the expectation associated with the loan payable account; however, because selling expenses increased by 25 percent, the accountant should inquire of the client and document the reason for that unexpected increase (actual increase does not correspond to expected increase).

Exhibit A

196 Exhibit A

Example 2—Expected Decrease in Revenue

An accountant is engaged to review the financial statements of a client that either owns or manages, or both owns and manages, a shopping mall. Due to a poor economy, the mall lost tenants during the year; as such, the accountant reasonably expects revenue to decrease. Using his or her knowledge of the client, the client's business, and the industry in which the client operates, the accountant expects a 5 percent to 10 percent decrease in revenue during the year. Further, the accountant expects that general and administrative expenses should increase due to an increase in leasing and sales expenses and that management fees should decrease due to a decrease in tenants in the building.

Sample documentation

Pearl River Mall
Analytical Procedures
For the year ended December 31, 20XX

Expectations

The following are factors that should affect the relationship between current and prior year amounts:

- Loss of tenants due to poor economy should result in a decrease in revenue. Expected decrease is between 5 percent and 10 percent.

- Because of the increased number of vacancies, general and administrative expenses are expected to increase because of an increase in leasing and sales expenses. Expected increase is between 5 percent and 10 percent (corresponds with the decrease in revenue).

- Because of the decrease in the number of tenants in the building, management fees are expected to decrease between 5 percent and 10 percent (corresponds with decrease in revenue).

Balance sheets and income statements are available for the current year and the two years prior to the current year.

Trend analysis

	Current Year	Prior Year	Change	% Change
Tenant revenue	$7,223,000	$8,603,000	$(1,380,000)	(16.04)%
Costs and expenses:				
Management fees	339,000	387,000	(48,000)	(12.40)%
General and administrative	583,000	511,000	72,000	14.09 %

Similar balance sheet analytics should be performed as those performed in Example 1 above.

The preceding documentation would be adequate; however, the results of the analytical procedures do not agree with the documented expectations associated with those procedures. Therefore, the accountant should inquire and document why the decrease in tenant revenue, the decrease in management fees, and the increase in general and administrative expenses exceeded expectations.

Exhibit A

Analytical Procedures in a Review Engagement

197

Example 3—No significant change in revenue or expenses expected

An accountant is engaged to review the financial statements of a small, privately held client in the candy store business. The accountant has performed a review of the financial statements of the candy store for each of the past five years with no significant change in revenue or expenses in any of those years. The accountant expects that trend to continue.

Sample documentation

Mom and Pop Candy Store
Analytical Procedures
For the year ended December 31, 20XX

Expectations

- Based on discussions with the owner and manager, no significant changes from prior year amounts are expected.

- All increases and decreases greater than 5 percent will be subjected to additional inquiries.

Trend analysis

	Current Year	*Prior Year*	*Change*	*% Change*
Sales	$44,000	$39,000	$5,000	12.82%
Cost of goods sold	32,500	31,000	1,500	4.84%
Gross margin	11,500	8,000		
Gross margin as a % of sales	26.14%	20.51%		
Operating expenses	5,200	4,500	700	15.56%
Net income	6,300	3,500		

Similar balance sheet analytics should be performed as those performed in Example 1 above.

The preceding documentation would be adequate; however, the results of the analytical procedures do not agree with the documented expectations associated with those procedures. Therefore, the accountant may deem it appropriate to inquire and document why sales increased by an amount greater than expected. In addition, the accountant should inquire as to why there was not a comparable increase in cost of goods sold. Also, the accountant should discuss with the owner and manager why there is a greater than expected increase in operating expenses and document the results of the discussion.

Example 4—Expected Changes in Construction Contracts

An accountant is engaged to review the financial statements of a general construction contractor primarily engaged in the construction of commercial office buildings. The accountant has performed the review of this company's financial statements for several years and expects that the current project in process should yield a 5 percent gross profit margin consistent with similar projects in the past and in accordance with the initial project estimate.

Exhibit A

198   Exhibit A

Sample documentation

ABC Construction Contractors
Analytical Procedures
For the year ended December 31, 20XX

Expectations

- Based upon discussions with the project manager, it is believed that the gross margin will be consistent with the 5 percent margin achieved in the past and in accordance with the initial project estimate.

- Any deviation in the margin greater than 1 percent will be subjected to additional inquiries.

Trend analysis

Building Contract	*Current Year*	*Prior Year*	*$ Change*	*% Change*
Contract value	$5.0 million	$5.0 million		
Estimated costs at completion	4.9 million	4.75 million	$150,000	3.15%
Planned profit	100,000	250,000	150,000	60.00%
Costs incurred	2.5 Million	1.0 million		
Profit recognized contract to date	50,000	50,000		

Exhibit A

AR Exhibit B
Going Concern Considerations

Notice to Readers

The purpose of this nonauthoritative exhibit is to help practitioners better understand the accounting concepts of going concern in performing a compilation or review engagement. This exhibit has been prepared and reviewed by AICPA staff; however, it has not been approved, disapproved, or otherwise acted upon by the Accounting and Review Service Committee or any senior technical committee of the AICPA.

Going Concern Consideration

Continuation of an entity as a going concern is assumed in financial reporting in the absence of significant information to the contrary. Ordinarily, information that indicates an uncertainty about the entity's ability to continue as a going concern for a reasonable period of time, typically not to exceed one year beyond the date of the financial statements, relates to the entity's inability to continue to meet its obligations as they become due without substantial disposition of assets outside the ordinary course of business, restructuring of debt, externally forced revisions of its operations, or similar actions.

Certain conditions or events, when considered in the aggregate, may indicate there could be substantial doubt about the entity's ability to continue as a going concern for a reasonable period of time. The significance of such conditions and events will depend on the circumstances, and some may have significance only when viewed in conjunction with others. The following are examples of such conditions and events:

- *Negative trends.* For example, recurring operating losses, working capital deficiencies, negative cash flows from operating activities, adverse key financial ratios.

- *Other indications of possible financial difficulties.* For example, default on loan or similar agreements, arrearages in dividends, denial of usual trade credit from suppliers, restructuring of debt, noncompliance with statutory capital requirements, need to seek new sources or methods of financing or to dispose of substantial assets.

- *Internal matters.* For example, work stoppages or other labor difficulties, substantial dependence on the success of a particular project, uneconomic long-term commitments, need to significantly revise operations.

- *External matters that have occurred.* For example, legal proceedings, legislation, or similar matters that might jeopardize an entity's ability to operate; loss of a key franchise, license, or patent; loss of a principal customer or supplier; uninsured or underinsured catastrophe such as a drought, earthquake, or flood.

Exhibit B

200 Exhibit B

After identifying adverse conditions and events, management's plans for dealing with the conditions or events may include the following:

- Plans to dispose of assets

  — Restrictions on disposal of assets, such as covenants limiting such transactions in loan or similar agreements or encumbrances against assets

  — Apparent marketability of assets that management plans to sell

  — Possible direct or indirect effects of disposal of assets

- Plans to borrow money or restructure debt

  — Availability of debt financing, including existing or committed credit arrangements, such as lines of credit or arrangements for factoring receivables or sale-leaseback of assets

  — Existing or committed arrangements to restructure or subordinate debt or to guarantee loans to the entity

  — Possible effects on management's borrowing plans of existing restrictions on additional borrowing or the sufficiency of available collateral

- Plans to reduce or delay expenditures

  — Apparent feasibility of plans to reduce overhead or administrative expenditures, to postpone maintenance or research and development projects, or to lease rather than purchase assets

  — Possible direct or indirect effects of reduced or delayed expenditures

- Plans to increase ownership equity

  — Apparent feasibility of plans to increase ownership equity, including existing or committed arrangements to raise additional capital

  — Existing or committed arrangements to reduce current dividend requirements or to accelerate cash distributions from affiliates or other investors

Financial Statement Effects

When management concludes there is substantial doubt about the entity's ability to continue as a going concern for a reasonable period of time, management should consider disclosing the following:

- Pertinent conditions and events giving rise to the assessment of the uncertainty about the entity's ability to continue as a going concern for a reasonable period of time

- The possible effects of such conditions and events

- Management's evaluation of the significance of those conditions and events and any mitigating factors

- Possible discontinuance of operations

- Management's plans (including relevant prospective financial information)

- Information about the recoverability or classification of recorded asset amounts or the amounts or classification of liabilities

Exhibit B

Going Concern Considerations

When management concludes that substantial doubt about the entity's ability to continue as a going concern for a reasonable period of time is alleviated, management should consider the need for disclosure of the principal conditions and events that initially caused it to believe there was an uncertainty. The consideration of disclosure may include the possible effects of such conditions and events, and any mitigating factors, including management's plans.

Exhibit B

AR Exhibit C

[Exhibit deleted, October 2009, to reflect conforming changes necessary due to the issuance of FASB ASC 855, which provides authoritative accounting guidance for subsequent events.]

AR

APPENDIXES

TABLE OF CONTENTS

	Page
Appendix A—[Reserved.]	207
Appendix B—Disposition of Accounting and Review Interpretations of Section 100	209
Appendix C—Schedule of Changes in Statements on Standards for Accounting and Review Services	217

AR Appendix A

[Reserved.]

———————————

AR Appendix B

Disposition of Accounting and Review Interpretations of Section 100

Statement on Standards for Accounting and Review Services (SSARS) No. 19, *Compilation and Review Engagements*, was issued in December 2009 and was effective for compilations and reviews of financial statements for periods ending on or after December 15, 2010. SSARS No. 19 superseded section 20, *Defining Professional Requirements in Statements on Standards for Accounting and Review Services*; section 50, *Standards for Accounting and Review Services*; and section 100, *Compilation and Review of Financial Statements*. The disposition of the interpretations to section 100 as a result of changes made to conform to SSARS No. 19 is outlined in the following table.

AR sec. 100 Interpretation No.	*Title*	*Disposition*
1	Omission of Disclosures in Reviewed Financial Statements	Withdrawn, December 2010, by the Accounting and Review Services Committee (ARSC)
[2]	[Financial Statements Included in SEC Filings]	Withdrawn, December 2008, by ARSC
3	Reporting on the Highest Level of Service	Withdrawn, December 2010, by ARSC
[4]	[Discovery of Information After the Date of the Accountant's Report]	Withdrawn, July 2007, by ARSC
5	Planning and Supervision	Withdrawn, December 2010, by ARSC
6	Withdrawal From Compilation or Review Engagement	Withdrawn, December 2010, by ARSC
7	Reporting When There Are Significant Departures From GAAP	Interpretation No. 1, "Reporting When There Are Significant Departures From the Applicable Financial Reporting Framework" of section 80, *Compilation of Financial Statements* (revised, December 2010, to conform to SSARS No. 19)

(continued)

Appendix B

210   Appendix B

AR sec. 100 Interpretation No.	Title	Disposition
		Interpretation No. 1, "Reporting When There Are Significant Departures From the Applicable Financial Reporting Framework" of section 90, *Review of Financial Statements* (revised, December 2010, to conform to SSARS No. 19)
[8]	[Reports on Specified Elements, Accounts, or Items of a Financial Statement]	Withdrawn, July 2005, by ARSC
9	Reporting When Management Has Elected to Omit All Disclosures	Withdrawn, December 2010, by ARSC
10	Reporting on Tax Returns	Interpretation No. 2, "Reporting On Tax Returns" of section 80 (revised, December 2010, to conform to SSARS No. 19)
		Interpretation No. 2, "Reporting on Tax Returns" of section 90 (revised, December 2010, to conform to SSARS No. 19)
[11]	[Reporting on Uncertainties]	Withdrawn, February 2007, by ARSC
[12]	[Reporting on a Comprehensive Basis of Accounting Other Than GAAP]	Withdrawn, July 2007, by ARSC
13	Additional Procedures	Interpretation No. 3, "Additional Procedures Performed in a Compilation Engagement," of section 80 (revised, December 2010, to conform to SSARS No. 19)
		Interpretation No. 3, "Additional Procedures Performed in a Review Engagement," of section 90 (revised, December 2010, to conform to SSARS No. 19)

Appendix B

Disposition of Interpretations of Section 100   **211**

AR sec. 100 Interpretation No.	Title	Disposition
[14]	[Reporting on Financial Statements When the Scope of the Accountant's Procedures Has Been Restricted]	Withdrawn, April 1990, by ARSC
15	Differentiating a Financial Statement Presentation From a Trial Balance	Interpretation No. 4, "Differentiating a Financial Statement Presentation From a Trial Balance," of section 80 (revised, December 2010, to conform to SSARS No. 19)
[16]	[Determining if the Accountant Has "Submitted" Financial Statements Even When Not Engaged to Compile or Review Financial Statements]	Withdrawn, November 1992, by ARSC
17	Submitting Draft Financial Statements	Interpretation No. 5, "Submitting Draft Financial Statements," of section 80 (revised, December 2010, to conform to SSARS No. 19) Interpretation No. 4, "Submitting Draft Financial Statements," of section 90 (revised, December 2010, to conform to SSARS No. 19)
[18]	[Special-Purpose Financial Presentations to Comply With Contractual Agreements or Regulatory Provisions]	Withdrawn, September 2005, by ARSC
19	Reporting When Financial Statements Contain a Departure From Promulgated Accounting Principles That Prevents the Financial Statements From Being Misleading	Interpretation No. 6, "Reporting When Financial Statements Contain a Departure From Promulgated Accounting Principles That Prevents the Financial Statements From Being Misleading," of section 80 (revised, December 2010, to conform to SSARS No. 19)

(continued)

Appendix B

212 Appendix B

AR sec. 100 Interpretation No.	Title	Disposition
		Interpretation No. 5, "Reporting When Financial Statements Contain a Departure From Promulgated Accounting Principles That Prevents the Financial Statements From Being Misleading," of section 90 (revised, December 2010, to conform to SSARS No. 19)
20	Applicability of Statements on Standards for Accounting and Review Services to Litigation Services	Interpretation No. 7, "Applicability of Statements on Standards for Accounting and Review Services to Litigation Services," of AR section 80 (revised, December 2010, to conform to SSARS No. 19)
21	Applicability of SSARS No. 1 When Performing Controllership or Other Management Services	Interpretation No. 8, "Applicability of Statements on Standards for Accounting and Review Services When Performing Controllership or Other Management Services," of section 80 (revised, December 2010, to conform to SSARS No. 19)
22	Use of "Selected Information—Substantially All Disclosures Required by Generally Accepted Accounting Principles Are Not Included"	Interpretation No. 9, "Use of the Label' Selected Information—Substantially All Disclosures Required by [the applicable financial reporting framework] Are Not Included' in Compiled Financial Statements," of section 80 (revised, December 2010, to conform to SSARS No. 19)
23	Applicability of Statements on Standards For Accounting and Review Services When an Accountant Engaged to Perform a Business Valuation Derives Information From an Entity's Tax Return	Withdrawn, December 2010, by ARSC

Appendix B

Disposition of Interpretations of Section 100   **213**

AR sec. 100 Interpretation No.	Title	Disposition
24	Reference to the Country of Origin in a Review or Compilation Report	Withdrawn, December 2010, by ARSC
25	Omission of the Display of Comprehensive Income in a Compilation	Interpretation No. 10, "Omission of the Display of Comprehensive Income in Compiled Financial Statements," of section 80 (revised, December 2010, to conform to SSARS No. 19)
[26]	[Communicating Possible Fraud and Illegal Acts to Management and Others]	Withdrawn, July 2005, by ARSC
27	Applicability of Statements on Standards for Accounting and Review Services to Reviews of Nonissuers Who Are Owned by or Controlled by an Issuer	Withdrawn, December 2010, by ARSC
28	Special-Purpose Financial Statements to Comply With Contractual Agreements or Regulatory Provisions	Interpretation No. 11, "Special-Purpose Financial Statements to Comply With Contractual Agreements or Regulatory Provisions," of section 80 (revised, December 2010, to conform to SSARS No. 19) Interpretation No. 6, "Special-Purpose Financial Statements to Comply With Contractual Agreements or Regulatory Provisions," of section 90 (revised, December 2010, to conform to SSARS No. 19)
29	Reporting on an Uncertainty, Including an Uncertainty About an Entity's Ability to Continue as a Going Concern	Interpretation No. 12, "Reporting on an Uncertainty About an Entity's Ability to Continue as a Going Concern," of section 80 (revised, December 2010, to conform to SSARS No. 19)

(continued)

Appendix B

Appendix B

214

AR sec. 100 Interpretation No.	Title	Disposition
		Interpretation No. 7, "Reporting on an Uncertainty About an Entity's Ability to Continue as a Going Concern," of section 90 (revised, December 2010, to conform to SSARS No. 19)
30	Considerations Related to Financial Statements Prepared in Accordance With International Financial Reporting Standards and Compilations and Reviews Performed in Accordance With International Standards	Interpretation No. 13, "Compilations of Financial Statements Prepared in Accordance With International Financial Reporting Standards," of section 80 (revised, December 2010)
		Interpretation No. 14, "Compilations of Financial Statements Prepared in Accordance With A Financial Reporting Framework Generally Accepted in Another Country," of section 80 (revised, December 2010)
		Interpretation No. 15, "Considerations Related to Compilations Performed in Accordance with International Standard on Related Services 4410, *Engagements to Compile Financial Statements*," of section 80 (revised, December 2010)
		Interpretation No. 8, "Reviews of Financial Statements Prepared in Accordance With International Financial Reporting Standards," of section 90 (revised, December 2010)

Disposition of Interpretations of Section 100   **215**

AR sec. 100 Interpretation No.	Title	Disposition
		Interpretation No. 9, "Reviews of Financial Statements Prepared in Accordance With A Financial Reporting Framework Generally Accepted in Another Country," of section 90 (revised, December 2010)
		Interpretation No. 10, "Considerations Related to Reviews Performed in Accordance with International Standard on Review Engagements 2400, *Engagements to Review Financial Statements*," of section 90 (revised, December 2010)
31	Preparation of Financial Statements for Use by an Entity's Auditors	Interpretation No. 16, "Preparation of Financial Statements for Use by an Entity's Auditors," of section 80 (revised, December 2010, to conform to SSARS No. 19)

Appendix B

AR Appendix C

Schedule of Changes in Statements on Standards for Accounting and Review Services

Section	Paragraph	Changes	Date of Change
20		SSARS No. 16 added	December 2007
20		Superseded by SSARS No. 19	December 2009
50		Added by SSARS No. 11	May 2004
50		Superseded by SSARS No. 19	December 2009
50	.01	Amended by SSARS No. 17	December 2008
60		Added by SSARS No. 19	December 2009
80		Added by SSARS No. 19	December 2009
90		Added by SSARS No. 19	December 2009
90	.01	Amended by SSARS No. 20	February 2011
100		Superseded by SSARS No. 19	December 2009
100	.01	Amended by SSARS No. 8	October 2000
100	.01	Amended by SSARS No. 15	July 2007
100	.01	Amended by SSARS No. 17	February 2008
100	.01	Amended by SSARS No. 18	February 2009
100	.02	Amended by SSARS No. 3	December 1981
100	.02	Amended by SSARS No. 8	October 2000
100	.02	Amended by SSARS No. 17	December 2008
100	.03	Amended by SSARS No. 8	October 2000
100	.03	Amended by SSARS No. 9	November 2002
100	.03	Amended by SSARS No. 17	February 2008
100	.04	Amended by SSARS No. 2	October 1979
100	.04	Amended by SSARS No. 8	October 2000
100	.04	Amended by SSARS No. 9	November 2002
100	.04	Amended by SSARS No. 15	July 2007
100	.04	Amended by SSARS No. 17	February 2008
100	.05	Amended by SSARS No. 8	October 2000
100	.05	Amended by SSARS No. 12	July 2005
100	.06	New paragraph added by issuance of SSARS No. 17; subsequent paragraphs renumbered	February 2008
100	.07	Amended by SSARS No. 8	October 2000
100	.08	Amended by SSARS No. 8	October 2000
100	.09	Amended by SSARS No. 8	October 2000
100	.10	Amended by SSARS No. 8	October 2000
100	.10	Amended by SSARS No. 9	November 2002
100	.10	Amended by SSARS No. 12	July 2005

(continued)

Appendix C

Appendix C

Section	Paragraph	Changes	Date of Change
100	.11	Amended by SSARS No. 8	October 2000
100	.12	New paragraph added by issuance of SSARS No. 17; subsequent paragraphs renumbered	February 2008
100	.13	Amended by SSARS No. 8	October 2000
100	.13	Amended by SSARS No. 9	November 2002
100	.14	Amended by SSARS No. 8	October 2000
100	.14	Deleted by SSARS No. 9	November 2002
100	.15–.16	Amended by SSARS No. 8	October 2000
100	.16	Amended by SSARS No. 15	July 2007
100	.17	New paragraph added by issuance of SSARS No. 15; subsequent paragraphs renumbered	July 2007
100	.18–.19	Amended by SSARS No. 3	December 1981
100	.20–.21	Amended by SSARS No. 8	October 2000
100	.21	Amended by SSARS No. 15	July 2007
100	.22	New paragraph added by issuance of SSARS No. 15; subsequent paragraphs renumbered	July 2007
100	.23–.27	Amended by SSARS No. 8	October 2000
100	.28	New paragraph added by issuance of SSARS No. 17; subsequent paragraphs renumbered	February 2008
100	.29	Amended by SSARS No. 9	November 2002
100	.29	Amended by SSARS No. 10	May 2004
100	.29	Amended by SSARS No. 17	February 2008
100	.30	New paragraph added by issuance of SSARS No. 17; subsequent paragraphs renumbered	February 2008
100	.31	Amended by SSARS No. 9	November 2002
100	.31	Amended and transferred, from former 100.32, by SSARS No. 10; subsequent paragraphs renumbered	May 2004
100	.31	Amended by SSARS No. 12	July 2005
100	.31	Amended by SSARS No. 17	February 2008
100	.32	New paragraphs added by issuance of SSARS No. 17; subsequent paragraphs renumbered	February 2008
100	.33	Amended by SSARS No. 10	May 2004
100	.36	New paragraphs added by issuance of SSARS No. 10; subsequent paragraphs renumbered	May 2004

Schedule of Changes in SSARS

Section	Paragraph	Changes	Date of Change
100	.36	Amended by SSARS No. 17	February 2008
100	.37–.38	New paragraphs added by issuance of SSARS No. 10; subsequent paragraphs renumbered	May 2004
100	.38	Amended by SSARS No. 10	May 2004
100	.39	New paragraph added by issuance of SSARS No. 9; subsequent paragraphs renumbered	November 2002
100	.39	Amended by SSARS No. 10	May 2004
100	.40	New paragraph added by issuance of SSARS No. 12; subsequent paragraphs renumbered	July 2005
100	.41	Amended by SSARS No. 9	November 2002
100	.41	Amended by SSARS No. 17	February 2008
100	.42	Amended by SSARS No. 10	May 2004
100	.43	New paragraph added by issuance of SSARS No. 10; subsequent paragraphs renumbered	May 2004
100	.44	Amended by SSARS No. 10	May 2004
100	.45	New paragraph added by issuance of SSARS No. 10; subsequent paragraphs renumbered	May 2004
100	.45	Amended by SSARS No. 12	July 2005
100	.46	Amended by SSARS No. 9	November 2002
100	.47	Deleted by SSARS No. 9	November 2002
100	.49	Amended by SSARS No. 15	July 2007
100	.50	New paragraph added by issuance of SSARS No. 15; subsequent paragraphs renumbered	July 2007
100	.51	Amended by SSARS No. 9	November 2002
100	.53	Amended by SSARS No. 3	December 1981
100	.54–.55	New paragraph added by issuance of SSARS No. 15; subsequent paragraphs renumbered	July 2007
100	.56	Amended by SSARS No. 5	July 1982
100	.56	Amended by SSARS No. 3	December 1981
100	.56–.58	Amended by SSARS No. 15	July 2007
100	.59–.68	New paragraphs added by SSARS No. 12; subsequent paragraphs renumbered	July 2005
100	.69–.76	New paragraphs added by SSARS No. 12; subsequent paragraphs renumbered	February 2008

(continued)

Appendix C

220 Appendix C

Section	Paragraph	Changes	Date of Change
100	.77	Amended by SSARS No. 9	November 2002
100	.77	Amended by SSARS No. 15	July 2007
100	.78–.82	New paragraphs added by issuance of SSARS No. 15; subsequent paragraphs renumbered	July 2007
100	.83	Amended by SSARS No. 17	February 2008
100	.84–.85	New paragraphs added by SSARS No. 12; subsequent paragraphs renumbered	July 2005
100	.85–.86	Amended by SSARS No. 17	February 2008
100	.92	Superseded by SSARS No. 2	October 1979
100	.93–.95	New paragraphs added by issuance of SSARS No. 9; subsequent paragraphs renumbered	November 2002
100	.94	Amended by SQCS 7	December 2008
100	.97	New paragraph added by issuance of SSARS No. 8; subsequent paragraphs renumbered	October 2000
100	.98	Amended by SSARS No. 10	May 2004
100	.98	Revised	December 2008
100	.99	Amended by SSARS No. 5	July 1982
100	.99	Amended by SSARS No. 17	February 2008
100	.100	New paragraph added by issuance of SSARS No. 8; subsequent paragraphs renumbered	October 2000
100	.100–.101	Amended by SSARS No. 17	February 2008
100	.102	Amended by SSARS No. 15	July 2007
100	.102	Amended by SSARS No. 17	February 2008
100	.103	New paragraphs added by SSARS No. 12; subsequent paragraphs renumbered	July 2005
100	.104	Deleted by SSARS No. 8	October 2000
100	.105	New paragraph added by issuance of SSARS No. 10; subsequent paragraphs renumbered	May 2004
100	.105	Amended by SSARS No. 15	July 2007
100	.106	New paragraph added by issuance of SSARS No. 15	July 2007
110		SSARS No. 13 added	July 2005
110	.01	Revised by SSARS No. 19	December 2010
110	.02	Revised by SSARS No. 19	December 2010
110	.04	Revised by SSARS No. 19	December 2010

Appendix C

Schedule of Changes in SSARS

Section	Paragraph	Changes	Date of Change
110	.05	Revised by SSARS No. 19	December 2010
110	.06	Revised by SSARS No. 19	December 2010
110	.07	Revised by SSARS No. 19	December 2010
110	.08	Revised by SSARS No. 19	December 2010
110	.09	Revised by SSARS No. 19	December 2010
110	.10	New paragraphs added by SSARS No. 19; subsequent paragraphs renumbered	December 2010
110	.11	Revised by SSARS No. 19	December 2010
110	.12	Revised by SSARS No. 19	December 2010
110	.13	Deleted by SSARS No. 19	December 2010
110	.14	Revised by SSARS No. 19	December 2010
110	.15	Amended by SSARS No. 17	May 2008
110	.15	Revised by SSARS No. 19	December 2010
110	.16	Revised by SSARS No. 19	December 2010
110	.17	Added by SSARS No. 19	December 2010
120		SSARS No. 14 added	July 2005
120	.01	Revised by SSARS No. 19	December 2010
120	.02	Revised by SSARS No. 19	December 2010
120	.06	Revised by SSARS No. 19	December 2010
120	.07	Revised by SSARS No. 19	December 2010
120	.09	Revised by SSARS No. 19	December 2010
120	.10	Revised by SSARS No. 19	December 2010
120	.11	Revised by SSARS No. 19	December 2010
120	.12	Revised by SSARS No. 19	December 2010
120	.13	New paragraphs added by SSARS No. 19; subsequent paragraphs renumbered	December 2010
120	.14	Revised by SSARS No. 19	December 2010
120	.15	Revised by SSARS No. 19	December 2010
120	.16	Deleted by SSARS No. 19	December 2010
120	.17	Revised by SSARS No. 19	December 2010
120	.18	Amended by SSARS No. 17	May 2008
120	.19	Revised by SSARS No. 19	December 2010
120	.20	Added by SSARS No. 19	December 2010
200	.01	Revised by SSARS No. 8	October 2000
200	.01	Amended by SSARS No. 17	February 2008
200	.01	Revised by SSARS No. 19	December 2010
200	.02	Amended by SSARS No. 3	December 1981
200	.02	Revised by SSARS No. 8	October 2000
200	.05	Amended by SSARS No. 15	July 2007
200	.05	Revised by SSARS No. 19	December 2010
200	.06	Revised by SSARS No. 19	December 2010

(continued)

Appendix C

222

Appendix C

Section	Paragraph	Changes	Date of Change
200	.09	Amended by SSARS No. 5	July 1982
200	.09	Amended by SSARS No. 7	November 1992
200	.09	Deleted by SSARS No. 19	December 2010
200	.10	Amended by SSARS No. 7	November 1992
200	.10	Deleted by SSARS No. 19	December 2010
200	.12	Revised by SSARS No. 19	December 2010
200	.15	Revised by SSARS No. 19	December 2010
200	.16	Amended by SSARS No. 4	December 1981
200	.17	Revised by SSARS No. 19	December 2010
200	.18	Revised by SSARS No. 19	December 2010
200	.19	Deleted by SSARS No. 19	December 2010
200	.22	Revised by SSARS No. 19	December 2010
200	.25–.26	Amended by SSARS No. 12	July 2005
200	.26	Revised by SSARS No. 19	December 2010
200	.27	New paragraph added by SSARS No. 12; subsequent paragraphs renumbered	July 2005
200	.27	Deleted by SSARS No. 19	December 2010
200	.28	Deleted by SSARS No. 19	December 2010
200	.29	Amended by SSARS No. 17	February 2008
200	.29	Revised by SSARS No. 19	December 2010
200	.30	Amended by SSARS No. 5	July 1982
200	.30	Amended by SSARS No. 7	November 1992
200	.30	Revised by SSARS No. 19	December 2010
200	.31	Revised by SSARS No. 19	December 2010
200	.32	Deleted by SSARS No. 19	December 2010
200	.33	Deleted by SSARS No. 8	October 2000
200	.33	Amended by SSARS No. 17	February 2008
200	.33	Deleted by SSARS No. 19	December 2010
200	.34–.35	Deleted by SSARS No. 8	October 2000
200	.38	Added by SSARS No. 19	December 2010
200	.39	Added by SSARS No. 19	December 2010
300	.01	Amended by SSARS No. 15	July 2007
300	.01	Revised by SSARS No. 19	December 2010
300	.01–.02	Amended by SSARS No. 17	February 2008
300	.02	Revised by SSARS No. 19	December 2010
300	.03	Amended by SSARS No. 5	July 1982
300	.03	Amended by SSARS No. 7	November 1992
300	.03	Amended by SSARS No. 17	February 2008
300	.03	Revised by SSARS No. 19	December 2010
300	.04	Revised by SSARS No. 19	December 2010
300	.05	Revised by SSARS No. 19	December 2010
300	.06	Added by SSARS No. 19	December 2010
400	.01	Amended by SSARS No. 7	November 1992

Appendix C

Schedule of Changes in SSARS

223

Section	Paragraph	Changes	Date of Change
400	.01	Amended by SSARS No. 9	November 2002
400	.01	Amended by SSARS No. 17	February 2008
400	.02	Amended by SSARS No. 9	November 2002
400	.03	Amended by SSARS No. 7	November 1992
400	.03–.06	Amended by SSARS No. 9	November 2002
400	.07	Deleted by SSARS No. 9	November 2002
400	.08	Revised by SSARS No. 19	December 2010
400	.08–.09	Amended by SSARS No. 9	November 2002
400	.09	Amended by SSARS No. 15	July 2007
400	.10	Amended by SSARS No. 9	November 2002
400	.10	Revised by SSARS No. 19	December 2010
400	.11–.12	New paragraphs added by issuance of SSARS No. 9	November 2002
400	.12	Revised by SSARS No. 19	December 2010
500	. . .	Deleted by SSARS No. 7	November 1992
600	.01	Revised by SSARS No. 19	December 2010
600	.02	Revised by SSARS No. 19	December 2010
600	.03	Revised by SSARS No. 19	December 2010
600	.05	Revised by SSARS No. 19	December 2010
600	.08	Added by SSARS No. 19	December 2010

Appendix C

AR TOPICAL INDEX

References are to AR section and paragraph numbers.

A

ACCOUNTANT, INDEPENDENT
- Association With Financial Statements 200.03
- Compilation Report 60.46; 80.13
- Continuing—See Continuing Independent Accountant
- Differentiating Between Financial Statement Presentation and Trial Balance 9080.10-.12
- Draft Financial Statements .... 9080.13-.14; 9090.10-.11
- Impaired Independence 80.62-.63; 90.02
- Lack of Independence 80.21
- Litigation Services 9080.17-.20
- Predecessor—See Predecessor Independent Accountant
- Reporting Obligation 200.08-.12; 200.29
- Reporting on Personal Financial Statements 600.01-.07
- Submission of Financial Statements to Client 9080.13-.14; 9090.10-.11
- Successor—See Successor Independent Accountant
- Tax Returns, Reporting .... 9080.05-.06; 9090.05-.06
- Understanding With Entity 600.03
- Understanding With Management and Others 80.02-.05; 90.03-.13
- Use of "Selected Information" Label 9080.25-.27

ACCOUNTING
- Changes—See Changes, Accounting
- Principles—See Generally Accepted Accounting Principles

ACCOUNTING SERVICES
- Applicability to Litigation Services 9080.17-.20
- Controllership Services—See Controllership Services
- Management Services—See Management Services

ACCOUNTS RECEIVABLE—See Receivables

ADVERSE OPINIONS
- Applicability 9080.02; 9090.02
- Prior Period Financial Statements 9200.02-.03

AMERICAN INSTITUTE OF CPAs
- Standards for Accounting and Review Services .... 80.03; 80.14; 80.17; 80.56-.57; 90.04

ANALYTICAL PROCEDURES
- Predecessor Accountant's Procedures 200.22
- Review Procedures .... 90.04; 90.14-.18; 90.26

APPLICABLE FINANCIAL REPORTING FRAMEWORK
- Disagreement With Management 400.05
- Omission of Disclosures ..... 200.05; 200.13; 200.30-.31; 300.01

ATTORNEYS—See Lawyers

AUDIT ENGAGEMENTS
- Adverse Opinion 9080.02; 9090.02
- Change in Engagement .... 80.56-.61; 90.63-.68
- Subsequent Period Compiled .... 200.29; 9200.01-.04
- Subsequent Period Reviewed 200.29

AUDITING STANDARDS—See Generally Accepted Auditing Standards

AUDITORS' OPINIONS—See Opinions, Auditors'

AUTHORITIES, REGULATORY—See Regulatory Agencies

AUTHORIZATION
- Client's Permission to Predecessor Accountant 400.04; 400.08
- Successor Accountant Acknowledgment Letter 400.12

C

CASH FLOWS—See Statements of Cash Flows

CHANGE OF ACCOUNTANTS
- Predecessor—See Predecessor Independent Accountant
- Successor—See Successor Independent Accountant

CLIENTS
- Accountant's Labeling of Financial Statement Notes 9080.25-.27
- Accountant's Submission of Written Personal Financial Plan With Unaudited Statements to a Client 9600.01-.03
- Authorization to Predecessor Accountant 400.04; 400.08
- Change in Engagement .... 80.56-.61; 90.63-.68
- Change of Accountants .... 200.16; 200.20-.27; 400.03
- Improper Use of Accountant's Name ... 200.03

CLI

226   AR Topical Index

CLIENTS—continued
- Subsequent Discovery of Facts 400.10-.11
- Understanding With Accountant 600.03;
- 9600.01-.03

**CODE OF PROFESSIONAL CONDUCT—See
Conduct, Code of Professional**

COMMUNICATION
- Audit Procedures 9080.09; 9090.09
- Between Predecessor and Successor
  Accountant 400.01-.12
- Change of Accountants...........400.01-.12
- Compilation Report 60.46; 80.13
- Establishing an Understanding With
  Management 80.02-.05; 90.03-.13
- Financial Statements Reported on By
  Predecessor Accountant.........400.10-.11
- Principal and Reporting Accountant ... 9400.05
- Successor Accountant Acknowledgment
  Letter 400.12
- Successor Accountant's Use of 400.09
- When Compiled Financial Statements
  Are Not Expected to Be Used by a Third
  Party........80.22-.24; 80.62; 9080.61-.62
- With Management and Others 80.02;
  ... 80.15; 80.54-.55; 90.03; 90.19; 90.26;
  .... 90.61-.62

COMPARABILITY
- Compiled Financial Statements 200.05

COMPARATIVE FINANCIAL STATEMENTS
- Compilation Each Period 9200.01-.04
- Definition.............................200.07
- Departures From GAAP............200.13-.15
- Omission of Disclosures..............200.05;
  .... 200.30-.31; 9080.51-.52; 9200.01-.04
- One Period Audited 200.29
- Prescribed Forms 200.02; 300.01
- Reference to Accountant's Report.....200.06;
  .... 9200.03-.04
- Uncertainties........................9200.04

COMPILATION ENGAGEMENT
- Audit Procedures 9080.07-.09
- Change From Audit Engagement 80.56-.61
- Communication Between
  Accountants 400.01-.12
- Communication of Possible Fraud and Illegal
  Acts 80.03
- Compilation Each Period 9200.01-.04
- Documentation.....................80.14-.15
- Elements 60.26
- Ethical Principles....................60.22-.23
- Limitations..........................60.05-.06
- Objectives 60.05-.06
- Prescribed Forms 300.01; 9300.01-.03
- Prior Period Audited 200.29; 9200.01-.04
- Pro Forma Financial Information—See
  Compilation of Pro Forma Financial
  Information
- Quality Control Standards....60.22; 60.24-.25
- Reports—See Compilation Reports

COMPILATION ENGAGEMENT—continued
- Reports on Application of Accounting
  Principles......................9400.01-.05
- Specified Elements, Accounts, or Items of a
  Financial Statement—See Compilation of
  Specified Elements, Accounts, or Items of a
  Financial Statement
- Subsequent Discovery of Facts 400.10-.11
- Subsequent Events ... 200.13-.15; 200.20-.23
- Successor Accountant Acknowledgment
  Letter 400.12
- Tax Returns, Reporting...........9080.05-.06
- Three Party Relationship............60.27-.36
- Uncertainties....................9080.41-.48
- Understanding with Management and
  Others...........................80.02-.05
- Withdrawal From Engagement ... 80.13; 80.29

COMPILATION OF FINANCIAL STATEMENTS
- Accountant's Responsibilities 80.03; 80.07
- Change of Accountants 400.02
- Comparative Financial
  Statements.......200.01-.39; 9200.01-.04
- Compliance With Contractual Agreement or
  Regulatory Provision 9080.32-.40
- Differences From a Review or Audit 80.03
- Departures From the Applicable Financial
  Reporting Framework................80.05;
  .... 80.27-.29300.01; 300.03-.04;
  .. 9080.01-.04; 9080.28-.40; 9090.01-.04;
  .... 9300.01-.03
- Documentation Requirements.........110.11;
  .... 120.13
- Draft Financial Statements 9080.13-.14
- Engagement Letters........80.03-.05; 80.15;
  .... 80.62
- Establishing an Understanding 80.02-.05
- Going Concern.....................80.40-.43
- Illustrative Engagement Letter 80.62
- Incomplete Presentation 9080.32-.40
- Management's Responsibilities..........80.03
- Omission of Disclosures—See Disclosure
- Performance Requirements.........80.06-.13
- Prescribed Forms ... 300.01-.06; 9300.01-.03
- Pro Forma Financial Information—See
  Compilation of Pro Forma Financial
  Information
- Reporting—See Compilation Reports
- Restricted Use..............80.23; 80.31-.38
- Specified Elements, Accounts, or Items of a
  Financial Statement—See Compilation of
  Specified Elements, Accounts, or Items of a
  Financial Statement
- Subsequent Discovery of Facts 400.10-.11
- Subsequent Events.................80.44-.46
- Successor Accountant Acknowledgment
  Letter 400.12
- Supplementary Information 80.05
- When Not Expected to Be Used by a Third
  Party...................80.62; 9080.61-.62
- Without a Report......................80.44

CLI

AR Topical Index

COMPILATION OF PRO FORMA FINANCIAL INFORMATION
- Conditions for Compiling 120.06-.08
- Distinguished From Historical Financial Information 120.05
- Engagement Letter 120.19
- Illustrations—See Illustrations
- Limitations 120.02
- Objectives 120.03-.04
- Performance Requirements 120.11-.12
- Reporting Requirements 120.14-.15
- Understanding With Management 120.09-.10

COMPILATION OF SPECIFIED ELEMENTS, ACCOUNTS, OR ITEMS OF A FINANCIAL STATEMENT
- Components 9080.11
- Conditions for Compiling 110.04-.05
- Engagement Letter 110.16
- Examples 110.03
- Illustrations—See Illustrations
- Included as Accompanying Information to Basic Financial Statements 110.04
- Limitations 110.02
- Performance Requirements 110.08-.09
- Reporting Requirements 110.11-.12
- Supplementary Information 110.01
- Understanding With Management 110.06-.07

COMPILATION REPORTS
- Accountant's Responsibility .... 60.46; 80.03-.05; 200.03; 200.11-.12
- Combined Reports 80.34
- Compilation Each Period 9200.01-.04
- Date of Report.............. 80.17; 80.47-.48
- Departures From the Applicable Financial Reporting Framework .... 80.63; 200.05; .... 200.13-.15; 200.30-.31; 300.01; .... 300.03-.05; 9080.01-.04; 9080.28-.31; 9200.04; 9300.01-.03
- Elements 80.17
- Emphasis of a Matter Paragraph....80.25-.26; 80.46; 9080.43; 9080.46
- Form and Content 110.11-.12; 120.14-.15
- General Use and Restricted Use.....80.30-.32
- Illustrations...80.63; 110.16-.17; 120.19-.20; ...... 200.38; 300.06; 9080.03; 9080.36; .... 9080.40; 9080.50; 9080.56; 9080.59; 9300.01-.02
- Impaired Independence.................80.63
- Inclusion of a Separate Restricted Use Report 80.35-.36; 80.38-.39
- Introductory Paragraph.................80.17
- Lack of Independence ....60.46; 80.21; 110.14; 120.17
- Modification .... 80.27-.29; 9080.01-.04; 9080.32-.48
- Omission of Disclosures .... 80.05; 80.20; .... 200.05; 200.30-.31; 9080.25-.27; ... 9080.28-.31; 9080.51-.52; 9200.01-.04

COMPILATION REPORTS—continued
- Omission of Display of Comprehensive Income........................9080.28-.31
- Preclusion From Issuance 80.59
- Predecessor Independent Accountant 200.16-.27
- Prepared in Accordance With OCBOA....80.19
- Prescribed Forms ... 300.01-.06; 9300.01-.03
- Prior Period Audited..... 200.29; 9200.01-.04
- Prior Period Reviewed .... 200.11-.12; 9200.01-.04
- Pro Forma Financial Information....120.14-.15
- Restricted Use 80.31-.32
- Signature of Firm or Accountant 80.17
- Special-Purpose Financial Statements.............9080.36; 9080.40
- Specified Elements, Accounts, or Items of a Financial Statement 110.11-.12
- Specified Parties 80.36-.39
- Subject Matter Based on Measurement or Disclosure Criteria Contained in Contractual Agreements, Regulatory Provisions....80.33
- Successor Independent Accountant 200.16-.27
- Supplementary Information 80.53
- Tax Returns 9080.05-.06
- Title......................................80.17
- Uncertainties 9080.41-.48
- Written Report.................60.46; 80.16

COMPREHENSIVE BASIS OF ACCOUNTING
- Disclosure of Basis 300.01
- Omission of Disclosures...............200.05

COMPREHENSIVE INCOME
- Omission of Display in a Compilation Report 9080.28-.31

CONDUCT, CODE OF PROFESSIONAL
- Disclosure of Confidential Information 400.04
- Engagement Documentation 400.08
- Interpretation 501-1 .... 400.08
- Litigation Services...............9080.17-.20
- Rule 202................60.16; 9090.29-.30
- Rule 203..........9080.15-.16; 9090.12-.13; 9090.29-.30

CONFIDENTIAL CLIENT INFORMATION
- Disclosure of Information.............400.04

CONTINGENCIES
- Communication With Predecessor Accountant 400.08

CONTINUING INDEPENDENT ACCOUNTANT
- Changed Reference in Report......200.13-.15
- Definition............................200.07
- Standard Reports 200.08-.12

CORPORATE JOINT VENTURES—See Jointly Owned Companies

CORRECTION OF ERROR
- Restatement of Prior Period 200.25-.27

COR

228 AR Topical Index

D

DATE OF REPORT
· Compilation Report 80.17; 80.37; 80.44;
.... 80.47-.48
· Review Report 90.24; 90.28; 90.44;
.... 90.54-.55
· Subsequent Period Compiled 9200.01

DEFINITIONS—See Terminology

DEPARTURES FROM ESTABLISHED PRINCIPLES
· Compilation of Financial Statements 80.05;
.... 200.05; 200.13-.15; 300.01;
.... 300.03-.04; 9080.01-.04; 9080.16;
.... 9080.28-.31; 9080.32-.40;
.... 9090.14-.22; 9200.04; 9300.01-.03
· Illustrations 9080.03; 9080.40; 9090.22;
.... 9300.01-.02
· Omission of Disclosures 80.05; 90.04-.06;
.... 200.30-.31; 300.01; 600.02;
... 9080.25-.27; 9080.28-.31; 9300.01-.03
· Omission of Display of Comprehensive
Income 9080.28-.31
· Personal Financial Statements 600.02
· Prescribed Forms 300.01; 300.03-.05;
.... 9300.01-.03
· Review of Financial Statements 200.13-.15;
...... 9090.01-.04; 9090.13; 9090.14-.22;
.... 9200.04; 9300.01-.03
· Unaudited Financial Statements 300.01;
.... 300.03

DISCLAIMER OF OPINION
· Prior Period Financial Statements 200.02;
.... 200.17; 200.33; 9200.02-.03

DISCLOSURE
· Comparative Information 9080.51-.52;
.... 9090.29-.30
· Controllership Services, When
Performing 9080.21-.24
· Departures From GAAP 300.01;
... 9080.01-.04; 9090.01-.04; 9300.01-.03
· Inadequate 80.12; 80.20; 90.34; 200.13
· Knowledge of the Client 80.10; 90.12
· Management Representations 90.23-.24
· Management Services, When
Performing 9080.21-.24
· Omission of Disclosures 80.05; 90.04-.06;
..... 200.05; 200.30-.31; 300.01; 600.02;
.. 9080.25-.27; 9080.28-.31; 9080.47-.48;
... 9080.51-.52; 9200.01-.04; 9300.01-.03
· Omission of Display of Comprehensive
Income 9080.28-.31
· Prescribed Forms 300.01; 9300.01-.03
· Privileged Communication 400.04
· Reporting 80.19-.21; 90.32-.35
· Review Procedures 90.19
· Subsequent Discovery of Facts 80.49-.52;
.... 90.54-.59
· Subsequent Events 80.44-.46; 90.51-.53;
.... 200.23
· Uncertainties 9080.41-.48; 9090.23-.28

DISCLOSURE—continued
· Use of "Selected Information"
Label 9080.25-.27

DISCOVERY
· Financial Statements of
Predecessor 400.10-.11
· Subsequent Discovery of Facts 80.47-.52;
.... 90.54-.59; 400.10-.11

DOCUMENTATION
· Compilation Engagement 80.14-.15
· Review Engagement 90.05; 90.25-.26

E

ELEMENTS OF FINANCIAL STATEMENTS—See Compilation of Specified Elements, Accounts, or Items of a Financial Statement

EMPHASIS OF A MATTER
· Departures From GAAP 9080.03-.04;
.... 9090.03-.04
· Prior Period Financial Statements 200.17;
.... 9200.03
· Required
· Review Procedures 90.33
· Separate Paragraph of the Accountant's
Report 80.25-.26; 80.46; 90.33
· Uncertainties 9080.43; 9080.46;
.... 9090.25; 9090.28

ENGAGEMENT
· Audit—See Audit Engagement
· Compilation—See Compilation Engagement
· Review—See Review Engagement

ENGAGEMENT DOCUMENTATION
· Predecessor Accountant 400.08
· Reviewed by Predecessor
Accountant 200.22
· Successor Accountant Acknowledgment
Letter 400.12

ENGAGEMENT LETTERS
· Compilation of Financial
Statements 80.03-.05; 9080.28-.31
· Compilation of Pro Forma Financial
Information 120.19
· Compilation of Specified Elements,
Accounts, or Items of a Financial
Statement 110.16
· Illustrations 80.62; 90.69
· Impaired Independence 80.62
· Review of Financial Statements 90.06;
.... 90.26

EVENTS
· Subsequent—See Subsequent Events

EXAMPLES—See Illustrations

F

FINANCIAL INFORMATION—See Financial Statements

DAT

AR Topical Index

229

FINANCIAL STATEMENTS
- Accountant's Responsibility...........200.03
- Accountant's Review.................9080.50
- Comparative—See Comparative Financial Statements
- Compilation—See Compilation of Financial Statements
- Controllership Services That Entail Submission of............................9080.21-.24
- Differentiating From Trial Balance.......................9080.10-.12
- Disclosures—See Disclosure
- Draft.............. 9080.13-.14; 9090.10-.11
- Elements—See Compilation of Specified Elements, Accounts, or Items of a Financial Statement
- Emphasis of Matter......... 80.25-.26; 90.33
- Evidence.......................... 60.43-.44
- Financial Information........... 9080.05-.06; 9090.05-.06
- Incomplete Presentation.........9080.32-.40; 9090.14-.22
- International Financial Reporting Standards.......9080.49-.59; 9090.29-.39
- International Standard on Related Service 4410...........................9080.53-.60
- International Standard on Review Engagements 2400..........................9090.33-.40
- Litigation Services and Service Engagements..................9080.17-.20
- Management Services That Entail Submission of..............................9080.21-.24
- Materiality.......................... 60.48-.50
- Misleading—See Misleading Financial Statements
- Nonissuer..............80.55-.56; 90.62-.63
- Omitted Disclosure.............. 9080.51-.52
- Personal—See Personal Financial Statements
- Pro Forma—See Compilation of Pro Forma Financial Information
- Reporting Framework..............60.37-.42; 80.27-.33; 80.42; 90.34-.40; 90.49
- Required Supplementary Information..... 9080.63-.68; 9090.41-.44
- Restatement of Prior Period....... 200.25-.27
- Review—See Review of Financial Statements
- Subsequent Discovery of Facts.... 400.10-.11
- Unaudited—See Unaudited Financial Statements
- Uncertainties—See Uncertainties
- U.S. Entity................ 9080.59; 9090.39

FOOTNOTES—See Notes to Financial Statements

FRAUD
- Communication to Management and Others.........................80.04; 90.04
- Definitions.......................80.04; 90.04

FUNDS STATEMENT—See Statements of Cash Flows

G

GENERAL STANDARDS, AUDIT
- Rule 203, Rules of Conduct......9080.15-.16; 9090.12-.13

GENERALLY ACCEPTED ACCOUNTING PRINCIPLES
- Departures—See Departures From Established Principles
- Disagreement With Management.......400.05
- Omission of Disclosures.........9080.28-.31; 9200.01; 9200.04; 9300.01-.02
- Omission of Display of Comprehensive Income.......................9080.28-.31
- Reports on Application..........9400.01-.05
- Required Supplementary Information..... 9080.63-.64; 9090.41-.42

GENERALLY ACCEPTED AUDITING STANDARDS
- Change of Auditors................... 400.03

GOING CONCERN
- Disclosure.........9080.41-.48; 9090.23-.28
- Emphasis of a Matter Paragraph.....9080.43; 9090.25
- Uncertainties.......... 80.40-.43; 90.47-.50; 9080.41-.48; 9090.23-.28

I

ILLEGAL ACTS
- Communication to Management and Others......................80.03; 90.04
- Definitions.......................80.03; 90.04

ILLUSTRATIONS
- Compilation Engagement Letter........ 80.62; 110.16; 120.19
- Compilation of Pro Forma Financial Information..................... 120.19-.20
- Compilation of Specified Elements, Accounts, or Items of a Financial Statement.......................110.16-.17
- Compilation Report........80.63; 110.16-.17; .... 120.20; 200.38; 300.06; 9080.03; .... 9080.36; 9080.40; 9080.50; 9080.56; 9080.59; 9300.01-.02
- Controllership Services, Required Communication When Performing...9080.23
- Departures From GAAP....9080.03; 9090.03; 9300.01-.02
- Emphasis of a Matter Paragraph.....9080.43; 9080.46; 9090.25; 9090.28
- Implementation of a Personal Financial Plan by Client's Advisers...................9600.03
- Management Services, Required Communication When Performing...9080.23
- Prior Period Audited.................. 200.29
- Report on Personal Financial Statements.........................600.05
- Representation Letters.............90.70-.71
- Review Engagement Letter............. 90.69
- Review Reports..... 90.72; 200.39; 9090.03; 9090.18; 9090.22; 9090.30

ILL

230   AR Topical Index

ILLUSTRATIONS—continued
- Specified Elements, Accounts, or Items of a Financial Statement 110.16-.17
- Successor Accountant Acknowledgment Letter 400.12
- Written Financial Plan Containing Unaudited Personal Financial Statements 600.08

INCOME TAX RETURNS—See Tax Returns

INDEPENDENCE
- Accountant Not Independent .... 60.46; 80.21; 110.14; 120.17
- Lack of Independence, Disclosure of 9080.22

INQUIRIES
- Acceptance of an Engagement 400.03-.06
- Compilation Procedures 9080.08
- Predecessor Accountant's Procedures 200.22
- Review of Engagement Documentation...................... 400.08
- Review Procedures .... 90.04; 90.14-.15; 90.19-.20; 9090.08
- Successor Accountant's Procedures ... 400.04

INSTITUTE—See American Institute of CPAs

INTERNATIONAL ACCOUNTING STANDARDS BOARD
- International Financial Reporting Standards........ 9080.49-.59; 9090.29-.39

INTERNATIONAL FINANCIAL REPORTING STANDARDS
- Accountant's Compilation 9080.50
- Accountant's Review................. 9090.30
- Financial Statements .... 9080.49-.59; 9090.29-.39

INTERPRETATIVE PUBLICATIONS
- Definition and Examples 60.18

IRREGULARITIES—See Fraud

J

JUDGMENT
- Materiality 60.48-.50
- Reports on Application of Accounting Principles 9400.05
- Use of "Selected Information—Substantially All Disclosures Required by Generally Accepted Accounting Principles Are Not Included" in Notes to Financial Statements 9080.25-.27

K

KNOWLEDGE
- Industry Accounting Practices.......... 80.07; 90.08-.09

L

LAWSUITS—See Litigation

LAWYERS
- Client's Improper Use of Statements ... 200.03
- Predecessor Independent Accountant 200.24
- Subsequent Discovery of Facts........ 400.11

LETTERS OF REPRESENTATION—See Representation Letters

LITIGATION
- Applicability of SSARS to Litigation Services................... 9080.17-.20
- Inquiries From Successor Accountant 400.06
- Responses From Predecessor Accountant 400.06

M

MANAGEMENT
- Change of Accountants 400.03
- Communication of Possible Fraud and Illegal Acts........................... 80.15; 90.26
- Controllership Services, Provision of............................... 9080.21-.24
- Disagreement With Predecessor Accountant 400.05
- Integrity............................... 400.05
- Management Services, Provision of............................... 9080.21-.24
- Omission of Disclosures............... 200.31
- Responsibility for Financial Statements 60.30; 80.03; 90.04

MATERIALITY
- Financial Statement 60.48-.50
- Judgment......................... 60.48-.50
- Misstatements 60.48

MEASUREMENT
- Prescribed Forms 300.01; 9300.01-.03

MISTAKES—See Fraud

N

NONISSUERS
- Comparative Financial Statements 200.01-.39
- Compilation of Financial Statements .... 80.55-.56; 400.01; 9300.01-.03
- Compilation or Review Engagement 60.15
- Definition 60.04
- Prescribed Forms ... 300.01-.05; 9300.01-.03
- Review of Financial Statements ..... 90.62-.63; 400.01; 9300.01-.03
- Tax Returns, Reporting .... 9080.05-.06; 9090.05-.06

NOTES TO FINANCIAL STATEMENTS
- Labeling When Client Includes More Than a Few Required Disclosures........... 9080.25-.27
- Omission of 9080.25-.27

ILL

AR Topical Index

231

O

OPINIONS, AUDITORS'
· Prior Period Audited 200.29

OTHER COMPILATION AND REVIEW PUBLICATIONS
· Definition and Examples 60.20

OTHER COMPREHENSIVE BASIS OF ACCOUNTING
· Examples 60.04
· Financial Statements Compiled in
Accordance 80.19; 90.32

P

PERFORMANCE REQUIREMENTS
· Knowledge of the Client 80.08-.11;
. . . . 90.10-.13
· Understanding of Accounting Principles and
Practices used by the Client 80.10
· Understanding of the Client's
Business 80.09-.10; 90.10-.11
· Understanding of the Industry 80.06-.07;
. . . . 90.08-.09

PERSONAL FINANCIAL STATEMENTS
· Departures From the Applicable Financial
Reporting Framework 600.02
· Omission of Disclosures—See Disclosure
· Reports 600.04-.06
· Unaudited Statements for a Written
Plan 600.03-.06; 9600.01-.03
· Understanding With Client 600.03;
. . . . 9600.01-.03
· Written Financial Plan Containing
Unaudited Personal Financial
Statements 600.08

PREDECESSOR INDEPENDENT ACCOUNTANT
· Availability of Engagement
Documentation 400.08
· Communication With Successor
Accountant 400.01-.12; 9400.01
· Compilation Engagements 400.01-.12
· Compilation Report Not
Presented 200.16-.19
· Compilation Report Reissued 200.16;
. . . . 200.20-.24
· Consultation With Successor 400.08
· Contingencies 400.08
· Definition 400.02
· Disagreement With Client 400.05
· Engagement Documentation 400.08
· Fees 400.06; 400.08
· Inquiries 400.03-.08
· Legal Advice on Reissuance of
Report 200.24
· Procedures for Reissuing Report 200.16;
. . . . 200.20-.24
· Representation Letters 200.23
· Responses to Successor
Accountant 400.01; 400.06

PREDECESSOR INDEPENDENT ACCOUNTANT—continued
· Restated Prior Period
Statements 200.25-.27
· Review Engagements 400.01-.12
· Review Report Not Presented 200.16-.19
· Review Report Reissued 200.20-.24
· Subsequent Discovery of Facts 400.10-.11

PRESCRIBED REPORT FORMS—See Special Reports

PRINCIPLES, ACCOUNTING—See Generally Accepted Accounting Principles

PRIVILEGED COMMUNICATION—See Confidential Client Information

PROFESSIONAL REQUIREMENTS
· Application Guidance 60.12-.14
· Unconditional Requirements 60.11
· Presumptively Mandatory
Requirements 60.11

Q

QUALIFIED OPINION
· Prior Period Financial
Statements 9200.02-.04

QUALITY CONTROL
· System of Quality Control—See System of
Quality Control

R

REGULATORY AGENCIES
· Filing for Sale of Securities 200.01
· Prescribed Forms 300.02

REPORTS
· Accountant's Reporting Obligation 200.08
· Compilation—See Compilation Reports
· Date of Reissued Report 200.23
· Personal Financial Statements 600.04-.06
· Reissued 200.07-.08; 200.11; 200.20-.24;
. . . . 200.29
· Review—See Review Reports
· Tax Returns 9080.05-.06; 9090.05-.06

REPRESENTATION LETTERS
· Illustrations 90.70-.71
· Information for Predecessor
Accountant 200.23

REVIEW ENGAGEMENT
· Audit Procedures 9090.07-.09
· Change From Audit Engagement 90.63-.68
· Change in Engagement 80.56-.61;
. . . . 90.63-.68
· Communication Between
Accountants 400.01-.12
· Documentation 90.25-.26
· Elements 60.26
· Ethical Principles 60.22-.23
· Limitations 60.07-.08
· Objectives 60.07-.08

REV

232   AR Topical Index

REVIEW ENGAGEMENT—continued
- Prescribed Forms 9300.03
- Prior Period Audited 200.29
- Quality Control Standards....60.22; 60.24-.25
- Reports—See Review Reports
- Reports on Application of Accounting
  Principles.......................9400.01-.05
- Subsequent Discovery of Facts 400.10-.11
- Subsequent Events ... 200.13-.15; 200.20-.23
- Subsequent Period Compiled 200.11-.12;
  .... 9200.01-.04
- Tax Returns, Reporting...........9090.05-.06
- Three Party Relationship............60.27-.36
- Uncertainties....................9090.23-.28
- Understanding with Management and
  Others 90.04-.06
- Withdrawal From Engagement 90.36

REVIEW OF FINANCIAL STATEMENTS
- Accountant's Responsibilities 90.04
- Analytical Procedures...............90.14-.18
- Change of Accountants 400.02
- Comparative Financial
  Statements........200.01-.37; 9200.01-.04
- Compliance With Contractual Agreement or
  Regulatory Provision 9090.14-.22
- Departures From the Applicable Financial
  Reporting Framework.........90.06; 90.21;
  .... 90.34-.36; 9090.14-.22
- Differences From an Audit 90.04
- Draft Financial Statements 9090.10-.11
- Engagement Letters........90.04-.06; 90.26;
  .... 90.69
- Establishing and Understanding 90.03-.13
- Going Concern..............90.47-.50; 90.70
- Illustrative Engagement Letter 90.69
- Illustrative Representation Letter....90.22-.26;
  .... 90.70-.71
- Impaired Independence.................90.02
- Incomplete Presentation 9090.14-.22
- Inquires and Other Procedures 90.19-.20
- Interim Financial Information
  Exceptions...........................90.01
- Management's Responsibilities..........90.04
- Objective.............................90.04
- Omission of Disclosures—See Disclosure
- Performance Requirements 90.07-.13
- Prescribed Forms ... 300.01-.05; 9300.01-.03
- Reporting—See Review Reports
- Required Supplementary
  Information 9080.63–.68; 9090.41–.44
- Restricted Use 90.37-.46
- Subsequent Discovery of Facts 400.10-.11
- Subsequent Events.............90.22; 90.33;
  .... 90.51-.53
- Subject Matter Based on Measurement or
  Disclosure Criteria Contained in Contractual
  Agreements, Regulatory Provisions....90.40
- Successor Accountant Acknowledgment
  Letter 400.12

REVIEW REPORTS
- Accountant's Responsibility 90.04;
  .... 90.07-.13; 200.03; 200.11-.12

REVIEW REPORTS—continued
- Combined Reports 90.41
- Date of Report..........90.24; 90.30; 90.44;
  .... 90.54-.55
- Departure From Rule 203 of Code of
  Conduct......................9090.12-.13
- Departures From GAAP....90.72; 200.13-.15;
  .... 9090.01-.04; 9200.04
- Elements..............................90.28
- Emphasis of a Matter Paragraph 90.33;
  .... 9090.25; 9090.28
- General Use and Resticted Use 90.37-.46
- Illustrations 90.69; 200.39; 9090.03;
  ... 9090.18; 9090.22; 9090.30; 9090.36
- Impaired Independence.................90.02
- Inclusion of a Separate Restricted Use
  Report............................90.37-.39
- Introductory Paragraph..................90.28
- Modification................90.28; 90.34-.36;
  ... 9090.01-.04; 9090.14-.28; 9300.01-.03
- Preclusion From Issuance 90.66
- Predecessor Independent
  Accountant 200.16-.27
- Prepared in Accordance With OCBOA....90.32
- Prescribed Forms 300.03; 9300.01-.03
- Prior Period Audited 200.29
- Restricted Use 90.37-.46
- Signature of Firm or Accountant on
  Report...............................90.28
- Specified Parties.....90.37; 90.41; 90.43-.44
- Subject Matter Based on Measurement or
  Disclosure Criteria Contained in Contractual
  Agreements, Regulatory Provisions....90.40
- Subsequent Period Compiled 200.11-.12;
  .... 9200.01-.04
- Successor Independent
  Accountant 200.16-.27
- Supplementary Information 90.60
- Tax Returns 9090.05-.06
- Uncertainties 9090.26-.28
- Written Report.................60.47; 90.27

S

SPECIAL REPORTS
- Application of Accounting
  Principles.......................9400.01-.05
- Comparative Financial Statements 200.02;
  .... 300.01
- Compilation of Financial
  Statements........300.01-.05; 9300.01-.03
- Departures From the Applicable Financial
  Reporting Framework...............300.01;
  .... 300.03-.05; 9300.01-.03
- Disclosure 300.01; 9300.01-.03
- Illustrations.......................9300.01-.02
- Measurement...........300.01; 9300.01-.03
- Nonissuer 300.02; 9300.01-.03
- Prescribed Forms........200.02; 300.01-.05;
  .... 9300.01-.03

REV

AR Topical Index — 233

SPECIAL REPORTS—continued
- Regulatory Agencies 300.02
- Unaudited Financial Statements 300.01;
  . . . . 300.03; 9300.01-.03

STANDARDS FOR ACCOUNTING AND REVIEW SERVICES
- Interpretative Publications 60.18
- Other Compilation and Review
  Publications 60.20
- Professional Requirements 60.09-.11

STANDARDS, GENERAL—See General Standards, Audit

STATEMENTS OF CASH FLOWS
- Omission in Compilation 80.05

STOCK—See Inventories

SUBSEQUENT DISCOVERY OF FACTS—See Discovery

SUBSEQUENT EVENTS
- Compilation Engagements 80.44-.46;
  . . . . 200.13-.15; 200.20-.23
- Review Engagements 200.13-.15;
  . . . . 200.20-.23

SUCCESSOR INDEPENDENT ACCOUNTANT
- Communication With Predecessor
  Accountant 400.01-.12; 9400.01
- Compilation Engagements 400.01-.12
- Consultation With Predecessor 400.08
- Contingencies 400.08
- Definition 400.02
- Engagement Documentation of
  Predecessor 400.08
- Inquiries 400.03-.08
- Reference to Predecessor's
  Report 200.16-.19; 200.21; 200.25-.27;
  . . . . 400.09-.11
- Relation to Predecessor Accountant . . . 200.16;
  . . . . 200.21-.22
- Restated Prior Period
  Statements 200.25-.27
- Review Engagements 400.01-.12
- Subsequent Discovery of Facts 400.10-.11

SUPPLEMENTARY FINANCIAL INFORMATION
- Compilation of Financial Statements 80.05;
  . . . . 80.53
- Review of Financial
  Statements 90.06; 90.60
- Required Supplementary
  Information 9080.63-.68; 9090.41-.44
- Separate Report 80.53

T

TAX RETURNS
- Relation to Compilation Report . . . 9080.05-.06
- Relation to Review Report 9090.05-.06

TERMINOLOGY
- Applicable Financial Reporting
  Framework 60.04
- Assurance Engagement 60.04

- Attest engagement 60.04

TERMINOLOGY—continued
- Comparative Financial Statements 200.07
- Continuing Accountant 200.07
- Contractual Agreement 80.32
- Error 80.12
- Financial Reporting Framework 60.04
- Financial Statements 60.04
- Fraud 80.03; 90.04; 120.09
- General Use 80.30
- Illegal Acts 80.03; 90.04; 120.09
- Interpretative Publications 60.18
- Management 60.04
- Other Compilation and Review
  Publications 60.20
- Other comprehensive basis of accounting
  (OCBOA) 60.04
- Predecessor Accountant 400.02
- Presumptively Mandatory
  Requirements 60.11
- Reasonable Period of Time 80.40
- Reissued Report 200.07
- Restricted Use 80.31; 80.38
- Review Evidence 60.04
- Submission of Financial Statements 60.04
- Successor Accountant 400.02
- Third Party 60.04
- Updated Report 200.07

THREE PARTY RELATIONSHIP
- Accountant in the Practice of Public
  Accounting 60.34
- Intended Users 60.35-.36
- Management 60.30-.33

TRIAL BALANCE
- Components 9080.11
- Differentiating From Financial
  Statements 9080.10-.12

U

UNAUDITED FINANCIAL STATEMENTS
- Accountant's Responsibility 200.03
- Disclaimer of Opinion 200.02
- Litigation Service
  Engagements 9080.17-.20
- Personal Financial Plans 600.03-.06;
  . . . . 9600.01-.03
- Prescribed Forms 300.01; 300.03;
  . . . . 9300.01-.03

UNCERTAINTIES
- Disclosure 9080.41-.48; 9090.23-.28
- Emphasis of a Matter Paragraph 9080.43;
  . . . . 9080.46; 9090.25; 9090.28
- Going Concern 9080.41-.48; 9090.23-.28
- Omission of Disclosure 9080.47-.48
- Other Than Going Concern 9080.44-.46;
  . . . . 9090.26-.28
- Prior Period Financial Statements 9200.04

UNC

AR Topical Index

UNDERSTANDING WITH MANAGEMENT
· Contents 110.06-.07; 120.09-.10
· Documentation 110.06
· Responsibilities 80.02-.05; 90.03-.06

V

VENTURES, JOINT—See Jointly Owned Companies

VIOLATIONS OF LAW—See Illegal Acts

W

WITHDRAWAL FROM COMPILATION ENGAGEMENT—See Compilation Engagement

WITHDRAWAL FROM REVIEW ENGAGEMENT— See Review Engagement

AICPA® Online Professional Library

Powerful Online Research Tools

The AICPA Online Professional Library offers the most current access to comprehensive accounting and auditing literature, as well business and practice management information, combined with the power and speed of the Web. Through your online subscription, you'll get:

- Cross-references within and between titles — smart links give you quick access to related information and relevant materials
- First available updates — no other research tool offers access to new AICPA standards and conforming changes more quickly, guaranteeing that you are always current with all of the authoritative guidance!
- Robust search engine — helps you narrow down your research to find your results quickly
- And much more…

Choose from two comprehensive libraries or select only the titles you need!

With the *AICPA Core Library*, you gain access to the following:
- AICPA Professional Standards
- AICPA Technical Practice Aids
- PCAOB Standards & Related Rules
- Accounting Trends & Techniques
- All current AICPA Audit and Accounting Guides
- All current Audit Risk Alerts
One-year individual online subscription
Item # ORS-XX

OR

AICPA Extended Library and get everything from the Core Library plus:
- AICPA Audit & Accounting Manual
- All current Checklists & Illustrative Financial Statements
- eXacct: Financial Reporting Tools & Techniques
- IFRS Accounting Trends & Techniques
One-year individual online subscription
Item # WAL-BY

You can also add the FASB *Accounting Standards Codification*™ and the GASB Library to either library.

Take advantage of a 30-day free trial!
See for yourself how these powerful online libraries can improve your productivity and simplify your accounting research.

Visit **cpa2biz.com/library** for details or to subscribe.